ISDN & SS7

Prentice Hall Series in
Advanced Communications Technologies

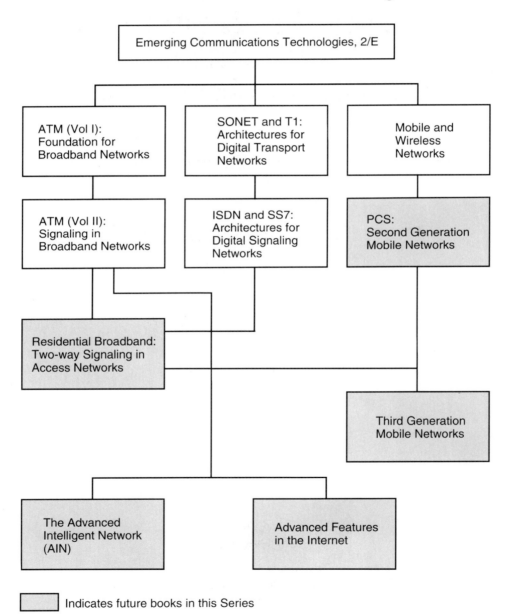

Emerging Communications Technologies, 2/E

ATM (Vol I):
Foundation for
Broadband Networks

SONET and T1:
Architectures for
Digital Transport
Networks

Mobile and
Wireless
Networks

ATM (Vol II):
Signaling in
Broadband Networks

ISDN and SS7:
Architectures for
Digital Signaling
Networks

PCS:
Second Generation
Mobile Networks

Residential Broadband:
Two-way Signaling in
Access Networks

Third Generation
Mobile Networks

The Advanced
Intelligent Network
(AIN)

Advanced Features
in the Internet

Indicates future books in this Series

ISDN & SS7

ARCHITECTURES
FOR DIGITAL
SIGNALING NETWORKS

UYLESS BLACK

To join a Prentice Hall PTR Internet mailing list, point to:
http://www.prenhall.com/mail_lists/

Prentice Hall PTR
Upper Saddle River, New Jersey 07458
http://www.prenhall.com

Library of Congress Cataloging-in-Publication Data

Black, Uyless D.
    ISDN & SS7 : architectures for digital signaling networks / Uyless
Black.
        p.   cm.
    Includes bibliographical references and index.
    ISBN 0–13–259193–6
    1. Integrated services digital networks.   I. Title.
TK5103.75.B53   1997
621.382—dc21   97–6009
                                                        CIP

Acquisitions editor: Mary Franz
Cover designer: Scott Weiss
Cover design director: Jerry Votta
Manufacturing manager: Alexis R. Heydt
Marketing manager: Dan Rush
Composition/Production services: Pine Tree Composition, Inc.

© 1997 by Uyless Black
 Published by Prentice Hall PTR
Prentice-Hall, Inc.
A Simon & Schuster Company
Upper Saddle River, New Jersey 07458

Printed in the United States of America
10 9 8 7 6 5 4 3 2 1

ISBN: 0-13-259193-6

Prentice-Hall International (UK) Limited, *London*
Prentice-Hall of Australia Pty. Limited, *Sydney*
Prentice-Hall Canada Inc., *Toronto*
Prentice-Hall Hispanoamericana, S.A., *Mexico*
Prentice-Hall of India Private Limited, *New Dehli*
Prentice-Hall of Japan, Inc., *Tokyo*
Simon & Schuster Asia Pte. Ltd., *Singapore*
Editora Prentice-Hall do Brasil, Ltda., *Rio De Janeiro*

This book is dedicated to my dear friends
Joe and Hilda Mitchell

The subject of this book is signaling systems in computer networks. It deals with how computers, which are called switches in this technology, find out about the existence of each other in a network, send signals to one another to establish a connection on behalf of two or more network users, then send user information through the connection to and from the users. Later, at the request of the users, the signaling system can terminate the connection.

This process sounds like the exchanges that take place in a conversation between humans, and indeed it is, for computer networks mimic human communications. And in a remarkably similar fashion, these systems also mimic the signaling of other creatures on this planet. In fact, some animals, birds, and fish have long possessed the signaling facilities that have recently been placed in computer-based signaling networks, albeit for these networks, with excruciating exactitude, and at enormous expense.

One of the most remarkable signaling creatures that I have come across is the fish, at least certain fish. While writing this book, I read some articles about how these fish have the ability, through electrically generated signals, to signal to other fishes some important facts, such as the type of fish that is sending the signal, the territory that the fish controls, whether the fish is going to fight or not, and for mating purposes, the sex of the fish. The "messages" that are exchanged between the fishes are much like those that are described in the first paragraph of this preface—they discover the existence of other fish; they establish communications, and so on.

In a remarkable display of versatility, some fish are ambulatory dipoles; they act as an antenna for sending and receiving low voltage signals. These signals, which are in the form of varying frequencies and voltages, convey a wide array of information. But the nuances of these signals are quite complex and are not fully understood by scientists.

Nonetheless, as computers and the associated software become more "intelligent," it is assumed by many people that they will someday be able to replicate not just the brains of fish, but the human brain. As Bill Gates stated in an interview, "All the neurons in the brain that make up perceptions and emotions operate in a binary fashion. We can someday replicate that on a machine. . . . Eventually, we'll be able to sequence the human genome and replicate how nature did intelligence in a carbon-based system."

This scenario may happen someday. But as a note of caution, it is appropriate to quote another noted individual, Albert Einstein, about this matter, "Try and penetrate with our limited means the secrets of nature and you will find that, behind all the discernible concatenations, there remains something subtle, intangible, and inexplicable. . . . The most beautiful and deepest experience a man can have is the sense of the mysterious."

But of course, Einstein did not have the computer, he had "only" his brain.

Contents

Chapter 7   **Signaling System Number 7 (SS7) Architecture**   **99**

Chapter 8   **MTP 1 and MTP 2**   **123**

Chapter 9	MTP 3	139

Chapter 14   Transaction Capabilities Applications Part (TCAP)   249

Chapter 15   Intelligent Networks   279

Appendix A   The OSI Model in ISDN and SS7   **303**

Appendix B   The OSI Presentation Layer and SS7   **312**

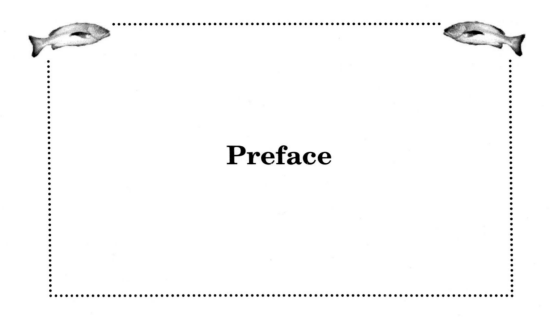

Preface

This book is one in a series titled *Advanced Communications Technologies,* and is written as a complement to this series. This particular book also has a close "companion" in this series, titled *SONET and T1: Architectures for Digital Transport Networks.*

In setting out to write this book, I established two goals. First, as with all the books in this series, I wish to complement the overall series, and avoid undue overlapping of the subject matter of the other books. Second, I wish to explain aspects of the subject matter that have not been provided in other reference books. I found that not much tutorial literature exists on narrowband signaling, especially the relationship of ISDN and SS7, and some of the new specifications for SS7. This information is provided in this book.

I hope you find this information useful. I look forward to your comments. I can be reached on the Internet at: 102732.3535@compuserv.com.

Note for the Reader

The material in this book has been derived from the specifications, standards and recommendations of the ITU-T, the ATM Forum, ANSI, ETSI, and Bellcore. In preparing the book, I studied scores of these documents and hundreds of pages of material. I have attempted to condense the material, yet provide sufficient detail to make the book a valuable tutorial and resource guide. I cite the relevant specification where appropriate, and recommend the reader study the source document if more detail is needed. You cannot design a system correctly is you do not read them.

I thank *Time* magazine for the interview with Bill Gates, and Mr. Gate's quote at the beginning of this book. The interview is published in *Time's* January 17, 1997 issue. I also thank Denis Brian for his wonderful biography of Albert Einstein, and the quotes I cite at the beginning of this book. Mr. Brian's book is *Einstein: A Life*, and is published by John Wiley & Sons, Inc.

1

Introduction to Digital Signaling Systems

INTRODUCTION

This chapter introduces the concepts of signaling systems and the operations of the Integrated Services Digital Network (ISDN) and Signaling System Number 7 (SS7). In-band and out-of-band signaling systems are compared, and a general review is provided of the telephone network and the local and interexchange carriers. The Open Systems Interconnection (OSI) Model is used to explain the layered architectures of ISDN and SS7.

PURPOSE OF SIGNALING SYSTEMS

The purpose of a signaling system is to transfer control information (signaling units) between elements in a telecommunications network. The elements are switches, operations centers, and databases. This information includes signaling units to establish and terminate connections and other information such as directory service and credit card messages.

Originally, signaling systems were designed to set up connections between telephone offices and customer premises equipment (CPE) in order to transport only voice traffic through a voice-oriented, analog network. Today, they are designed to set up connections between service provider offices and CPE in order to transport not only voice but also video or data signals through either an analog or a digital network. The focus of this book is on digital signaling systems.

Early signaling systems carried the control signals on the same circuit as the user traffic;[1] for example, the older in-band analog systems use this approach. The newer signaling systems, such as SS7, use a separate channel for signaling information. These systems are called common channel signaling (CCS) systems because a separate (common) channel is used for signaling. Some people call this approach out-of-band signaling and it is preferred to in-band signaling because it is more efficient and robust. Later discussions will amplify and reinforce this general statement.

PHYSICAL OUT-OF-BAND AND PHYSICAL IN-BAND/LOGICAL OUT-OF-BAND SIGNALING

Two types of out-of-band signaling exist today. SS7 is an example of the first type—physical out-of-band signaling—in which a separate physical channel is used for signaling. ISDN is an example of physical in-band/logical out-of-band signaling.[2] With this latter approach, signaling and user traffic share the same physical channel, but part of the channel capacity[3] is reserved only for signaling traffic; the remainder of the bandwidth is reserved for user traffic, such as the telephone call. ISDN uses the term B channel to describe the user channel, and the term D channel to describe the signaling channel. SS7 makes none of these distinctions, since it uses separate physical channels for signaling.

Figure 1–1 shows the differences between these two methods of signaling. In Figure 1–1(a), two physical links are used between two nodes, which are switches in this example. This is the approach taken with SS7.

---

[1]The term circuit is used to describe the physical communications channel. Other terms are also used. Some organizations use the terms link, line, or trunk to describe this channel. Unless otherwise noted, all these terms are used synonymously. Other terms to describe the link are cable-pair and wire-pair, which consist of a pair of copper wires, one for traffic and one for return.

[2]The term logical channel means that different types of traffic share a physical channel. Each of these signals is called a logical channel.

[3]This book uses the term bandwidth to describe capacity. Unless noted otherwise, bandwidth describes how many bits per second (bit/s) are provided for an application. In some descriptions, bandwidth is used to describe frequency spectrum, but I will alert the reader for this second use of bandwidth.

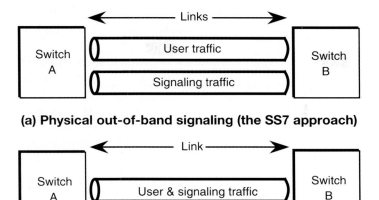

(a) Physical out-of-band signaling (the SS7 approach)

(b) Physical in-band/logical out-of-band signaling (the ISDN approach)

Figure 1–1   Comparison of signaling systems

In Figure 1–1(b), one physical link is used between two nodes, with the signaling traffic allotted reserved bandwidth on the link. This is the approach taken with ISDN.

If physical out-of-band signaling is so effective, why does ISDN not use the concept? The answer is that ISDN is usually implemented on the local subscriber loops running between a customer's home or office and the telephone office. Generally, it is not practical or cost-effective to use two separate links (two separate wire-pairs) for each customer (or a few customers). This would entail installing more cable in the local distribution plant. Consequently, the ISDN approach represents a compromise; the physical channel is shared, but some bandwidth is dedicated to the logical signaling channel.

In addition, ISDN is designed to support a limited set of users, and it does not provide for the redundant links that are used in the SS7 technology. If the link fails, the user or a few users are denied service, but the failure does not affect a large population.

In contrast, SS7 is usually deployed as a separate network within the complete telephone network architecture for the purpose of establishing and terminating telephone calls. If a user link fails, the signaling link is still operable and can continue to support other user calls.

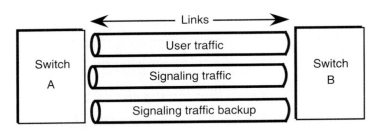

Figure 1–2   Redundant signaling links to provide robustness.

But what happens if the signaling link fails? As shown in Figure 1–2, SS7 is designed to support more than one signaling link; if one link fails, another link is available to take over, without the loss of any signaling traffic. Since SS7 signaling links may support many users (in fact, millions of users), physical signaling with redundant links is an absolute necessity.

We can take this discussion one step farther and pose another question: What happens if an SS7 switch (or some other SS7 node) fails? SS7 is sufficiently concerned with downtime (SS7 unavailability) that the SS7 network also has redundant nodes, as well as redundant links between the nodes. These topologies are explained in more detail in subsequent chapters. For this discussion, keep in mind that a key goal of an SS7 network is "no downtime."

PLACEMENT OF ISDN AND SS7 IN THE NETWORK

Figure 1–3 shows that the most common placement of ISDN and SS7 is to operate ISDN between the customer premises equipment (CPE) and the network node (such as a switch) and to operate SS7 inside the network as the signaling protocol between switches. The first interface (between the user and the network) is called a user-network interface (UNI), and ISDN is designed to function as a UNI. The second interface (between SS7 nodes) is called a network node interface (NNI), and SS7 is designed to function as an NNI.

While this placement is the common practice, it does not preclude running SS7 between the CPE and the network node. Moreover, SS7 does not require ISDN to operate at the UNI. Indeed, at this stage in the evolution from analog-to-digital interfaces, conventional analog signaling (with dial tone) is much more prevalent than the ISDN interface.

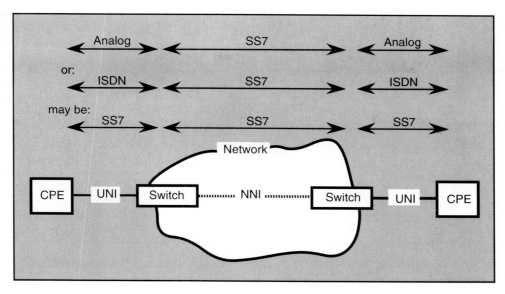

where:
    CPE   Customer premise equipment
    NNI   Network node interface
    UNI   User-network interface

Figure 1–3   Placement of ISDN and SS7.

ISDN, SS7, AND THE OSI MODEL

Figure 1–4(a) shows the relationship of the OSI layers to the layers of ISDN, and SS7. I have also added two other technologies to this discussion, the T1 family and the Synchronous Optical Network (SONET). If the OSI Model is not familiar to the reader, please see Appendix A.

The first observation is that T1 and SONET operate at the physical layer of the OSI Model; the second is that ISDN operates at the lower three layers of the model; and the third is that SS7 operates at all layers, with the exception of the session layer.[4] It is certainly possible for the ISDN and SS7 physical layer to be implemented with the T1 or SONET technology. Indeed, this configuration is common in many systems.

---

[4]Later chapters will reveal that the use of the application and presentation layers varies, depending upon what SS7 is doing. SS7 does not use the OSI session layer. The SS7 transport layer is derived from the OSI Model, with added features. The lower three layers of SS7 are modeled on the lower three layers of OSI.

OSI	T1	SONET	ISDN	SS7
Application				Application
Presentation				Presentation
Session				Session
Transport				Transport
Network			Network	Network
Data link			Data link	Data link
Physical	Physical	Physical	Physical	Physical

(a) Comparison of the layers in regard to OSI (Session layers is null)

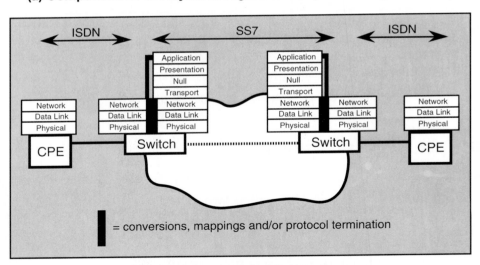

= conversions, mappings and/or protocol termination

(b) Relationship of ISDN and SS7

Figure 1–4   System placement in relation to the OSI Model.

The relationship of the ISDN layers and the SS7 layers is a bit more complex and Figure 1–4(b) shows this relationship. Once again, we assume in this figure that ISDN operates between the CPE and the network and SS7 operates within the network. Therefore, the network node (a switch) has two stacks of protocols. On the user side, it operates the ISDN layers and on the network side it operates the SS7 layers.

The job of this network node is to translate the ISDN network layer header to an associated header corresponding to an SS7 application layer header, which is symbolized in the figure with the **Ⴑ**. We shall see that this operation is performed through an SS7 application called the ISDN User Part (ISUP)

As a general rule, the invocation at the CPE of the physical and data link layers are performed solely to transfer the network layer header to the switch and vice versa. Afterwards, these layers are terminated; that is to say, they do not proliferate past the switch into the network.

The reader may wonder about the upper four layers of SS7, since there are no corresponding four layers running on top of the ISDN layers. How these layers are invoked is a function of how the ISDN network layer header is interpreted when it is received at the switch. The parameters in the ISDN network layer header affect the invocation of these layers. Subsequent chapters will expand considerably on these concepts.

PROGRESS IN ISDN PENETRATION INTO THE MARKETPLACE

After ISDN was introduced in 1984 (in the ITU-T Red Book), it then languished in the marketplace, unable to find a niche. Some people joked that the initials ISDN meant: "I still don't know" what ISDN is supposed to do.

Several reasons can be cited for the slow acceptance of this technology. First, in affluent countries that might have been able to afford the implementation of ISDN, the existing analog infrastructure was quite satisfactory. Second, a 64 kbit/s bandwidth was not needed by most applications in the early 1980s. After all, personal computers were just appearing and most workstations had no disk storage, so data transfer rates were no faster than the speed of a person entering traffic through a keyboard. Third, in the United States, AT&T had just been broken up, and (for several years), the national telecommunications infrastructure was not focused on a national plan for any new technology; the new Baby Bells, AT&T, MCI, and Sprint were preoccupied with adjusting to a new environment.

This situation began to change in the late 1980s and early 1990s, because the analog modems of 9600 or 14400 bit/s were not providing enough bandwidth for many applications, such as file transfer and electronic mail. In addition, the Regional Bell Operating Companies (RBOCs) and Bellcore as a unified group decided to launch "National ISDN", an ambitious project to bring ISDN into most of the telephone end offices by 1994. These two factors converged to foster the rapid ascendancy of ISDN in the U.S.

Figure 1–5 illustrates just how successful ISDN has become in the United States in a short time. Granted, the ISDN service is still relatively expensive, especially when compared to a traditional analog dial-up service. However, it offers 64 kbit/s bandwidth services (known as the basic rate interface, or BRI) and is viewed as effective from the standpoint of cost versus performance. An ISDN customer can also obtain higher bandwidth services (known as the primary rate interface or PRI) of 1.544 Mbit/s. This figure shows the growth of BRI and PRI ISDN and forecasts usage through 1999.

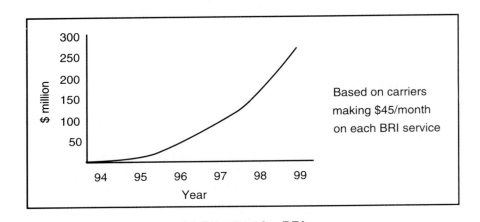

(a) Forecast for BRI

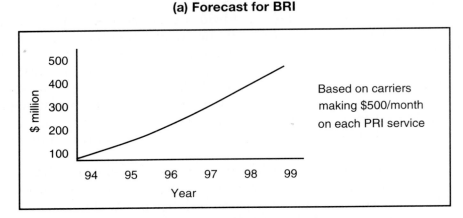

(b) Forecast for PRI

Figure 1–5   ISDN market penetration in United States.

However, some people view ISDN as "too little, too late." The BRI rate of 64 kbit/s does not provide enough bandwidth for many applications, especially the rapidly growing market for multimedia services supporting integrated voice, video, and data applications.

While these thoughts have merit, not everyone needs bandwidth beyond 64 kbit/s. It is likely ISDN will continue to grow, as suggested in Figure 1–5. It is also likely that as several physical layer local loop technologies mature to provide more bandwidth (such as asymmetrical digital subscriber line [ADSL]), cable modems, and hybrid fiber coaxial cable [HFC]), the other two layers of ISDN (layers two and three) will be modified and placed onto these new physical layer (layer one) technologies.

PROGRESS IN SS7 PENETRATION INTO THE MARKETPLACE

SS7 has had a much easier task in being accepted in the marketplace than ISDN. Indeed, its installation began almost as soon as the ITU-T published the specification. In the past, telephone networks used interoffice trunk signaling (signaling within the network) in a manner that required the call set up between the stations to follow the same path as the actual connected call. This approach was deemed reasonable to avoid separate transmission channels for signaling control and the call.

This per-trunk system is inefficient for several reasons. First, the call is initiated without a priori knowledge of a probable successful connection. Second, during periods of heavy traffic, calls originating form the external users seize resources inside the network. Even though a telephone user has not received a connection, the user is reserving resources on a piecemeal basis from the network. In essence, partially completed calls satisfy no one, but still consume network resources.

Several years ago, telephone companies recognized the inefficiency of integrating its control signals on the same channel with voice traffic. Consequently, it devised the Common Channel Interoffice Signaling (CCIS) system, a first-generation signaling system, which transmitted the signaling information for a group of trunks over a separate channel from the user communications channel, a technique also known as clear channel signaling.

CCIS was based on the CCITT (now named ITU-T) Signaling System No. 6 (SS6). AT&T/Bell designed its CCIS protocol to be consistent with CCITT Signaling System No. 6 (with this exception: The CCIS version used a 4.8 kbit/s rate, in contrast to the international system of 2.4 kbit/s). However, today, most systems utilize the digitally oriented Signaling System No. 7.

CCIS and SS6 performed well enough, but the link speeds of 2.4 and 4.8 kbit/s and the limited size of the service unit (SU) limit their capabilities. Also, the routing operations were awkward to manage. With a few exceptions, these older systems have been replaced with SS7.

Most industrialized countries have migrated to SS7, and it is only a matter of time before SS7 (or some other common channel signaling (CCS) system) becomes the sole way of performing signaling operations. What is more, SS7 is finding its way into networks other than the fixed-wire telephone network. As examples, a variation of SS7 has been adapted for use in the Asynchronous Transfer Mode (ATM) technology. Other variations of SS7 are now employed in all the new mobile, wireless networks such as the Global System for Mobile Communications (GSM) and Personal Communications System networks (PCS).[5]

ARRANGEMENT OF THE TELEPHONE NETWORK

It will be helpful to devote some time in this chapter to an explanation of some basic telephony concepts. These concepts will be used throughout the book. To start this discussion, telephone users, either in homes or offices, connect through the telephone system into the central office (CO), local exchange, or end office (EO). Thousands of these offices may be installed around a country. I described earlier that the connection is provided to the CO through a pair of wires (or four wires) called the local loop or subscriber loop.

Figure 1–6 depicts several lines, types of equipment, and types of "offices" found in the public network. Most of the terms in this figure are self-explanatory, but some of them warrant amplification:

- *Trunk:* A communication channel between two switching systems.
- *Tandem office:* A broad category of office that represents systems that connect trunks to trunks. Local tandem offices connect trunks within a metropolitan area. Toll offices connect trunks in the toll part of the network.
- *Toll connecting trunk:* A trunk between an end office (local office) and a toll office.

---

[5]SS7 is not used at the mobile air interface (the UNI), but between the nodes that support the air interface (the NNI).

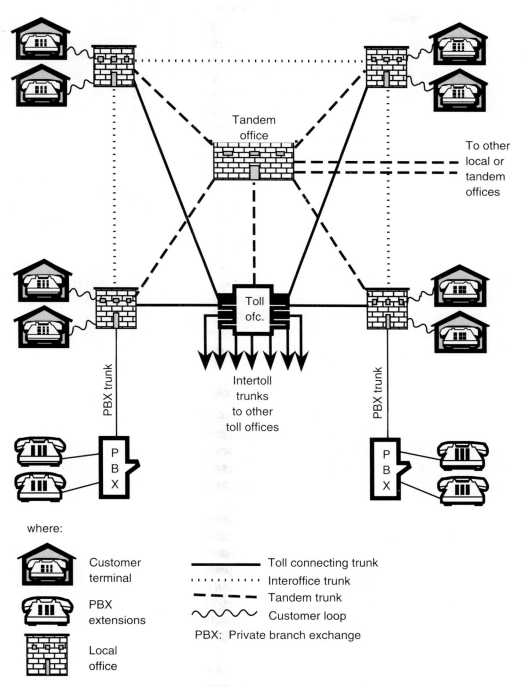

To other
local or
tandem
offices

Tandem
office

Toll
ofc.

Intertoll
trunks
to other
toll offices

PBX trunk

PBX trunk

where:

Customer
terminal

PBX
extensions

Local
office

—————— Toll connecting trunk
· · · · · · · · · · · Interoffice trunk
– – – – – – Tandem trunk
〰〰〰〰 Customer loop
PBX: Private branch exchange

Figure 1–6   Offices and trunks.

The use of direct or indirect connections between offices with tandem trunks or other tandem switching systems depends on several factors: distances between offices, the traffic volume between offices, and the potential for sharing facilities among the customers within the geographical area. In the case of intermediate traffic volumes or longer distances, the telephone system generally establishes a combination of direct and tandem lengths.

The system is built around high-usage trunks (or high-volume trunks) that carry the bulk of the traffic. High-usage trunks are established when the volume of calls warrants the installation of high-capacity channels between two offices. Consequently, trunk configurations vary, depending on traffic volume between centers.

Local Exchange and Interexchange Carriers

When the divestiture of AT&T occurred in 1984, the local bell operating companies were divided into the Regional Bell Operating Companies (RBOCs), and were required to confine their operations to local exchange carrier (LEC) functions (see Figure 1–7).

Prior to divestiture, an exchange area was the term used to describe a geographical area in the United States where a single, uniform set of service was provided by "Ma Bell". The Modification of Final Judgment (MFJ) established 160 areas based on the United States Government Standard Metropolitan Statistical Areas. These areas are named local access and transport areas (LATAs). These LATAs may span a metropolitan area or a state, since they are based on population density. The most important part of this part of deregulation was the restriction on both LECs and the now-called interexchange carriers (ICs or IXCs). The LECs offered service within the LATA, and the ICs offered service between the LATAs.

Points of Presence (POP)

With divestiture in 1984, points of presence (POP) were designated within each LATA for the interconnection of the IC equipment with the LEC facilities. The locations of the POPs vary depending on the LATAs and agreements between the ICs and the LECs, but the most common approach is to house the POP in the same building that houses the ICs' facilities. The only hard and fast rule is that the POP must be located within the LATA that the IC serves. For high-density and/or large LATAs, it is not unusual to have more than one POP within the LATA.

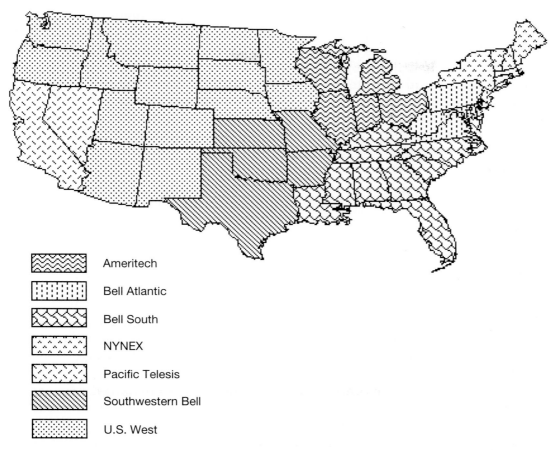

	Ameritech
	Bell Atlantic
	Bell South
	NYNEX
	Pacific Telesis
	Southwestern Bell
	U.S. West

Notes:
- The 1984 divestiture divided system in to these regions and into local access and transport areas (LATAs) within these regions.
- The LECs offered service within the LATA, and the IXCs offered service between the LATAs.
- In 1996, several of these RBOCs merged or were purchased by another RBOC.

Figure 1–7 Local exchange carriers (LECs) and the Regional Bell Operating Companies (RBOCs), as of February 1996.

Each POP must have designated with it a physical point of termination (POT). The POT acts as the demarcation between the LEC and ICs' functions and the IC is required to provide the POT in accordance with the LEC's technical and operational specifications.

The physical implementation of the POT is usually a conventional distributing frame, or some other piece of equipment that terminates the LEC's access lines. The particular piece of equipment is not specified, but it must allow cross-connections and the testing and service verification of the interfaces.

The Dialing Plan

The current dialing plan in North America is a seven-digit address to identify each network station (telephone). The address takes the form:

$$NXX\text{-}XXXX$$

where: N can be any digit 2 through 9 and X can be 0 through 9. The arbitrarily assigned NXX portion of the address identifies the customer location where the station is homed. It cannot be the same as the NXX digits assigned to the same switch for public network use. The XXXX digits are the numbers of the individual station at the customer location.

This address is preceded with a three-digit area code, and for dialing since the 1984 divestiture, the full dialing address is:

$$10XXX \text{ (to be expanded to } 101XXXX) \text{ carrier access code}$$

where: XXX identifies the specific carrier. The dialing sequence is 10XXX+(0/1)+7/10 digits (D), where X can be any digit from 0 to 9. The 7/10 digits dialed must conform to the North American Numbering Plan (NANP).

In the local exchange carrier (LEC) network, the complete convention for "Dial 0" services is as follows:

Intra-exchange:	0	or	0 + /10D
Interexchange (inside world zone 1):	10 XXX + 0 + 7/10D	or	0 + 7/10D*
Outside world zone 1:	10 XXX + 01 + CC + NN	or	01 + CC + NN*
No call address	10 XXX + 0	or	00*

where: CC = country code and NN = network number; * represents presubscribed numbers.

TELECOMMUNICATIONS ACT OF 1996

The passage of the 1996 Telecommunications Bill (signed by President Clinton in February 1996) represents the most significant legislation concerning the U.S. communications industry since the 1984 divestiture legislation. Essentially, many of the barriers have been removed for the various players to move into each other's market.

Mergers and acquisitions began the day after the bill was signed into law. Nevertheless, it will take quite a while before all issues are sorted out, and the Federal Communications Commission (FCC) has the huge task of interpreting some of the broad statements of the law into specific rules. It is expected that all of FCC's rules will not be finished for several years.

Regardless of how some of the specific rules are written, the U.S. telecommunications industry changes will affect all citizens, as well as the services and products of vendors, manufacturers, and service providers.

As the final nail in the coffin to the past environment, Judge Harold Greene terminated the Modification of Final Judgment (MFJ), the antitrust consent decree (1984 Divestiture). He agreed that 1996 Telecommunications Act has rendered the MFJ moot.

CHALLENGE OF SUPPORTING CUSTOMER CALLS

Before we close this chapter and move on to our examination of ISDN and SS7, it will prove helpful to discuss the subject of telephone traffic. It should come as no surprise to note that the customers' traffic load on the public network is highly variable when measured across the business day and the early evening. Figure 1–8(a) illustrates the traffic pattern for calls from businesses, residences, and coin-operated telephones.

The load on the network for business calls has two peaks, one at mid-morning and one at mid-afternoon. Not surprisingly, the load on the network for coin-operated systems peaks during the lunch period, with a moderate increase just after the work day, with a moderate peak also occurring around 9–10 PM.

Residential calls peak in the mid-morning with a steady decline throughout the day and early evening, with a slight peak in the mid-evening hours.

From the preceding discussion, it is evident that customers exhibit a variable, but somewhat predictable load on the network. Nonetheless,

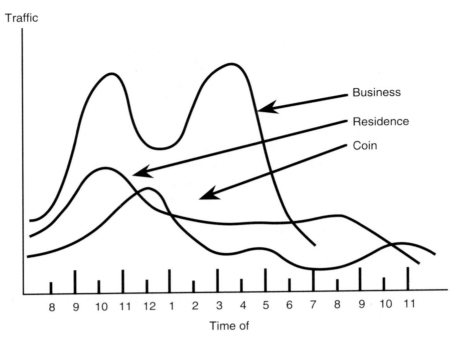

(a) Traffic variations

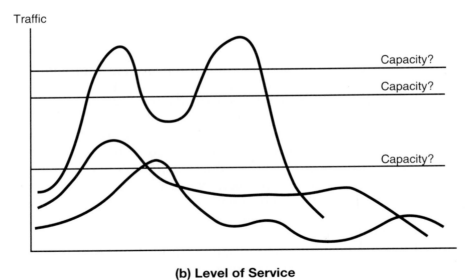

(b) Level of Service

Figure 1–8   Traffic profiles and capacity issues.

the challenge is to support all applications from the customer. Due to variable traffic profiles, it may be imperative to refuse calls from users if the network experiences congestion problems. This situation is illustrated in Figure 1–8(b). For a brief period of time the user requirements exceed the transfer rate permitted in the network. Of course, a network provider (AT&T, MCI, Sprint, etc.) cannot refuse calls often. That will result in the loss of the customer.

ISDN and SS7 play key roles in the support of these call requirements. SS7 is especially critical due to its role as the signaling system within the network. How these challenges are met by ISDN and SS7 is the subject of several discussions in this book.

SUMMARY

ISDN and SS7 are based on digital technology. Both have signaling capabilities: ISDN can also transport user traffic in its B channels, whereas SS7 carries only signaling traffic. Both technologies were introduced in the mid-1980s, and both have been deployed in many systems and products.

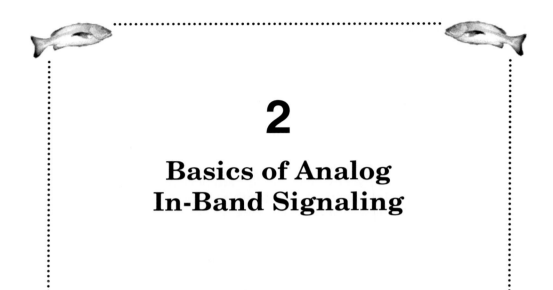

2

Basics of Analog In-Band Signaling

INTRODUCTION

Even though ISDN an SS7 are digital signaling systems and do not use dial tone or multifrequency pulsing, they must be able to interwork with these analog technologies, since analog operations are the most prevalent form of signaling in the local loop.

In recognition of this fact, this chapter examines analog control signaling. In later chapters (especially Chapter 13, where we will show how an ISDN/SS7 gateway interworks the analog control signals with the digital control signals).

If the reader is not using nor interested in analog, in-band signaling, this entire chapter can be skipped with no ill-effects.

THE BASIC OPERATIONS OF ACCESS LINE SIGNALING

Access line signaling defines the operations to connect the CPE to the switching system. The signaling can take place across a two-wire or four-wire interface, and signaling is transmitted in various modes, depending on the specific implementation by the network provider. Regardless of the mode of operation, six classes of signals are used during access line operations:

- *Supervisory.* These signals are used to initiate or terminate connections. From the sending customer, the initiator requests a service. From the standpoint of the receiver, they represent the initiation of a connection.
- *Address.* These signals provide information to the network about the destination user. In so many words, they are the called party (and maybe the calling party) numbers.
- *Alerting.* These signals are provided by the network to the receiving customer that an incoming call is taking place, or to alert that some need is being signaled (flashing, recall, etc.).
- *Call progress.* These signals inform the user about the progress or lack of progress of a call that has been initiated by this user.
- *Control.* These signals are used for functions that usually remain transparent to the end customer. They are usually associated with network connections to the point-of-termination (POT) or the demarcation point. One example of a control signal is the requirement for party identification.
- *Test signals.* These signals are used for a wide array of circuit validation and quality checks.

The supervisory signals convey the following service conditions:

- *Idle circuit.* Indicated by the combination of an on-hook signal and the absence of any connection in the switching system between loops.
- *Seizure (request for service).* Indicated by an off-hook signal and the absence of any connection to another loop or trunk.
- *Disconnect.* Indicated by an on-hook signal in the presence of a connection to a trunk or another loop.
- *Wink start.* Indicated by an off-hook signal from the called office after a connect signal is sent from the calling office.

LOOP-START SIGNALING

Access line signaling can be implemented in a number of ways. The most common scheme used in the public telephone network is known as loop-start signaling. It is employed in the BOC's Message Telecommunications Service (MTS) for residence and business lines, the public telephone service, data/facsimile service, and private branch exchange (PBX) or automatic call distributor (ACD) service.

Loop-start signaling requires that the network connect the "tip" connector to the positive end and the "ring" connector to the negative end of the power supply for an on-hook (idle) state. The voltage supply is usually 48 volts (V), but different line conditions may cause the voltage to vary from as low as 0 V to as high as 105 V.

Telephony Standards impose stringent requirements on vendors' systems with regard to access line signaling. Nonetheless, within the confines of the standards, variations do exist. The variations are well documented and well understood and do not usually present a major problem to the end-user customer. Figure 2–1 shows a schematic representation of loop-start signaling and the directions of the major signals that are sent from the user equipment or the network. The following material explains Figure 2–1 in more detail.

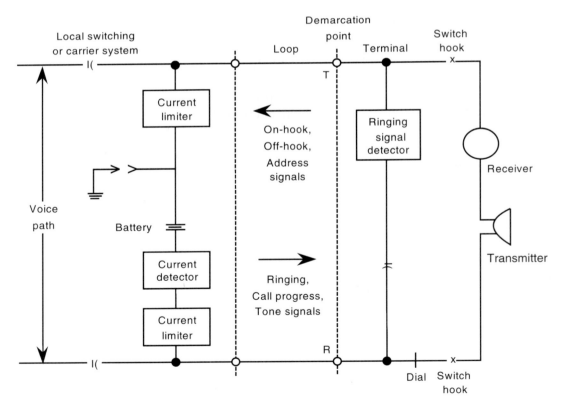

Figure 2–1   Loop-start signaling arrangement.

Most vendors' products establish a timer upon placing dial tone on the line until the detection of the first address signal. While implementations vary, if an address signal is not received between 5 and 40 seconds, the loop is connected either to an announcement and/or to a receiver-on-hook (ROH) tone and then to an open-circuit condition.

After all the address signals have been sent to the network, the calling party may hear call-progress tones and, of course, audible ringing signals that indicate a successful connection. At the calling end, the ringing signal is comprised of a 88 V, 20 Hz signal superimposed upon a 48 V nominal DC voltage. The ringing signal detector usually detects this signal, which is followed by about 4 seconds of silence. Because of this operation, a central office line may be seized up to 4 seconds before the seizure is detected by the user station. The possible outcome of this situation is that a person may attempt to establish a call during this period. This is not a big problem since the person that originates the call from that station is the person to whom the call is intended anyway. You may have experienced this situation when you picked up the phone and the party you wanted to call was already connected to you. It is not a poltergeist in action—there is really a practical explanation for it.

When the called party answers the call, the off-hook action removes the ringing signal and cuts through the talking path. This removal is called a tripping interval and usually lasts 200 ms, although ringing can continue for longer intervals before it is tripped.

Of course, either party can end the call by going on-hook. This forces the telephone instrument to an idle state and no DC-loop current flows to the circuit. During this disconnect operation, the network does not send any type of signal to the called or calling terminal.

GROUND-START SIGNALING

The ground-start signaling for a two-way dial system is an old technology (introduced in the 1920s). It is used typically on two-way PBX central office trunks with direct outward dialing (DOD) and attendant-handled incoming call service. The ground-start line conductors transmit common battery-loop supervision, dual-tone multifrequency (DTMF) address signaling or loop dial pulses, alerting signals, and voiceband electrical energy.

Even though ground-start lines are an old technology, they may be used in place of loop-start because: (1) They provide a signal that can act as a start-dial signal (it is not necessary to detect dial tone in most situations); (2) they provide a positive indication of a new call; (3) they help prevent unauthorized calls; and (4) they provide an indication to the calling or called party of distant-end disconnect under normal operation.

OPEN SWITCHING INTERVALS (OSIs)

OSIs are generated on lines by switching systems as the call is switched from one call state to another. An OSI removes battery and ground from the line for a period of time. OSIs occur on loop-start and ground-start.

Systems vary on the use of OSI, even products within a manufacturer (AT&T, Nortel, etc.). Installers should check the specifications carefully. Regardless of the specific piece of equipment. Here are typical call state changes that cause OSIs:

- Placing a call on hold
- Transferring a call
- Connecting a calling line to dial tone
- Completion of dialed digit by calling line
- Start and removal of ringing
- Switching to call-waiting tone

TESTING THE CIRCUIT

Tests must be applied to the circuit to ensure that it is operating correctly. These tests are made when the circuit is idle and during the process of connecting or disconnecting a call.

While the local loop is idle, the central office periodically applies test signals—either on a loop-start or ground-start. During a call setup or disconnect, tests are also conducted. The following tests are conducted.[1]

- *Power cross test.* This test is made before originating and terminating the calls. The tests vary, depending on the equipment. For example, in an AT&T 1/1AESS, an OSI of 25 to 50 ms precedes the

---

[1]These tests are defined in ANSI T1.401-1988 and ANSI/EIA 470-A-1987 Specifications. Also see Bellcore SR-TSV-002275, Issue 2, April 1994.

test. The test detects ac or positive dc voltages over 16 V as a power cross on loop-start or ground-start lines. To make this test, detectors are placed tip-to-ground and ring-to-ground. The input resistance of each detector is about 18 kΩ on calls originating from the line. For calls terminating to the line, the ring detector resistance is about 18kΩ, while the tip detector resistance is about 36 kΩ. The test lasts about 50 to 100 ms. If the test is successful, dial tone, battery on the ring, and ground on the tip are connected to the line immediately after the power-cross test.

- *Low line resistance test.* This test is performed on all switching systems and is used to prevent false charging if line irregularities exist on the line. The test is performed prior to ringing in the terminating call sequence. In the 1/1A ESS system on loop-start lines, the test is made by applying approximately a 250 Ω ground to the tip and approximately 250 Ω from battery to the ring. On ground-start lines, the battery and ground are reversed.

- *Restore and verify test.* This test is made on a line just before it is idled after supporting a connection. It is used to determine if supervision has been returned to the line and if the cutoff contact has been closed. As an example, the 1/1A ESS system places a 1000 or 2000 Ω resistor from the tip to the ring for a loop-start line or between ring and ground for a ground-start line. The test takes about 50 to 100 ms.

COMMON CONTROL SIGNALS

This section provides a brief explanation of several control signals used with in-band analog signaling systems. Many other signals are used by the telephone network, but the described here are sufficient to understand this type of signaling in the context of interworking with SS7.

On-Hook and Off-Hook Signals

The terms on-hook and off-hook were derived from the old telephone that use a hook to hold the telephone. When the handset was removed to make or answer a call, it was *off-hook*. Otherwise, it was *on-hook*. In modern networks, a station is on-hook if the conductor loop between the user station and the end office is open, with no current flowing. The off-hook has a dc shunt across the line, and current is flowing between the station and the end office.

For the discussion in this section, we use these terms to designate the two signaling conditions of a trunk. Typically, if a trunk between these offices is idle (not in use) the offices send on-hook signals to each other. Trunk seizure occurs at the calling end by sending an off-hook signal to the called end. If the trunk then is awaiting an answer from the called end, the called end sends on-hook signals to the calling end. The calling end receives an off-hook signal when the called end answers the call.

Off-hook and on-hook signals are used to convey a wide variety of control signals, which are identified by the duration of the off-hook/on-hook conditions.

Connect (Seizure)

Connect (seizure) is a sustained off-hook signal that is sent from the calling end of a trunk to the called end following the trunk seizure. The purpose of this signal is to provide a means for the calling end to request service. As long as the connection is up, this signal continues to exist.

Disconnect

The *disconnect*, as its name implies, is used to terminate the call. Several forms of disconnect operations are available. The first disconnect described is known as calling-customer control of disconnect. This is also known as forward control of disconnect, forward disconnect, or calling-party control. It is used by the calling end to signify that the connection is no longer needed. Forward disconnect is an on-hook signal. In order to distinguish this on-hook signal from other on-hook signals, the forward-disconnect signal must exceed 150 ms. Typically, this signal ranges from 150 to 400 ms.

The second form of disconnect is called calling-customer control of disconnect with forced disconnect. As this name implies, even though the customer may disconnect at any time, the call may also be disconnected when an on-hook signal is received from the network.

Yet another form of disconnect is known as operator control of disconnect. Once again as the name implies, the operator controls the disconnect on outgoing trunks to operator-services systems. The end-offices are designed to support customer control of disconnect, until the operator office returns off-hook supervision to indicate that the operator office is ready to accept the call. For the duration of the call, this off-hook signal remains in the system, which essentially locks the calling customer to the operator office. Eventually, the operator office recognizes an on-hook from either a called or calling party and reverts to on-hook toward the end office, and this forces a disconnect of the customer.

Signaling Integrity Check

During the call setup, the network performs a signaling integrity check to test the ability of the trunk to handle the connection. The test detects, identifies, and records troubles and ensures a caller is not "suspended" with no activity from the service provider.

While the exact type of check varies between systems, the most common types are a delay-dial or wink-start signal, which is called an integrity check. The second type, used on wire trunks only, is called a continuity and polarity check. SS7 uses the initial COT to describe a continuity check. The integrity check is some form of a wink-start signal or delay-dial signal. The COT requires circuit continuity and the correct polarity on the tip and ring of the trunk.

Wink-Start Signaling

Wink-start and delay-start signals are off-hook signals of varying durations. They are used from the called end to control the calling end's operations, usually the beginning of pulsing the address digits of a called party number. The duration of the wink ranges between 140 ms and 290 ms, but due to transmission delays and distortion occurrences, the wink may range between 100 ms and 350 ms in duration.

Figure 2–2 shows an example of the use of wink-start signaling. Notice that it is sent by the receiving end. The end of the wink-start signal must not occur until 210 ms after the receipt of the incoming seizure signal.

MULTIFREQUENCY (MF) PULSING

To this point in the chapter, we have discussed several types of signals and tests that are used on in-band, analogy systems. Most of these signals are represented with the off-hook/on-hook operations or the measurement of a voltage level on the circuit.

In addition to these simple arrangements, most analog telephone systems in use in modern countries use multifrequency (MF) pulsing. This type of signaling consists of combinations of frequencies to send other kinds of information over trunks. The combinations of two frequencies represents a pulse and as depicted in Table 2–1, where each combination represents a digit. These signals fall within the speech bandwidth, so they can be sent over regular voice channels. MF pulses are used to transfer information to the control equipment that sets up the connections through the switches.

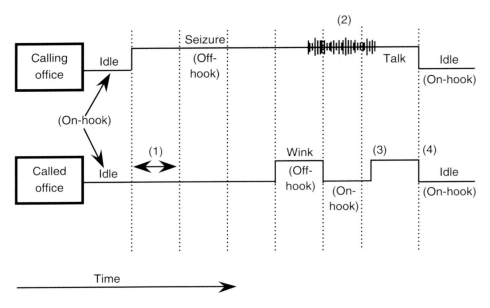

1. Transmission delay
2. Multifrequency pulses
3. Answer
4. Disconnect

Figure 2–2   Wink-start signaling.

MF pulsing is also used to send information on the call in a BOC Centralized Automatic Message Accounting-Automatic Number Identification (CAMA-ANI) procedure. The calling number is transmitted from the originating end office to the CAMA office after the sending of the called number. For equal access arrangements to an IC, the calling number is sent first, followed by the called number.

Two control signals listed in Table 2–1 are of particular interest because they must be interpreted by an SS7 gateway and mapped into SS7 messages (signaling units). They are the key pulse signal and the start signal.

A key pulse (KP) signal is a multifrequency tone of 1100 + 1700 Hz ranging from 90 to 120 ms. Its function is to indicate the beginning (the start) of pulsing, that is, the dialed number follows the KP signal. The start (ST) signal does not mean the start of the signal. It indicates the end of the pulsing—that is, the end of the dialed telephone number. From the perspective of the telephone exchange, it represents the beginning of the processing of the signal.

Table 2–1   Multifrequency Codes

Frequencies (Hz)	Digit and Control
700 + 900	1
700 + 1100	2
700 + 1300	4
700 + 1500	7
700 + 1700	
900 + 1100	3
900 + 1300	5
900 + 1500	8
900 + 1700	
1100 + 1300	6
1100 + 1500	9
1100 + 1700	KP
1300 + 1500	0
1300 + 1700	
1500 + 1700	ST

DUAL-TONE MULTIFREQUENCY (DTMF) PULSING

For customer stations, another signaling arrangement is used called dual-tone multifrequency (DTMF) signaling. DTMF is provided for the pushbuttons on the telephone set. This form of signaling provides sixteen distinct signals, and each signal uses two frequencies selected from two sets of four groups. Table 2–2 shows the arrangement for the DTMF pairs.

Table 2–2   DTMF Pairs

		High Group (Hz)			
		1209	1336	1477	1633
	697	1		3	A
Low	770	4	5	6	B
Group	852	7	8	9	C
(Hz)	941	*	0	#	D

EXAMPLES OF TELEPHONE CALLS

In the introduction to this chapter, I stated that digital signaling systems must support (interwork with) the older analog signaling systems because analog is still the pervasive technology used in the local loop. In Chapter 13, several examples are provided to the interworking operations. If you are not interested in analog control signaling, you can skip this section, as well as the section in Chapter 13 titled "CCS Call Setup without ISDN."

These examples are not all-inclusive, but they represent common implementations. For the reader who needs information on each service option offered by the U.S. BOCs, I refer you to Bellcore Document SR-TSV-002275, Issue 2, April 1994.

Example One: Feature Group B (FGB)

The BOCs classify several of their access arrangements with the title "Feature Group." This example (Figure 2–3) is feature group B, which specifies an access agreement between an LEC end office (EO) and an interexchange carrier (IC).

With this arrangement, the calls to the IC must use the initial address of:

$$(I) + 950 + WXXX$$

where: W = 0/1.

Figure 2–3 is largely self-explanatory, but some rules for the signaling sequences shown in the figure should be helpful. For calls from EOs or an access tandem: (1) The carrier returns a wink signal with 4 seconds of trunk seizure, and (2) the carrier returns an off-hook signal within 5 seconds of completion of the address outpulsing. For calls from a carrier to an EO or access tandem: (1) The end office or access tandem returns the wink-start signal within 8 seconds of trunk seizure; (2) the carrier starts outpulsing the address with 3.5 seconds of the wink; and (3) the carrier completes sending the address sequence within 20 seconds.

Example Two: Operator Service Signaling (OSS)

OSS signaling is similar to one of the feature groups (FGC, not explained in this book), but it has some characteristics that may be more familiar to the reader. Figure 2–4 shows these operations with six events.

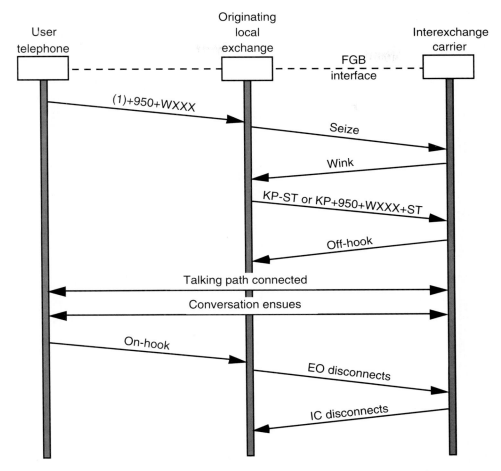

User telephone

Originating local exchange

Interexchange carrier

FGB interface

(1)+950+WXXX

Seize

Wink

KP-ST or KP+950+WXXX+ST

Off-hook

Talking path connected

Conversation ensues

On-hook

EO disconnects

IC disconnects

Figure 2–3   Example of trunk-side access arrangement.

In event 1, the customer dials 10XXX+(1)+7 or 10, or 10XXX+0+7 or 10. Upon receiving these signals, the EO (event 2) seizes an outgoing trunk. In event 3, the OS facility responds with a wink. Upon receiving the wink signal, in event 4 the EO outpulses the called number after a delay of 40 to 200 ms. The outpulsing is KP + 7/10 digits + ST (STP, ST2P, ST3P), or KP+STP(ST3P)

In event 5, the OS facility will go off-hook (any time of the start of the ST pulse. Off-hook indicates its ability to receive ANI.

In event 6, the EO sends the ANI (after a delay of 40–200 ms). The signals are KP + 02 + ST (STP).

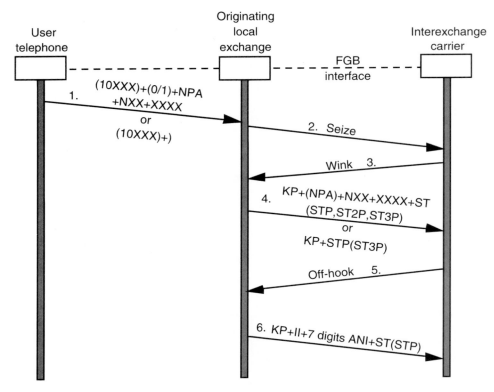

Figure 2–4   Operator service signaling (OSS).

SUMMARY

Analog in-band control signaling does not exist in an all-digital out-of-band signaling system. Nonetheless, an SS7-based system must support this older technology due to is continued wide use throughout the world.

3

The Integrated Services Digital Network (ISDN) Architecture

INTRODUCTION

This chapter introduces the Integrated Services Digital Network (ISDN) architecture. The ISDN reference points and functional groups are explained with examples of typical implementations. ISDN logical and physical channels are introduced, as well as the D and B channels. At the end of the chapter, the ISDN terminal adapter (TA) is introduced, with an explanation of how a TA supports existing non-ISDN equipment.

GOALS OF ISDN

Chapter 1 introduced ISDN and explained some of its features. As a brief review, recall that ISDN is a digital transport and signaling system that conveys both user traffic and control signaling across the same physical channel. This type of technology is classified as a physical in-band/logical out-of-band system.

Although other standards groups and enterprises are involved in publishing ISDN-related standards, the ITU-T is the authoritative standards body that develops and publishes the ISDN specifications. From the perspective of the ITU-T and the other standards groups, ISDN was created to:

- Provide a worldwide, uniform digital user network interface (UNI) to support a wide range of services.
- Provide a uniform set of standards for digital transmission between different vendors' equipment, and, insofar as possible, use the same standards across different countries.
- Keep internal changes to a public digital network transparent to the end user.
- In conjunction with the last objective, provide for end-user application independence—no consideration is made as to the applications' characteristics in relation to the ISDN itself.
- As an adjunct to the last two goals, provide portability of user stations and applications.

ISDN is centered on three main areas: (1) the standardization of services offered to subscribers in order to foster international compatibility; (2) the standardization of user-to-network interfaces in order to foster independent terminal equipment and network equipment development; and (3) the standardization of network capabilities in order to foster user-to-network and network-to-network communications.

ASPECTS OF ISDN

Figure 3–1 shows some important aspects of ISDN. The ISDN operations occur between the user equipment (telephones, PBXs, personal computers, workstations) and the network. Typically, the network is provided by the public telephone companies. The operations inside the network are not defined by ISDN, and as we learned in Chapter 1; SS7 is the prevalent technology there. Thus, ISDN provides a standardized, digital interface to the network. This interface is vendor and application independent.

Well, perhaps it is independent, but vendor independence depends upon how well the actual implementations of ISDN have been standardized and if the vendors' products have been tested for conformance. In the United States and Europe, standardized implementations and conformance testing have been quite successful. In the United States, this effort was achieved through the Bellcore and BOC's National ISDN, described in Chapter 6.

Application independence depends on how the ISDN service provider establishes services on the ISDN interface, and how much band-

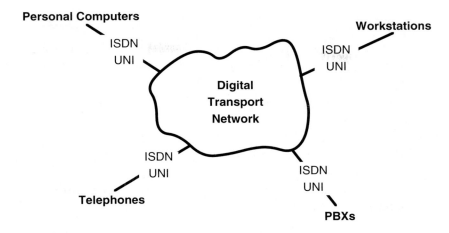

UNI: Standard interface; all digital; application independent; vendor independent

Figure 3–1   The Integrated Service Digital Network (ISDN).

width is provided. Ideally, ISDN does not care about the application, but it is important to keep in mind that ISDN was designed primarily for circuit-switched voice traffic, and secondarily, for anything else. These points will be revisited later in the chapter.

INTERFACES AND FUNCTIONAL GROUPINGS

The user interface to ISDN is a very similar arrangement to that of X.25. An end-user device connects to an ISDN node through a UNI protocol. Of course, the ISDN and X.25 interfaces are used for two different functions. The X.25 UNI provides a connection to a packet-switched data network; while ISDN provides a connection to an ISDN node, which can then connect to a voice, video, or data network.

Two definitions are in order (refer to Figure 3–2). Functional groupings (TE, TA, NT2, etc.) are a set of capabilities needed in an ISDN user-access interface. Specific functions within a functional grouping may be performed by multiple pieces of equipment or software. Second, reference points (R, S, T, and U) are the interfaces dividing the functional groupings. Usually, a reference point corresponds to a physical interface between pieces of equipment. The reference points labeled R, S, T, and U

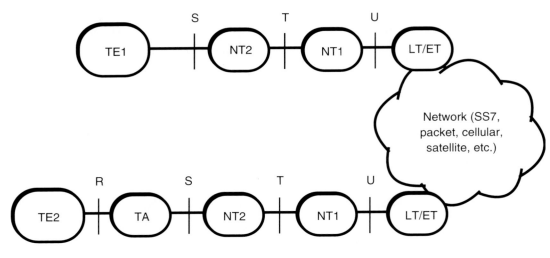

where:
ET   Exchange termination
LT   Line termination
NT   Network termination
TA   Terminal adapter
TE   Terminal equipment

Figure 3–2   ISDN model: Interfaces and functional groupings.

are logical interfaces between the functional groupings, which can be either a terminal type 1, a terminal type 2, or a network termination grouping. The purpose of the reference points is to delineate where the responsibility of the network operator ends or begins.

The U reference point is the reference point for the two-wire side of the NT1 equipment. It separates a NT1 from the line termination (LT) equipment. The R reference point represents non-ISDN interfaces, such as RS-422 or V.35.

The end-user ISDN terminal is identified by the ISDN term TE1. The TE1 connects to the ISDN through a twisted-pair four-wire digital link. The TE2 connects to a terminal adapter (TA), which is a device that allows non-ISDN terminals to operate over ISDN lines. The TA and TE2 devices are connected to either an ISDN NT1 or NT2 device. The NT1 is a device that connects the four-wire subscriber wiring to the conventional two-wire local loop. ISDN allows up to eight terminal devices to be addressed by NT1. The NT1 is responsible for the physical layer functions, such as signaling synchronization and timing. NT1 provides a user with a standardized interface.

The NT2 is a more intelligent piece of equipment. It is typically found in a digital PBX and contains the layer 2 and 3 protocol functions. It can multiplex 23 B+D channels onto the line at a combined rate of 1.544 Mbit/s or 31 B+D channels at a combined rate of 2.048 Mbit/s. NT2 is optional and not often found in actual implementation.

Reference Points

Figure 3–3 provides a more detailed view of the ISDN reference points. The purpose of the reference points is to: define (1) the mechanical connectors, (2) the electrical signals, and (3) the procedures (protocols) that take place between the functional groups. As stated earlier, the S & T reference points are standardized internationally, and the U reference point is based on national standards within countries.

Depending on national or vendor implementations, network provider responsibilities end at the S, T, or U reference points: (1) At the S reference point, the network provider is responsible for NT2 and NT1; (2) at the T reference point, the network provider is responsible for NT1 only; and (3) at the U reference point, the network provider is responsible for neither NT1 nor NT2. The S and T reference points may be the same (combined), if functional group NT2 is not implemented (that is, no NT2 is used, known as zero NT2). For this arrangement, reference point S operates at reference point T.

The R reference point defines conventional interfaces, such as the ITU-T V-Series Recommendations, EIA-232-E, RS-442, etc. As shown in Figure 3–3 and Table 3–1, the R reference point delineates the boundary between the non-ISDN world and the ISDN world.

Functional Groups

Figure 3–4 and Table 3–2 provides more information on the ISDN functional groups. The end user device is identified by the ISDN term TE1 (terminal equipment, type 1). The TE1 connects to the ISDN through a twisted-pair four-wire digital link. This link uses time division

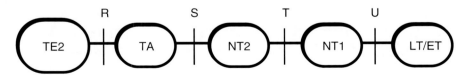

Figure 3–3   Reference points.

Table 3–1   Explanation of Reference Points

Purpose of reference points is to define:
- (a) Mechanical connectors
- (b) Electrical signals
- (c) Protocols between functional groups

Reference point types:
- S & T reference points: Standardized internationally

    S: 4 wires, 144 kbit/s

    T: same as S for BRI (basic rate interface)

    U reference point: Based on national standards

    In United States, a subscriber loop interface of two wires
- Depending on national or vendor implementations, network carrier responsibilities end at S, T, or U:
- (a) At S: Responsible for NT2 and NT1
- (b) At T: Responsible for NT1 only
- (c) At U: Responsible for neither NT1 or NT2
- S and T: May be the same (combined)
- R: Conventional interfaces, such as V Series, EIA-232-E

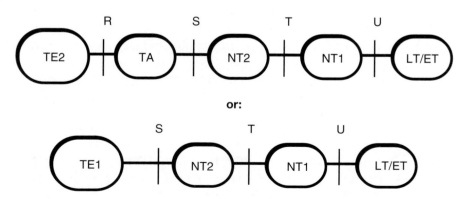

Figure 3–4   Functional groups.

Table 3–2   Explanation of Functional Groups

Purpose of functional groups is to define the role of ISDN machines:

- TE1: ISDN terminal equipment
- TE2: Non-ISDN equipment
- TA: Terminal adapter to map ISDN and non-ISDN operations
- NT1: Layer one functions
- NT2: Layer two and three functions

multiplexing (TDM) to provide three channels, designated as the B, B, and D channels (or 2 B+D). The B channels operate at a speed of 64 kbit/s; the D channel operates at 16 kbit/s. The 2 B+D is designated as the basic rate interface (BRI). ISDN also allows up to eight TE1s to share one 2 B+D channel.

The TE2 device is the current equipment in use such as terminals, workstations, and devices. The TE2 connects to the terminal adapter (TA), which is a device that allows non-ISDN terminals to operate over ISDN lines. The user side of the TA typically uses a conventional physical level interface such as EIA-232, or the V-series specifications. It is packaged like an external modem or as a board that plugs into an expansion slot on the TE2 devices. The EIA or V-series interface is called the R interface in ISDN terminology.

The TA and TE2 devices are connected through the basic access to either an ISDN NT1 or NT2 device (NT is network termination). Figure 3–4 shows several of the options. The NT1 is a customer premise device that connects the three-wire subscriber wiring to the conventional two-wire local loop. ISDN allows up to eight terminal devices to be accessed by NT1.

The NT1 is responsible for the physical layer functions, such as signaling, synchronization, and timing. It provides a user with a standardized interface.

The NT2 is a more intelligent piece of customer premise equipment (CPE). It is typically found in a digital PBX, and contains the layer 2 and 3 protocol functions. The NT2 device is capable of performing concentration services, meaning it multiplexes 23 B+D channels onto the line at a combined rate of 1.544 Mbit/s. This function is called the ISDN primary rate access, or interface as is referred to as the PRI.

The NT1 and NT2 devices maybe combined into a single device called NT12. This device handles the physical, data link, and network layer functions.

In summary, the TE equipment is responsible for user communications and the NT equipment is responsible for network communications.

A PRACTICAL VIEW

Figure 3–5 shows a typical implementation of a installation. The R reference point may be implemented with a conventional EIA-232 connector, although this interface is not common because it is restricted to transmission rates of 20 kbit/s. A more common arrangement is the use of RS-422 or V.35, which allows the exploitation of the 64 B or 128 ISDN B+B transfer rates.

The TA performs gateway services. It accepts the signals across the R interface, which are not coded in accordance with the ISDN standards. First, they do not use the same electrical conventions; and second, the digital encoding scheme is different. So, the TA translates and maps these signals into the ISDN standards. NT1 is a small piece of hardware that terminates the S/T four-wire loop with the U interface two-wire loop, which is terminated into the telephone central office.

ISDN LOGICAL CHANNEL CONCEPT

ISDN employs time division multiplexing (TDM) operations on its physical channels. The TDM slots contain user traffic (such as a voice signal or data signal), or control traffic (such as a call setup or network

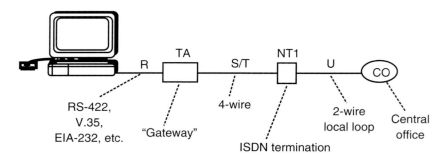

Figure 3–5   Typical ISDN installation.

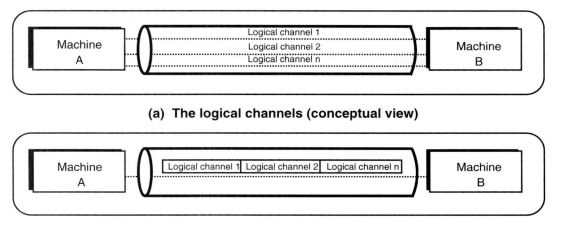

(a) The logical channels (conceptual view)

(b) The logical channels on the physical channel

Figure 3–6   ISDN logical channels.

management message). These slots are structured in accordance with concise rules to keep the traffic on the physical channel organized into discrete, identifiable signals. This approach is quite important, because it enables the receiving machine to discern the type of traffic in each of the received slots, and react accordingly.

As depicted in Figure 3–6, each slot is part of a "logical channel" that resides on the physical channel. The term logical channel is used to convey the idea of a logical association of TDM slots. On the physical media, the slots are discrete binary 1s and 0s. For ISDN, these slots are called D or B channels. Examples are shown in Table 3–3.

Each D channel is used to carry control/signaling information or user data. The B channels carry user voice, video, or data traffic. As shown in the figure, a D channel can operate at 16 or 64 kbit/s. The B

Table 3–3   Examples of ISDN Logical Channels

- D Channel: 16 or 64 kbit/s
- B Channel: 64 kbit/s
- H Channel: Aggregates of B channels
    - H0:   384 kbit/s (6 B channels)
    - H11:   1536 kbit/s (24 B channels)
    - H12:   1920 kbit/s (30 B channels) etc.

channel operates at 64 kbit/s, although a number of B channels can be aggregated together to provide a user application more transmission capacity. For example, an H0 channel is an aggregation of six B channels, and operates at 384 kbit/s

TYPICAL ISDN CONFIGURATION

The TE1 connects to the ISDN through a twisted-pair four-wire digital link (see Figure 3–7). This link uses TDM to provide three channels, designated as the B, B, and D channels (or 2 B+D). The B channels operate at a speed of 64 kbit/s; the D channel operates at 16 kbit/s. The 2 B+D is designated as the basic rate interface (BRI). ISDN also allows up to eight TE1s to share one 2 B+D link. The purpose of the B channels is to carry the user payload in the form of voice, compressed video, and data. The purpose of the D channel is to act as an out-of-band control channel for setting up, managing, and clearing the B channel sessions.

In other scenarios, the user DTE is called a TE2 device. As explained earlier, it is the current equipment in use such as IBM 3270 terminals and telex devices. The TE2 connects to a TA, which is a device that allows non-ISDN terminals to operate over ISDN lines. The user side of the TA typically uses a conventional physical layer interface such as EIA-232-D, RS-422 or the V-series specifications. It is packaged like

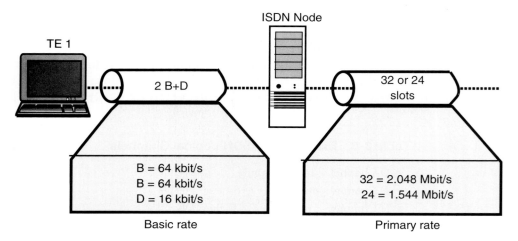

Figure 3–7   An ISDN configuration.

an external modem or as a board that plugs into an expansion slot on the
TE2 devices.

THE ISDN LAYERS

The ISDN approach is to provide an end user with full support
through the seven layers of the OSI Model, although ISDN confines itself
to defining the operations at layers 1, 2, and 3 of this model, as shown in
Figure 3–8. In so doing, ISDN is divided into two kinds of services: the
bearer services, responsible for providing support for the lower three layers of the seven-layer standard; and teleservices (for example, telephone,
message handling), responsible for providing support through all seven
layers of the model and generally making use of the underlying lower-

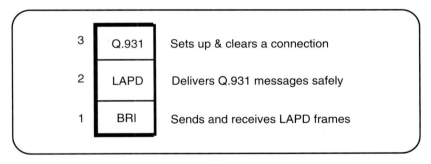

(a) Functions of the layers

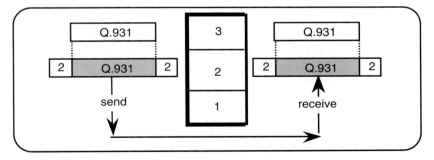

(b) Layer interaction

Figure 3–8   The ISDN layers.

layer capabilities of the bearer services. The services are referred to as low-layer and high-layer functions, respectively.

Figure 3–8 shows the ISDN layers and provides a brief description of their functions. Layer 1 (the physical layer) uses either BRI, utilizing 2 B+D concepts, or PRI, utilizing either 23 B+D or 31 B+D channel concepts. These standards are published in ITU-T's I Series as I.430 and I.431, respectively. Layer 2 (the data link layer) consists of LAPD and is published in the ITU-T Recommendation Q.921. Layer 3 (the network layer), is defined in the ITU-T Recommendation Q.931.

BRI CONFIGURATION OPTIONS

The BRI is configured as a point-to-point or multipoint topology at the S/T reference point. The U reference point does not support multipoint connections (nor do the PRI or B-ISDN interfaces). The point-to-point arrangement is a common implementation for dial-up services; for example, from a home to an Internet service provider. The multipoint arrangement is useful in situations where multiple terminals must share one physical channel, for example in a business office.

Terminal Endpoint Identifiers (TEIs)

We shall see later that the traffic on the BRI is placed into a LAPD frame. The address field in the frame contains a terminal endpoint identifier (TEI) and a service access point identifier (SAPI). The TEI and SAPI fields are known collectively as the data link connection identifier (DLCI). These entities are discussed in the following paragraphs (see Figure 3–9).

The TEI identifies either a single terminal (TE) or multiple terminals that are operating on the BRI link. The TEI value can be assigned automatically by a separate assignment procedure. A TEI value of all 1s identifies a broadcast connection. TEI values ranging from 0 through 63 make up the fixed TEIs and are assigned prior to a terminal logging on and accessing the ISDN channel. TEI values ranging from 64 through 126 make up the values that are assigned automatically by the network during the logon procedure. TEI 127 is used during this assignment procedure.

As a general practice, fixed TEIs are used with point-to-point configurations, and multipoint configurations use the automatic assignment procedure.

(a) Point-to-point

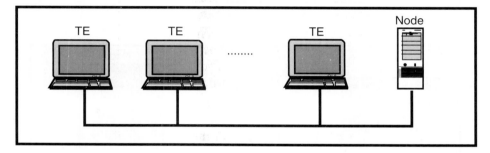

(b) Multi-point

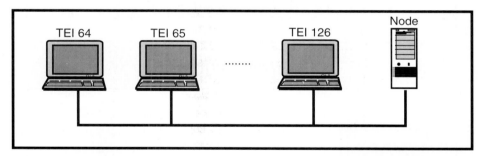

(c) Using TEIs to identify terminals

Figure 3–9   BRI configurations.

Service Access Point Identifiers (SAPIs)

The service access point identifier (SAPI) identifies the entity where the data link layer services are provided to the layer above (that is, layer 3). The SAPI is based on the OSI service access point concept and is shown in Figure 3–10.

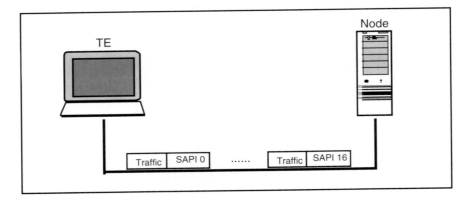

(a) SAPI usage

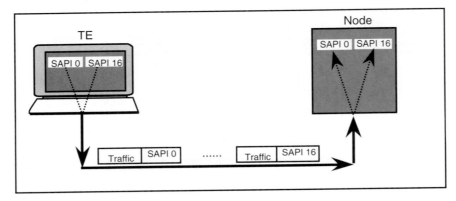

(b) From TE to node

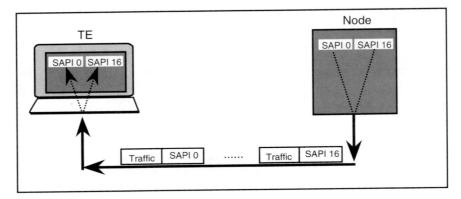

(c) From node to TE

Figure 3–10   Identifying processes with SAPIs.

The services invoked at a layer are dictated by the upper layer (e.g., ISDN's layer 3) passing primitives (transactions) to the lower layer (e.g., ISDN's layer 2).

Services are provided from the lower layer to the upper layer through a service access point (SAP). The SAP is nothing more than an identifier that identifies the entity in the layer that is performing a defined service.

It is the responsibility of the receiving lower layer (in concert of course with the operating system in the receiving machine) to pass the traffic to the proper destination SAP in the upper layer. If multiple entities (e.g., processes) exist in the machine, the SAP serves to properly identify the process.

One way to view the SAP concept is to consider it to be a software "port." It is akin to the socket concept found in the UNIX operating system environment. At the present time, these SAPIs are defined in ISDN:

SAPI Value	Frame Carries
0	Signaling (call control) information
1–15	Reserved
16	User traffic
17–31	Reserved
63	Management information
Others	Not available for layer 2 operations

Service Profiles

In addition to the TEI and SAPI, a service profile is available to identify and characterize a service that is offered by the network to a user. ISDN service providers offer different features to a customer and uses this operation to identify them.

The service profile is carried in a layer 3 Q.931 message and consists of:

- *Service profile ID (SPID)*. This value (used in United States) is sent in a Q.931 message from the user to the network to identify and invoke the user's specific service profile. This value is provided to the user at subscription time.
- *User service ID (USID)*. This value uniquely identifies a provider's service profile.

THE ISDN TERMINAL ADAPTER (TA)

The ITU-T recognizes that the V and X Series interface recommendations, and the EIA interfaces will be prevalent for many years. From the perspective of ITU-T, it is desirable to evolve quickly to all digital systems using the ISDN interface standards. From the perspective of the end users, this may not be quite as desirable. Nonetheless, the ITU-T has published several specifications to aid in the transition from the V and X Series, and the EIA interfaces to an all digital system using the ISDN standards (I and Q Series). To this end, the ISDN rate adapter (RA) and the ISDN terminal adapter (TA) provide conversions to/from the X, V, EIA, and ISDN protocol stacks and physical interfaces. They allow end users to retain their current equipment, yet obtain the services of the ISDN BRI. Figure 3–11 shows an arrangement using a terminal adapter (which includes the rate adapter).

The rate adapter is so named because it translates between the R interfaces transmission rates and ISDN S/T interface transmission rates. The R rates range from 300 bit/s to 56 kbit/s, whereas the S/T rates operate at 64 kbit/s.

The ISDN standards for terminal adapters define a wide variety of operations and options. For the reader who wishes to delve into detail on

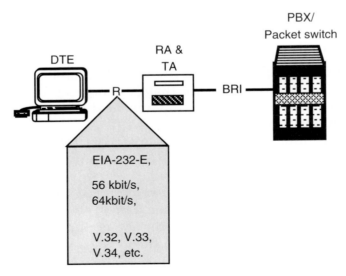

Figure 3–11   ISDN rate adapter (RA) and terminal adapter (TA).

some of the major operations, I refer you to Appendix C of this book. For the reader who wishes to know more about how a terminal adapter supports Internet access, I refer you to Chapter 6.

SUMMARY

ISDN is designed as an all-digital UNI. It is intended to be vendor and application independent. It supports user traffic on its B channels and allocates part of its bandwidth for signaling and control with its D channel. Through the use of TEIs and SAPIs, it can support and identify multiple workstations on the link, and applications within the workstations. And through the use of the TA, it can support non-ISDN interfaces.

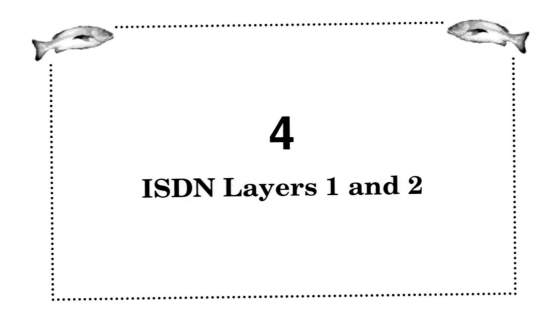

4

ISDN Layers 1 and 2

INTRODUCTION

This chapter examines the lower two layers of ISDN, known as the physical and data link layers. The electrical, coding, and framing conventions are described for layer 1. For layer 2, the link access procedure for the D channel (LAPD) is explained.

ISDN LAYER 1

Figure 4–1 shows the placement of the ISDN physical layer (layer 1) in the ISDN protocol stack. Physical layer protocols and interfaces are so named because (in ISDN links) the stations attached to the link are physically connected with wires and cables. Layer 1 is responsible for defining the connectors between equipment as well as the signals that traverse the link.

ISDN layer 1 describes these attributes of the interface: electrical, functional, mechanical, and procedural. The electrical attributes describe the voltage levels, the timing of the electrical signals, and all other electrical characteristics (e.g., capacitance, signal rise time). The functional attributes describe the functions to be performed by the physical interface, such as control, timing, data, and ground. The mechanical attributes describe the dimensions of the connectors and the number and type

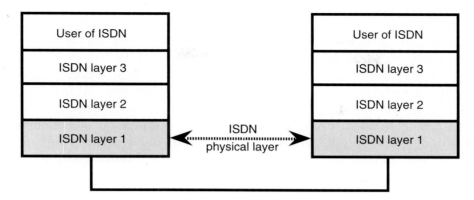

Figure 4–1   Layer 1 of ISDN.

of wires on the interface. The procedural attributes describe what the connectors must do and the sequence of events required to effect actual transfer of signals across the interface.

Location of the Interfaces

The wiring in the user premises is one continuous cable run with jacks for the TEs and NT attached directly to the cable. The jacks are located at interface points I_A and I_B (in Figure 4–2). One interface point, I_A, is adjacent to each TE. The other interface point, I_B, is adjacent to the NT. In some applications, the NT may be connected to the wiring without the use of a jack or with a jack that accommodates multiple interfaces.

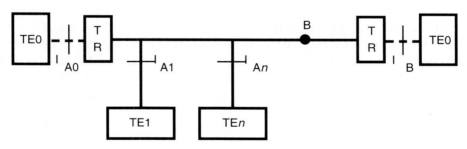

where:
  TR   Terminating resistor
  I   Electrical interface
  B   Location of IB when the terminating resistor (TR) is included in the NT

Figure 4–2   Configuration for wiring at the user premises.

Line Code

For both directions of transmission (TE↔NT), pseudo-ternary coding is used with 100 percent pulse width as shown in Figure 4–3. A binary 1 is represented by no line signal. A binary 0 is represented by a positive or negative pulse. The first binary 0 following the framing bit-balance bit is of the same polarity as the framing bit-balance bit. Subsequent binary 0s must alternate in polarity. A balance bit is a binary 0 if the number of binary 0s following the previous balance bit is odd. A balance bit is a binary 1 if the number of binary 0s following the previous balance bit is even.

Physical Layer Framing Conventions

The formats for the frames exchanged between the TE and the NT (over reference points S and T) are shown in Figure 4–4. The formats vary in each direction of transfer but are identical for point-to-point or multipoint configurations. The frames are 48 bits in length and are transmitted by the TE and NT every 250 microseconds (μs). The first bit of the frame transmitted to the NT is delayed by two bit periods with respect to the first bit of the frame received from the NT.

The 250 microsecond frame provides 4000 frames a second (1 second/.000250 = 4000) and a transfer rate of 192 kbit/s (4000 * 48 = 192,000). However, 12 bits in each frame are overhead, so the user data transfer rate is 144 kbit/s (4000 * [48 – 12] = 144,000).

The first two bits of the frame are the framing bit (F) and the DC balancing bit (L). These bits are used for frame synchronization. In addition, the L bit is used in the NT frame to electrically balance the frame and in the TE frame to electrically balance each B channel octet and each D channel bit. The auxiliary framing bit (F_a) and the N bit (in NT frame only) are also used in the frame alignment procedures. Bit A (in the NT frame only) is used for TE activation and deactivation. The echo bits ensure the link is free before a TE attempts the transmission of traffic.

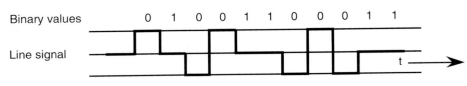

Figure 4–3   Pseudo-ternary code.

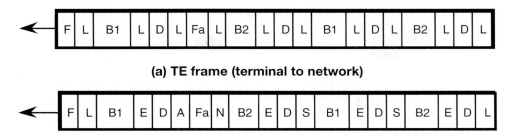

(a) TE frame (terminal to network)

(b) NT frame (network to terminal)

where:
F   Framing bit
L   DC balancing bit
B1   B1 channel bits
B2   B2 channel bits
D   D channel bits
Fa   Auxiliary training bit
E   Echo bits

Figure 4–4   Basic rate format.

The bit positions and their groups are summarized in Tables 4–1 and 4–2. Table 4–1 pertains to the TE frame and Table 4–2 pertains to the N7 frame.

Electrical Requirements for the Basic Access

Table 4–3 provides a summary of the physical layer characteristics in accordance with the ITU-T Recommendations.

THE 2B1Q LINE CODING SCHEME

After the 1988 release of ISDN was published, the ANSI T1D1.3 working group established a specification for local loop basic access signaling that ameliorated the problem of signal loss on the channel.

The ISDN uses the local loops currently in existence. Replacing the many millions of miles of unshielded copper wires comprising the local loop would entail unacceptable costs. The voice signal is carried on the local loop over a frequency range from approximately 50 Hz to 4 kHz. The ISDN basic rate access operates at much higher frequencies, in the range of about 200 kHz.

Signal loss increases with higher frequencies, so the high frequency signal loss is quite significant for loops of medium to long distances. For

Table 4–1   Physical Layer Framing

Bit position	Group
1 and 2	Framing signal with balance bit
3 to 11	B1-channel (first octet) with balance bit
12 and 13	D-channel bit with balance bit
14 and 15	F_a auxiliary framing bit or Q bit with balance bit
16 to 24	B2-channel (first octet) with balance bit
25 and 26	D-channel bit with balance bit
27 to 35	B1-channel (second octet) with balance bit
36 and 37	D-channel bit with balance bit
38 to 46	B2-channel (second octet) with balance bit
47 and 48	D-channel bit with balance bit

Table 4–2   Physical Layer Framing (*continued*)

Bit position	Group
1 and 2	Framing signal with balance bit
3 to 10	B1-channel (first octet)
11	E, D-echo-channel bit
12	D-channel bit
13	Bit A used for activation
14	F_a auxiliary framing bit
15	N bit
16 to 23	B2-channel (first octet)
24	E, D-echo-channel bit
25	D-channel bit
26	M, multiframing bit
27 to 34	B1-channel (second octet)
35	E, D-echo-channel bit
36	D-channel bit
37	S, the use of this bit is for further study
38 to 45	B2-channel (second octet)
46	E, D-echo-channel bit
47	D-channel bit
48	Frame balance bit

Table 4–3 Electrical Characteristics for Basic Access

Description	Characteristics
Interchange circuit characteristics:	
Terminating resistor	$100\ \Omega \pm 5\%$
Maximum attenuation (at 96 kHz) in the point-to-point configuration	6 dB
Minimum longitudinal conversion loss (at 96 kHz)	43 dB
Upper limit value for NT-TE-NT round trip delay	$42.0\ \mu s$
Transmitter characteristics:	
Voltage-limited current or voltage feeding	
Pulse amplitude at $50\ \Omega^c$	$750\ mV \pm 10\% = V_{nom}$
400 Ω	90^e to 160% V_{nom}
5.6 Ω	$\leqslant 20\%\ V_{nom}$
Output impedance	
when transmitting a pulse	$\geqslant 20\%\ \Omega$
during a space	Specified values depend on frequency
Jitter in NT output signal (peak-to-peak)	$\leqslant 0.26\ \mu s$
Jitter in TE output signal	$\leqslant \pm0.36\ \mu s$
Phase displacement in the TE between input and output	$-0.36\ \mu s$ to $+0.78\ \mu s$
Frame offset between TE input and TE output	$10.4\ \mu s$
Receiver characteristics:	
Input impedance	Specified values depend on frequency

example, a test by NYNEX several years ago revealed the following performances, on local loops using 26-gauge wire:

- 3700 feet: Loss of 15 dB (decibels)
- 9000 feet: Loss of 30 dB
- 18000 feet: Loss of 40 to 50 dB

Since the majority of local loops are longer than 9000 feet, it is obvious that the high frequency ISDN signals presented problems. Moreover, the NYNEX test demonstrated that noise and crosstalk creates significant distortion of ISDN frequencies.

Binary	Quaternary	
10	+3	
11	+1	
01	−1	
00	−3	

Figure 4–5   2B1Q line code.

A partial solution to this problem was offered by a new coding scheme. It is called 2 binary 1 quaternary (2B1Q) (see Figure 4–5). With 2B1Q, each signal change represents two binary bits. Consequently, a signaling rate of 80 kHz provides a bit transfer rate of 160 kbit/s. The lower frequencies provide better performance over the loops.

ISDN LAYER 2

The ISDN provides a data link protocol (layer 2) for devices to communicate with each other across the D channel. This protocol is LAPD, which is a subset of high level data link control (HDLC), a widely used international standard. The LAPD implementation of HDLC protocol is independent of a transmission bit rate and it requires a full duplex, bit-transparent, synchronous channel.

Figure 4–6 shows the position of LAPD in the ISDN layers. An end user may obtain the services of LAPD directly, without going through

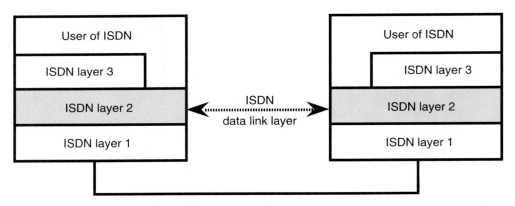

Note: As an option, the user layer can reside directly on top of layer 2.

Figure 4–6   Layer 2 of ISDN.

layer 3. This option is available for data applications but not voice connections. The idea behind this concept is that the D channel is reserved for control signaling, such as setting up and tearing down a connection; consequently, it is not used continuously. During periods of inactivity, the D channel is available for the transport of bursty, asynchronous data traffic. This option is not provided for voice calls, because they use the B channel and, as Chapter 5 explains, must invoke layer 3 to set up the call.

LAPD is responsible for providing the following support to layer 3, or to an end user's data application:

- Provides safe delivery of the traffic across the link.
- Uses special codes (a specific stream of bits) to distinguish the beginning and ending of the traffic.
- Provides for flow control mechanisms to prevent buffer overflow at a receiver.
- Supports the TEI and SAPI to permit multiple terminals and applications to share on BRI link (Chapter 3 explains these identifiers).
- Maintains an awareness of link conditions, such as distinguishing between data and control signals, and determining if the link is operating properly.

LAPD Architecture

In order to understand LAPD, it is necessary to explain several concepts that are part of HDLC. First, HDLC provides for a number of options to satisfy a wide variety of user requirements. It supports both half-duplex and full-duplex transmission, point-to-point and multipoint configuration, as well as switched or nonswitched channels. LAPD is used on a full duplex, point-to-point, or multipoint channel, so it does not use all the HDLC options.

The Combined Station Approach. A LAPD station is called an HDLC combined station. This term can be explained by first describing primary and secondary stations and using these terms to explain the LAPD station.

A *primary station* is in control of the link. This station acts as a master and transmits command frames to the secondary stations on the channel. In turn, it receives response frames from those stations. If the link is multipoint channel, the primary station is responsible for maintaining a separate session with each station connected to the link. The *secondary station* acts as a slave to the primary station. It responds to the commands from the primary station in the form of responses.

The *combined station* approach is used by LAPD. Communicating stations on the same ISDN link can transmit and receive commands and responses to/from each other without waiting for a solicitation for data. This approach is clearly preferred over a primary/secondary link configuration, because the ISDN channel is full duplex. It makes no sense to wait for permission to send data when a path is available in each direction.

Remember, the ISDN physical layer (layer 1) runs a protocol that ensures the attached multipoint stations do not transmit at the same time, which, of course, is what a combined mode of operation permits.

The Balanced Mode of Operation. An HDLC balanced configuration consists of two combined stations connected point-to-point only, operating at half duplex or full duplex, on switched or nonswitched links. The combined stations have equal status on the link and may send unsolicited traffic to each other. Each station has equal responsibility for link control. Typically, a station uses a command in order to solicit a response from the other station. The other station can send its own command as well. LAPD uses the balanced option of HDLC, but only on full duplex, point-to-point, or multipoint links.

In conjunction with the balanced configuration, LAPD uses the asynchronous balanced mode (ABM) feature of HDLC. This simply means that the combined station may initiate transmissions without receiving prior permission from the other combined station.

Sequence Numbers and State Variables. LAPD maintains accountability of the traffic and controls the flow of frames by state variables and sequence numbers. Sequence numbers are coded in the control field of the LAPD frame, which is discussed shortly.

The N(S) (send sequence) number indicates the sequence number associated with a transmitted frame. The N(R) (receive sequence) number indicates the sequence number that is expected at the receiving site. The value of N(R) also serves to acknowledge all frames that were transmitted previously.

The traffic at both the transmitting and receiving stations are controlled by counters that are called state variables. The transmitting site maintains a send state variable [V(S)], which is set to the value of the sequence number of the next frame to be transmitted. The receiving site maintains a receive state variable [V(R)], which contains the number that it expects to be in the sequence number of the next frame. The $V(S)$ is incremented with each frame transmitted, and placed in the $N(S)$ field in the frame.

Upon receiving the frame, the receiving station checks the $N(S)$ with its $V(R)$. If the cyclic redundancy check (CRC) passes and if the $V(R)$ value equals the $N(S)$ in the received frame, then it increments $V(R)$ value by one, places this value in the receive sequence number field $N(R)$ in the next frame to be sent, and sends it to the transmitting site to complete the acknowledgment for the transmission.

If the $V(R)$ value does not match the sending sequence number in the received frame (or the CRC does not pass), an error has occurred, and a reject frame with the value in $V(R)$ is sent to the transmitting site. The $V(R)$ value informs the originator of the next frame that it is expected to send, that is, the number of the frame the originating site is to retransmit. With the reject feature, the rejected frame and all succeeding frames must be retransmitted

The LAPD Frame

Figure 4–7 depicts the LAPD frame and its relationship to the ISDN layer 3, Q.931 specification. The Q.931 message is carried within the LAPD frame in the I (information) field. LAPD ensures that the Q.931 messages are transmitted across the link, after which the frame fields are stripped and the message is presented to the network layer. The principal function of the link layer is to deliver the Q.931 message error-free despite the possible error-prone nature of the communications link.

The LAPD frame is constructed of address, control, information, and a frame check sequence fields with a flag field placed before and after these fields.

The LAPD frame format is similar to HDLC, but LAPD utilizes the TEI and SAPI concepts in the address field (as we learned in Chapter 3). Also, by certain conventions regarding the bit sequence of the SAPI and TEI octets, these fields can be used to advise the recipient of the frame as to how the frame is to be interpreted. A few points should be made about the TEI and SAPI. First, a TEI set to all 1s is a broadcast TEI, and all stations on the link will process the frame that contains this value in the TEI. Second, TEIs of 0 to 63 are selected by the user; TEIs of 64 to 126 are automatically assigned by the network to a station. Third, a SAPI of 63 is used for management operations on the link, principally for the identification of the users on the link. For the reader who wishes more details on the SAPI = 63 procedures, I refer you to ITU-T's Blue Book, X.921, Volume VI, Fascicle V1.10, Chapter 5.

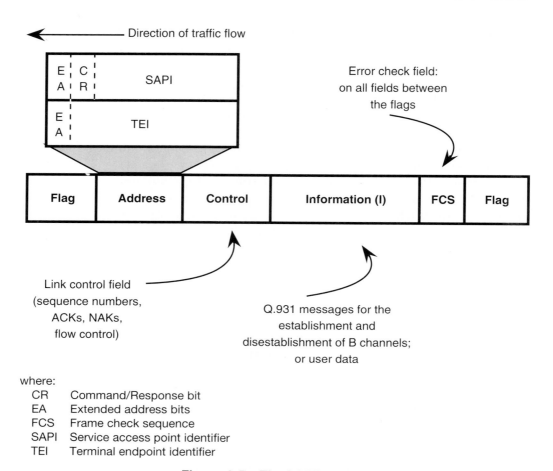

Figure 4–7   The LAPD frame.

The first bit of the TEI and SAPI octet is the extended address (EA) bit. The extended address (EA) bits can be used to stipulate a larger address field if the data link connection identifier (TEI/SAPI) needs to be expanded. The second bit of the SAPI is the C/R bit.

When the command/response (C/R) bit is set to one, it indicates that the address frame is to be interpreted as a command; or when set to a zero, it indicates a response. The receipt of a command frame dictates certain actions at the receiver, such as responding immediately by sending back a certain type of frame. The rules for the use of the C/R bit are as follows:

Command: Network side to user side, C/R = 1
Command: User side to network side, C/R = 0

Response: Network side to user side, C/R = 0

Response: User side to network side, C/R = 1

The frame check sequence field (FCS) is used to detect errors (damaged bits) that occurred during transmission of the frame across the link. The hardware implementation of the LAPD FCS is accomplished with a shift register. The transmitter initializes the register to all 1s and then changes the register contents by the division of the generator polynomial on the A, C, and I fields. The 1s complement of the resulting remainder is then transmitted as the FCS field. At the receiver, the register is also set to all 1s, and the A, C, I, and FCS fields are subjected to the calculation and checked for errors.

LAPD uses a convention in which the calculation by the generator polynomial $x^{16} + x^{12} + x^5 + 1$ is always 0001110100001111 (7439 decimal), if no bits have been damaged during the transmission between the transmitter and receiver.

The FCS field is created by a cyclic redundancy check (CRC) of the frame. The transmitting station performs Modulo 2 division (based on an established polynomial) on the A, C, and I fields plus sixteen leading zeros and appends the remainder as the FCS field. In turn, the receiving station performs a division with the same polynomial on the address, control, information, and FCS fields. If the remainder equals a predetermined value, the chances are quite good that the transmission occurred without any errors. If the comparisons do not match, it indicates a probable transmission error, in which case the receiving station sends a negative acknowledgment. This requires a transmitting station to retransmit the frame.

Bit Stuffing

LAPD is a code-transparent protocol. It does not rely on a specific code (ASCII/IA5, EBCDIC, etc.) for the interpretation of line control. For example, bit position n within a control field has a specific meaning, regardless of the other bits in the field. However, on occasion, a flag-like field, 01111110, may be inserted into the user data stream (I field) by the application process. More frequently, the bit patterns in the other fields may appear "flag-like." To prevent "phony" flags from being inserted into the frame, the transmitter inserts a zero bit after it encounters five continuous 1s anywhere between the opening and closing flag of the frame. Consequently, zero insertion applies to the address, control, information, and FCS fields. This technique is called *bit stuffing*. As the frame is stuffed, it is transmitted across the link to the receiver. The receiver performs a complementary function and removes the stuffed bits before any further processing of the frame.

Commands and Responses

Table 4–4 lists the HDLC commands and responses that are used with LAPD and Table 4–5 provides a summary of their operations. A connection is set up through the sending of a set asynchronous balanced

Table 4–4   Commands and Responses in the LAPD Control Field

Format	Control Field Bit								Commands	Responses
	Encoding									
	1	*2*	*through*	*8*	*9*	*10*	*through*	*16*		
Information	0	—	N(S)	—	•	—	N(R)	—	I	
	1	*2*	*3*	*4*	*5*	*9*	*through*	*16 (4–8 are all 0s)*		
Supervisory	1	0	0	0	•	—	N(R)	—	RR	RR
	1	0	0	1	•	—	N(R)	—	REJ	REJ
	1	0	1	0	•	—	N(R)	—	RNR	RNR
	1	*2*	*3*	*4*	*5*	*6*	*7*	*8*		
Unnumbered	1	1	0	0	•	0	0	0	UI	
	1	1	0	0	•	0	1	0	DISC	
	1	1	0	0	•	1	1	0		UA
	1	1	1	0	•	0	0	1		FRMR
	1	1	1	1	•	0	0	0		DM
	1	1	1	1	•	1	1	0	SABME	
	1	1	1	1	•	1	0	1	XID	XID

where:
I	Information
RR	Receive Ready
REJ	Reject
RNR	Receive Not Ready
UI	Unnumbered Information
FRMR	Frame Reject
DISC	Disconnect
XID	Exchange Identification
DM	Disconnect Mode
SABME	Set ABM Extended Mode
•	The P/F Bit

Table 4–5   LAPD Frame Types

- *Information (I).* Used to send the LAPD I field, which contains an ISDN layer three Q.931 message, or user data traffic.
- *Receive Ready (RR).* Indicates station is ready to receive traffic and/or acknowledge previously received frames by using the N(R) field.
- *Receive Not Ready (RNR).* Indicates the transmitting station that the receiving station is unwilling to accept additional incoming data. The RNR frame may acknowledge previously transmitted frames by using the N(R) field.
- *Reject (REJ).* Requests the retransmission of frames starting with the frame numbered in the N(R) field.
- *Unnumbered Information (UI).* Allows for transmission of user data in an unnumbered (i.e., unsequenced) frame.
- *Disconnect (DISC).* Places the station in the disconnected mode.
- *Disconnect Mode (DM).* Transmitted to indicate a station is in the disconnect mode (not operational).
- *Set Asynchronous Balanced Mode Extended (SABME).* Sets SABM with two octets in the control field for extended sequencing.
- *Reset (RESET).* Used for reinitialization. Previously unacknowledged frames remain unacknowledged.
- *Unnumbered Acknowledgment (UA).* Acknowledges frames that do not contain an I field, for example, the SABME frame.
- *Frame Reject(FRMR).* Rejects a frame that passed the CRC check, but is otherwise not intelligible (usually, because of a field that is not coded correctly).
- *Exchange Identification (XID).* Used to exchange an I field without the use of sequence numbers. Not used for delivery of Q.931 traffic.

mode, extended frame (SABME), and the receipt of an unnumbered acknowledgment frame (UA). After this connection is established, ongoing traffic is exchanged with information frames (I), and unnumbered information frames (UI). The information frame mode uses sequence numbers, ACKs, NAKs, and retransmissions of errored frames. The UI frame mode does not employ these services.

The flow control capabilities are implemented with the receive ready (RR) and receive not ready (RNR) frames. Negative acknowledgments are signaled with the reject (REJ) frames. Upon the receipt of a REJ frame, the terminal must initiate retransmission procedures.

The disconnect frame (DISC) logically disconnects the LAPD session. It means that the terminal will no longer acknowledge frames. The disconnect mode (DM) frame informs the recipient of the frame that the station does not acknowledge.

Table 4–5 summarizes all of the LAPD command and response frames.

The flow control capabilities are implemented with the receive ready (RR) and receive not ready (RNR) frames. Negative acknowledgments are signaled with the reject (REJ) frames. Upon the receipt of a REJ frame, the terminal must initiate retransmission procedures.

The disconnect frame (DISC) logically disconnects the LAPD session. It means that the terminal will no longer acknowledge frames. The disconnect mode (DM) frame informs the recipient of the frame that the station does not acknowledge.

The exchange identification (XID) frame is used for ongoing link administration. The frame reject (FRMR) frame is used to reject a frame that has completed the FCS operation but could not be processed further (usually, because the address or control field could not be interpreted.

Examples of LAPD Operations

Figure 4–8 provides several examples of LAPD operations and the exchange of frames between two machines, a TE and an NT. The full contents of the frames are not shown for purposes of simplicity. The LAPD retransmission timer (T200)[1] is also introduced in this figure. The process begins in event 1 by the TE sending a set asynchronous balanced extended frame (SABME) to the NT; the NT responds with an unnumbered acknowledgment frame (UA) in event 2. The effect of this initial "handshake" is to set up a layer 2 connection by reserving buffer space for the receipt of frames, and initializing several counters, variables, and sequence numbers that are used to keep track of the frames as they are sent across the channel. This handshake also invokes a process in each machine to govern the upcoming dialogue.

Notice that the T200 timer is turned on when frames are sent and turned off when an acknowledgment is received. This operation (and the T200 timer) pertains to the control frames and the information frames. In addition, if a satisfactory response is not received before T200 expires, the station will resend the outstanding frame a given number of times. The number of retries is set by a retry parameter stored at each machine.

After the SABME and UA are exchanged successfully, the ISDN stations can exchange frames. The remainder of Figure 4–8 shows these ex-

---

[1]LAPD uses other timers to manage link activities. This example illustrates the most common timer.

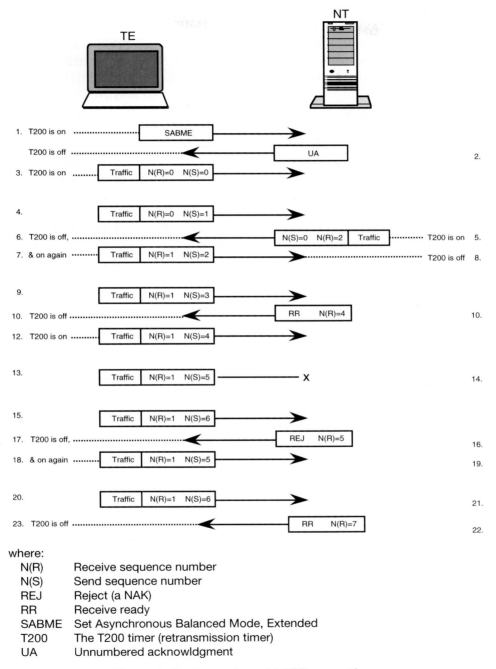

1. T200 is on ············· | SABME |
   T200 is off ············· | UA | 2.
3. T200 is on ········· | Traffic | N(R)=0 N(S)=0 |

4. | Traffic | N(R)=0 N(S)=1 |
6. T200 is off, ············· | N(S)=0 N(R)=2 | Traffic | ············ T200 is on   5.
7. & on again ········· | Traffic | N(R)=1 N(S)=2 | ···················· T200 is off   8.

9. | Traffic | N(R)=1 N(S)=3 |
10. T200 is off ············· | RR   N(R)=4 | 10.
12. T200 is on ··········· | Traffic | N(R)=1 N(S)=4 |

13. | Traffic | N(R)=1 N(S)=5 | ─── X   14.

15. | Traffic | N(R)=1 N(S)=6 |
17. T200 is off, ············· | REJ   N(R)=5 | 16.
18. & on again ·········· | Traffic | N(R)=1 N(S)=5 | 19.

20. | Traffic | N(R)=1 N(S)=6 | 21.
23. T200 is off ············· | RR   N(R)=7 | 22.

where:
N(R)	Receive sequence number
N(S)	Send sequence number
REJ	Reject (a NAK)
RR	Receive ready
SABME	Set Asynchronous Balanced Mode, Extended
T200	The T200 timer (retransmission timer)
UA	Unnumbered acknowldgment

Figure 4–8   Examples of LAPD operations.

changes. In events 3 and 4, the TE begins the exchange of traffic by sending its first two frames to the NT; the first frame is sequenced with $N(S) = 0$, and the second frame is sequenced with $N(S) = 1$. The $N(R)$ fields in these frames are set to 0 to indicate to the NT that the TE is expecting a frame from the NT with the $N(S)$ set to 0. (During the SABME/UA operations, both stations set their $N(S)$ and $N(R)$ fields to 0.)

In event 5, the NT sends a frame, with its $N(S) = 0$ (its first frame of the session). It also acknowledges TE's frames, by coding its $N(R) = 2$. In effect, this value means that the NT has received and has acknowledged all frames numbered up to 1, and is expecting the TE to send its next frame with the $N(S)$ set to 2. In this manner, the two stations keep their traffic in proper sequential order. The receipt of this frame at the TE turns off the T200 timer (event 6).

Operations in events 7 to 9 proceed normally, and in event 10, the NT responds by sending an RR frame to the TE. This is sent in lieu of traffic (if a station has no traffic to send) to (1) acknowledge traffic and (2) satisfy the T200 timer, which in event 10 is turned off when it receives the RR.

In events 12, 13, and 15, the TE continues to send frames. However, as noted in event 14, one frame's contents (the frame with $N(S) = 5$) are damaged enroute (symbolized with a X). To recover from this error, the NT in event 16 sends a reject frame (REJ) to the TE with the $N(R)$ set to 5. This is a negative acknowledgment, and requires that the TE resend this frame (event 18). With the REJ convention, all subsequent frames to $N(S) = 5$ (if any) must be resent. In this example, the frame with $N(S) = 6$ must be resent (and is in event 20).

The two retransmitted frames are received successfully by the NT and it so indicates by sending another RR to the TE (in event 22). The $N(R) = 7$ in this frame inclusively acknowledges the TE's frames of $N(S) = 5$ and $N(S) = 6$. With the action in event 23, all traffic has been acknowledged and all timers are turned off.

D-CHANNEL BACKUP PROCEDURE

The term *associated signaling* means the D-channel signaling entity can only assign calls to channels on the physical interface containing the D-channel. *Nonassociated signaling* means the D-channel signaling entity can assign calls to channels on more than one interface (including the one containing the D-channel).

With nonassociated signaling, the reliability of the signaling performance for the ISDN interfaces controlled by the D-channel may be unacceptable. To improve the reliability, a D-channel backup procedure employing a standby D-channel can be employed.

When two or more interfaces connect a network and a user, a primary D-channel (labeled "one") is always present on one interface. On a different interface, a secondary D-channel (labeled "two") is present that can also send signaling packets.

D-channel one is used to send signaling packets across the user-network interface for multiple interfaces, including the interface containing D-channel two. D-channel two has a standby role and is active at layer 2 only. All SAPI groups (e.g., 0, 16 and 63) are alive and can send packets. At periodic intervals, determined by the appropriate layer 2 timer associated with SAPI 0, a link audit frame is sent on the point-to-point signaling link with DLCI = 0 of D-channel two.

Since D-channel two is in a standby role, load sharing between D-channels one and two is not possible. Furthermore, D-channel two cannot serve as a B-channel when it is in a standby role. Lastly, D-channel two can only back up the signaling functions provided by D-channel one and not some other D-channel on a different interface.

SUMMARY

Layer 1 of ISDN defines the physical layer that describes four attributes of the interface: electrical; functional; mechanical; and procedural.

Layer 2 of ISDN is LAPD. Its primary job is to manage link activities and ensure the safe delivery of traffic across the channel.

The purpose of layers 1 and 2 is to support layer 3, which is concerned with setting up and terminating connections on the B channels.

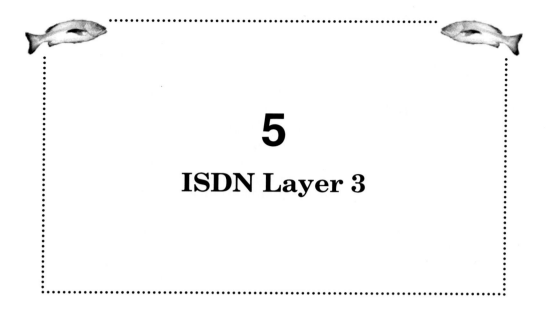

5

ISDN Layer 3

INTRODUCTION

This chapter examines layer 3 of ISDN, which is called the network layer. The emphasis in this chapter is on the ITU-T Q.931 Recommendation, which describes the procedures to set up, manage, and terminate a connection in an ISDN system. Each ISDN message is examined, as well as the parameters in the message. After these subjects have been explained, several examples of ISDN layer 3 operations are provided.

LOCATION OF Q.931 IN THE PROTOCOL STACK

Figure 5–1 shows the placement of Q.931 in the ISDN protocol suite. Because the layer 2 LAPD is a service provider to Q.931 (and performs error checks with possible retransmissions), Q.931 assumes the traffic given to it from LAPD has not been damaged during its transit across the link. Other than performing edits on the fields of the received messages, it relies on LAPD for reliable link transfer of the Q.931 messages.

The support operations of LAPD occur only on the D channel, for it is in this channel that Q.931 is operating. The B channels do not use LAPD nor Q.931 and, therefore, do not have access to LAPD's services.

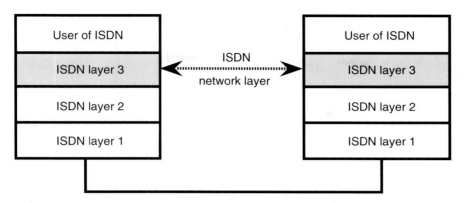

Figure 5–1   Location of the ISDN layer 3.

It is not desirable to use the LAPD services on the B channel because of the overhead and delay associated with the acknowledgments and possible retransmissions of LAPD traffic. LAPD traffic (in the I field of the LAPD frame) is signaling traffic (or maybe user data traffic). By its nature, it is asynchronous and bursty, and does not require tight timing constraints. In contrast, the B channels are designed to support synchronous, nonbursty traffic.

Q.931—USE IN OTHER TECHNOLOGIES

Even if the reader is not particularly interested in ISDN's layer 3 and Q.931, it is a good idea to have a concept of its characteristics, because it is used in many other systems. Although it was first published in 1984 for ISDN, it has been modified and adapted for use in such diverse technologies as frame relay and wireless, mobile networks. It is also the basis for SS7's ISDN User Part (ISUP), a subject discussed in Chapter 10. Figure 5–2 provides a view of its position in these and other technologies (not all inclusive).

Once the basic Q.931 operations are understood, its use in other systems is not very difficult to grasp. Therefore, the reader may wish to study Q.931 in more detail as a way to learning more about other signaling protocols.

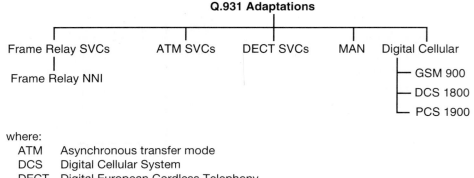

Figure 5–2   Use of ISDN's Q.931 in other technologies (not all inclusive).

PRINCIPAL FUNCTIONS OF ISDN LAYER 3

ISDN layer 3 is implemented with the ITU-T Q.931 Recommendation and other support protocols. Q.931 is responsible for setting up connections between the user station and the network, providing a limited number of support features during the connection, and terminating the connection when one of the parties in the connection issues a disconnect request (such as going on-hook). With most implementations of ISDN, the connections are mapped into the B channels, although it is also possible to send a limited amount of data traffic in the D channel when it is not being used for signaling operations.

Before proceeding further, the ISDN messages are examined. After this activity, we will analyze some examples of how ISDN establishes and manages a call between two parties.

ISDN MESSAGES

It has been emphasized that the ISDN layer 3 messages are used to manage ISDN connections on the B channels. Table 5–1 lists the messages used for this purpose. The table represents the ITU-T Blue Book specification. The messages noted with an asterisk (*) means they have

Table 5–1   ISDN Layer 3 Messages

Call Establishment Messages	Call Disestablishment Messages
ALERTING	DISCONNNECT
CALL PROCEEDING	RELEASE
CONGESTION CONTROL	RELEASE COMPLETE
CONNECT	RESTART*
CONNECT ACKNOWLEDGE	RESTART ACKNOWLEDGE*
PROGRESS	
SETUP	
SETUP ACKNOWLEDGE	

Call Information Phase Messages	Miscellaneous Messages
RESUME	CONGESTION CONTROL
RESUME ACKNOWLEDGE	FACILITY
RESUME REJECT	INFORMATION
SUSPEND	STATUS
SUSPEND ACKNOWLEDGE	STATUS ENQUIRY
SUSPEND REJECT	NOTIFY*
USER INFORMATION	

(Note: Use of these messages varies across vendors and national boundaries)

been added to the ANSI T1.607 (1990) standards. For consistency, the ITU-T specifications will be emphasized in this chapter, but I will also explain the ANSI messages.

Message Format

All Q.931 messages use a format depicted in Figure 5–3. The message contains several parameters to define the connection and the attributes of the connection. The parameters are examined by the called party (and, if applicable, the intervening network nodes) to determine the exact nature of the call.

As an example, the parameters in the message can request services from the network and/or called party, such as a transfer rate (in bit/s), the type of voice encoding (PCM, adaptive PCM), and so on.

Every Q.931 message exchanged between the user and the network must contain these three parameters:

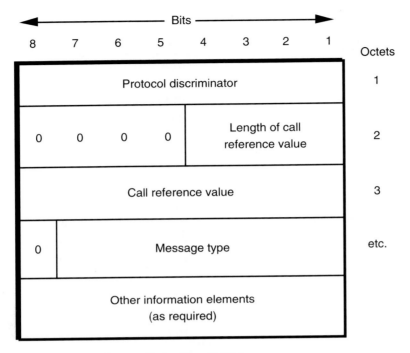

Figure 5–3   The Q.931 message.

- *PROTOCOL DISCRIMINATOR.* This parameter distinguishes between ISDN user-network call control messages and other messages, for example, in other technologies that use Q.931 (such as ATM, and frame relay). The field is coded as 00001000 for Q.931 messages.
- *CALL REFERENCE.* This parameter identifies a specific ISDN call at the local UNI. It is a unique identifier of each call on a UNI and, with its use, a call can be distinguished from other calls. Call references are also used in SS7 in a similar fashion to that of ISDN, but SS7 allows the call reference to be used across more interfaces. If you want to know more about the SS7 operation, refer to the section titled "Reference Numbers" in Chapter 10.
- *MESSAGE TYPE.* This parameter identifies the message function, such as a SETUP, DISCONNECT, and so on.

Figure 5–3 shows the *information elements (IEs)* field(s) residing behind the three mandatory parameters in the Q.931 message. The information element may consist of many entries (fields), and its contents depend on the message type. Later, we explain each message type and its associated information element(s).

Functions of the Messages

This section provides a description of the functions of the Q.931 messages. For ease of reference, they are listed in alphabetical order. Examples and explanations of the commonly used messages are provided later in the chapter. (You might find it useful to refer to Figure 5–5 while reading about the messages.)

- *ALERTING.* This message is sent to indicate that the called user party has been "alerted" and the call is being processed. This message is sent in response to an incoming SETUP message, and it is sent in the backward direction (backwards from the called end to the calling end) after the called exchange has placed ringing signals on the line to the called party.
- *CALL PROCEEDING.* This message is sent to the call initiator to indicate that the call establishment procedures have been initiated. It also indicates that all information necessary to set up the connection has been received and that any other call establishment information will not be accepted. In ISDN-conformant implementations, the CALL PROCEEDING message is exchanged only at the originating end of the connection.
- *CONGESTION CONTROL.* This message is employed only on USER INFORMATION messages. As the name implies, it is used to govern the flow of USER INFORMATION messages. In most implementations, congestion control is not used or, if it is used, it is rarely invoked.
- *CONNECT.* When the called party picks up the telephone and goes off-hook, this action precipitates the invocation of this message. The message is sent in the backward direction (from the called party to the calling party) to signal the call acceptance by the called party.
- *CONNECT ACKNOWLEDGE.* This message is sent in response to the CONNECT message. Its invocation means that the parties have been awarded the call.
- *DISCONNECT.* This message is sent when either party (calling or called) hangs up the telephone (goes on-hook). It is a trigger to the network that the end-to-end connection is to be cleared and the re-

sources reserved for the connection are to be made available for another call.

- *INFORMATION*. As the name implies, this message is sent by either the user or the network to provide more information about a connection. For example, the message may be invoked by an exchange if it wishes to provide additional information about a connection to another exchange.

- *NOTIFY*. This message is not often used, but is available for the user or the network to provide information regarding a connection. The NOTIFY message contains a field called the notification indicator, which is described in the next section of this chapter.

- *PROGRESS*. The progress message is part of the call establishment procedure, although it is not invoked in a typical implementation. However, it is available to indicate the progress of a call and it is invoked in situations where interworking is required or where the exchanges need to provide information about in-band information. This information is provided through a field in the message called the progress indicator, which is described in the next section.

- *RELEASE*. This message is invoked in response to the reception of a DISCONNECT message. It is sent by the network or the user to notify its recipient that the equipment has disconnected the circuit that had been reserved for the connection. In essence, it tells the receiver that it should also release the circuit. The RELEASE message is designed also to free and make available the call reference numbers (and the associated resources) associated with the call.

- *RELEASE COMPLETE*. As the name implies, this message is sent in response to the RELEASE message and it indicates by its invocation that the sender has released the circuit, the call reference, and, of course, the resources associated with the connection. The combination of the RELEASE and RELEASE COMPLETE messages means that the circuit has been completely cleared and made available for other calls, and that the call reference is no longer valid.

- *RESUME*. This message is used for a relatively simple operation, which is to request that the network resume a suspended call. The arrangements for resuming a suspended call vary between network providers, but the idea is to allow users to change their minds (within a brief period of time) upon hanging up.

- *RESUME ACKNOWLEDGE.* This message is sent by the network in response to the RESUME message. It indicates the completion of a request to RESUME a suspended call.
- *RESUME REJECT.* This message is sent by the network to indicate that it cannot fulfill the request to resume a suspended call.
- *SETUP.* The setup message contains more information elements than any of the other Q.931 messages. It is used to begin the call setup procedure. The SETUP message is always issued by the calling user to the network at the originating end and by the network to the called user at the terminating end.
- *SETUP ACKNOWLEDGE.* This message is sent in response to the SETUP message to indicate that the SETUP message has been received correctly. It is used to indicate that call establishment has been initiated. It may also indicate that additional information may be required to complete the call. For the latter case, the recipient of the SETUP ACKNOWLEDGE is required to send the additional information, which is coded in an INFORMATION message.
- *STATUS.* This message is sent in response to a STATUS INQUIRY message. It may also be sent in the event of certain error conditions that occur at a network node.
- *STATUS ENQUIRY.* This message is sent by either the user or the network to inquire about the status of an ongoing operation, such as a call in progress. Both the STATUS and STATUS ENQUIRY messages are intended to be flexible enough to allow implementors latitude in their implementations. The only information element in these messages is the display information element, described later in this chapter.

ISDN permits calls to be suspended. The reason for the suspensions are not defined in the specifications. Whatever the reasons, Q.931 provides several messages to support these operations. They are as follows:

- *SUSPEND, SUSPEND ACKNOWLEDGE, and SUSPEND REJECT.* The SUSPEND message is sent from the user to request that the network suspend the call. The direction of the message is important in that the network is not allowed to send this message; so, call suspension can only be initiated by the user. SUSPEND ACKNOWLEDGE is an acknowledgment by the network of the reception of the SUSPEND message; it also indicates the completion of the call suspension. SUSPEND REJECT is an acknowledgment by the network of the reception of the SUSPEND message, but it indicates that the network did not suspend the call.

- *USER INFORMATION.* This message is slightly different from the INFORMATION message described earlier, in that it contains different parameters than the INFORMATION message. The major aspect is the existence of the user-user field, which does not reside in the INFORMATION message. As the next section will explain, the user-user field is passed transparently by ISDN to ISDSN users.

- *FACILITY.* This message is used by either the user or the network to provide additional information about a call. Examples are keypad facility and display information, described in the next section.

- *RESTART.* This message is sent by the user or the network to request a restart of a connection. It returns the identified channel to an idle state.

- *RESTART ACKNOWLEDGE.* This message acknowledges the RESTART message.

Information Elements (Parameters) in the Message

Most ISDN messages contain only a few parameters, with the exception of SETUP, which may contain several parameters. It is up to the judgment of the ISDN implementor if the optional parameters should be included in an operational system. Other parameters are mandatory; they must be in the message. If they are not present, the system is considered to be "non-conforming" to the ISDN specifications.

Two tables are provided to aid in understanding the Q.931 messages and the information elements that are coded in the messages. Table 5–2 contains a list of the ISDN layer 3 message types and the information elements that are contained in the messages. The message types are shown as row entries and the columns are the information elements. Table 5–3 reverses the row-column entries of Table 5–2.

The use of the "x" in these tables does not indicate if the information element is mandatory or optional; it means that it may be (or may not be) present in the message. I have purposely avoided the mandatory/optional entries in these tables because implementations vary on which information elements are used (or not used). The reader should check the manufacturer and service provider to determine which information elements are used in an operating system.

The field in the Q.931 message in Figure 5–3 titled "Other information elements" contains one or more of the information elements listed in

Tables 5–2 and 5–3. Each information element in the message is preceded with a unique code, followed by the contents of the information element. The information elements described below are listed in alphabetical order.

- *Bearer capability*. This information element is used to request a service from the network (in accordance with ITU-T I.231). However, even though the service is furnished as a result of the request from the calling party, this information element is passed to the called party (or the called party's exchange termination, if the called party is non-ISDN). After all, the requested services usually affect both parties, due to the types of services that may be provided.

  For example, at the originating end of the connection in the analog-to-digital (A/D) process, the analog voice signal is coded into a digital representation through a specific encoding algorithm. The transmitted digital signals represent algorithms operations. (The A/D algorithm is not the same in all networks. The ITU-T differs from the North American algorithm.) In order for the receiving end to be able to decode the digital signal correctly and convert it back to an analog audio signal, it must know how the signal was coded at the transmitting end. Here are some examples of services that can be requested in the bearer capability information element:

  - Request for an information transfer capability, such as speech, 3.1 kHz audio, or 7 kHz audio.
  - Request for circuit or packet transfer mode.
  - Request for a specific transfer rate, such as 64 kbit/s, 384 kbit/s, and so on.
  - Identification of user's encoding and compression algorithm (A-law, μ-law).
  - Request for a data transfer rate, if data are to be transmitted during the connection.
  - Request for rate adaptation (see Appendix C for more information on this procedure).

- *Call identity*. This information element is used to identify a suspended call. It is assigned at the start of the call suspension operation.

- *Call state*. Q.931 is a connection-oriented protocol, and uses call states (and timers) to govern its actions. This information element is used to describe the current status (state) of a call. It identifies states such as call initiated, call received, call present, and so on.

Table 5–2   Information Elements for Message Types

1. Protocol discriminator	7. Call state
2. Call reference	8. Repeat indicator
3. Message type	9. Bearer capability
4. Sending complete	10. Channel identification
5. Congestion level	11. Facility
6. Cause	12. Progress indicator

Message Type	Direction*	Information Elements								
		1	2	3	4	5	6	7	8	9
Alerting	B	x	x	x						
Call proceeding	B	x	x	x						
Congestion control	B	x	x	x		x	x			
Connect	B	x	x	x						
Connect Ack	B	x	x	x						
Disconnect	B	x	x	x			x			
Information	B	x	x	x	x		x			
Notify	B	x	x	x						x
Progress	B	x	x	x			x			
Release	B	x	x	x			x			
Release complete	B	x	x	x			x			
Resume[1]	U-N	x	x	x						
Resume Ack	N-U	x	x	x						
Resume Reject	N-U	x	x	x			x			
Setup	B	x	x	x	x				x	x
Setup Ack	B	x	x	x						
Status	B	x	x	x			x	x		
Status Enquiry	B	x	x	x						
Suspend[1]	U-N	x	x	x						
Suspend Ack	N-U	x	x	x						
Suspend Reject	N-U	x	x	x			x			
User Information[2]	B	x	x	x						

*B indicates direction both ways; N-U = network to user; U-N= user to network
[1]Also contains *call identity* information element
[2]Also contains *more data* information element

13. Notification indicator	19. Feature activation/ indication
14. Network specific facilities	20. Calling/called party number
15. Display	21. Calling/called party subaddress
16. Keypad facility	22. Transit network selection
17. Signal	23. Low layer /high layer capability
18. Switchhook	24. User-user

Information Elements

10	11	12	13	14	15	16	17	18	19	20	21	22	23	24
X	X	X			X		X		X					X
X		X			X									
					X									
X	X	X			X		X	X	X				X	X
X					X		X							
	X	X			X		X		X					X
					X	X	X	X	X	X				
			X		X									
		X			X				X					X
	X				X		X		X					X
	X				X		X		X					X
X					X									
					X									
X	X	X		X	X	X	X	X	X	X	X	X	X	X
X		X			X		X							
					X									
					X									
					X									
					X									
														X

Table 5–3   Message Types for Information Elements

1. Alerting	7. Information
2. Call proceeding	8. Notify
3. Congestion control	9. Progress
4. Connect	10. Release
5. Connect ACK	11. Release complete
6. Disconnect	12. Resume

Information Element	Message Type								
	1	2	3	4	5	6	7	8	9
Protocol discriminator	x	x	x	x	x	x	x	x	x
Call reference	x	x	x	x	x	x	x	x	x
Message type	x	x	x	x	x	x	x	x	x
Sending complete							x		
Congestion level			x						
Cause			x			x	x		x
Call state									
Repeat indicator								x	
Bearer capability									
Channel identification	x	x		x	x				
Facility	x			x		x			
Progress indicator	x	x		x		x			x
Notification indicator								x	
Network specific facilities									
Display	x	x	x	x	x	x	x	x	x
Keypad facility							x		
Signal	x			x	x	x	x		
Switchhook				x			x		
Feature activation	x			x			x		
Feature indication	x			x		x	x		
Calling party number									
Calling party subaddress									
Called party number							x		
Called party subaddress									
Transit network selection									
Low layer capability				x					
High layer capability									
Call identity									
More data									
User-user	x			x		x			x

13. Resume ACK	19. Suspend
14. Resume reject	20. Suspend ACK
15. Setup	21. Suspend reject
16. Setup ACK	22. User Information
17. Status	
18. Status enquiry	

Message Type

10	11	12	13	14	15	16	17	18	19	20	21	22
X	X	X	X	X	X	X	X	X	X	X	X	X
X	X	X	X	X	X	X	X	X	X	X	X	X
X	X	X	X	X	X	X	X	X	X	X	X	X
					X							
X	X			X			X				X	
							X					
					X							
					X							
			X		X							
X	X				X							
					X	X						
					X							
X	X		X	X	X	X	X	X		X	X	
					X							
X	X				X	X	X					
					X							
X	X				X							
					X							
					X							
					X							
					X							
					X							
					X							
					X							
					X							
		X							X			
												X
X	X				X							X

- *Called and calling party numbers.* These numbers can be coded in several forms. The most common form is in accordance with the national numbering plan in a country, which is usually compatible with the ITU-T E.164 and E.163 numbering plans. These ITU-T Recommendations define the ISDN/telephone numbering plan. Other numbering plans may be used, such as X.121 (a common numbering plan used in data networks), F.69 (the telex numbering plan), or even a private numbering plan. This information element also identifies if the numbering plan is a international number, a national number, a network-specific number, or others.

- *Called and calling party subaddress.* These information elements identify the subaddress of the called and calling party addresses. This approach allows one party address to identify multiple entities, which would be coded as subaddresses. For example, if multiple applications are running concurrently in a machine, the machine is identified with a party number and each application is identified with a party subaddress.

- *Cause.* This information element is used primarily to report a problem, but it is used also to provide status information about a call. For the first use, it can be coded to indicate that a specified transit network cannot be reached, the called user is busy, the called user has not answered, the dialed number is invalid, the user dialed a 1 or 0, which is not allowed on this exchange, and many others. For the second use, it can indicate that the called number has too many digits, but the call is still proceeding, the call is being delivered in an established channel, or others. Currently, ANSI defines 98 cause codes and the ITU-T defines 51 cause codes.

- *Channel identification.* A call must be associated with a channel (logical channel) on a physical channel (which are called interfaces in this information element description). This information element is used for this purpose. The following additional information is coded in this field: (a) a BRI or PRI channel, (b) identified channel is (or is not) a D channel, (c) the channel is a B1 or B2 channel, (d) the identified channel is an H0, H10, H11, and so on channel unit.

One method of indicating a channel for DS1 systems is the use of a slot map, as depicted in Figure 5–4. Each DS0 slot is identified in a three-octet field, one bit per DS0 channel. This arrangement is shown in Figure 5–4(a). In Figure 5–4(b), six B channels have

24	23	22	21	20	19	18	17
16	15	14	13	12	11	10	9
8	7	6	5	4	3	2	1

(a) The 24 slots at an interface

0	0	0	0	0	0	0	1
0	1	1	0	1	0	0	1
0	1	0	0	0	0	0	0

(b) Six B channels identified to form an H0 channel

Figure 5–4   The slot map.

been identified in slots 7, 9, 12, 14, 15, and 17. These aggregated B channels form an ISDN H0 channel.

- *Congestion level.* This information element is used to describe the congestion level of the call as viewed by the user or the network. In effect, it is a flow control mechanism, and is coded as "receiver ready" or "receiver not ready" (RR or RNR).
- *Display.* This information element contains ASCII/IA5 characters, which are supplied to the user for display on a terminal screen or printer.
- *Facility.* Under network-specific conditions, supplementary services may be invoked. The ITU-T version of Q.931 (ANSI does not publish a facility information element) uses this field to code messages to support a special remote procedure call (RPC) at layer 3. This protocol is based on the Remote Operations Service Element (ROSE) and the Transaction Capabilities Applications Part (TCAP) and is described in the TCAP chapter.
- *Feature activation/indication.* These two information elements are defined in Q.932 and are used to support supplementary services, which are network-specific.
- *High layer compatibility.* The users and the network use this information element to check for compatibility of the OSI high (upper)

layer capabilities. Compatibility checking can be performed at (a) the user-network interface on the calling side, (b) the network-user interface on the called side, or (c) between the users. A code in this information element identifies the specific capabilities; examples are (a) fax profile, (b) X.400 Message Handling Services (MHS), or (c) videotext.

- *Keypad facility*. This information element conveys ASCII/IA5 characters, which are entered through a terminal keypad. It can support an operation in which a user requests a service from the network by coding this information element in an INFORMATION message. The network responds with an INFORMATION message with the Display or Signal information element to inform the user that it is accommodating the request. The user can then enter more keypad information, if necessary, to allow the network to complete the service request. The ITU-T also uses this information as part of a keypad protocol. This protocol can be used to establish a second call while holding the first one. A later section in this chapter shows an example of this protocol.

- *Low layer compatibility*. This information element is used for the same purpose as the high layer compatibility information element, except it checks for compatibility at the lower OSI layers. The checks are performed only between the calling party and the addressed entity (the called party, gateway, etc.). Examples of the capabilities checked are those described in the bearer capability information element.

- *More data*. As the name implies, this information element indicates to the network that the user is sending additional information. It is used in the USER INFORMATION message to indicate that another USER INFORMATION message will follow.

- *Network-specific facilities*. For many years, the ITU-T has published standards on facilities to be used in various types of networks (circuit switched networks, packet switched networks, maritime networks, etc.). The facilities are quite diverse and include operations such as reverse charging, hunt groups, call redirection, and closed user groups. This information element identifies these facilities and also indicates if they are (a) user specified, (b) based on a national plan, (c) based on an international plan. It includes a field to identify a specific service provider (carrier), or an X.121 address of a network.

- *Notification indicator.* This information element provides the following information about a call: (a) user suspended the call, (b) user resumed the call, or (c) a bearer service is changed.
- *Progress indicator.* If a event occurs during the life of a call, it can be indicated by data-filling this information and sending it in one of several messages (see Tables 5–2 and 5–3). The information indicates the location of the entity that is reporting the event (private or public network serving the local or remote user), the nature of the event (destination address is non-ISDN, call is not end-to-end ISDN, call has returned to the ISDN, etc.)
- *Repeat indicator.* Some of the information elements may be repeated in a message. If they are, this information element indicates how to interpret them.
- *Restart indicator.* In case a restart of a connection or connections is required, this information element indicates if the restart is a single interface, all interfaces, or certain channels on an interface. For the latter information, the channel identification information element is used.
- *Segmented message.* It may be necessary to segment a message into smaller parts due to limitations on the physical channel or buffer restraints in a machine. This information element indicates if segmentation has been performed, how many segments are involved, and the length of the segments.
- *Sending complete.* This information element is sent (optionally) to indicate the completion of a called party number.
- *Signal.* Since the calling and called parties are using a conventional telephone handset that employs dial tones, busy tones, and other control signals, ISDN must have a mechanism to convey information about these signals. The signal information element is used for this purpose. A one-octet field is coded in accordance with the rules in Table 5–4.
- *Switchhook.* This information element indicates that the status of the telephone terminal switchhook is either on-hook or off-hook.
- *Transit network selection.* A user is allowed to stipulate a transit network, if appropriate. In the United States, this information element can be used to select an interexchange carrier.
- *User-user.* This information element is not processed nor examined by the network. It is passed between end users and may contain anything the users wish to convey to each other.

Table 5–4   Coding for the Signal Information Element

Bits	Meaning	North American Practice
8765 4321		
0000 0000	Dial tone on	Continuous 350 Hz tone added to a 440 Hz tone
0000 0001	Ring back tone on	440 Hz tone added to a 480 Hz tone, repeated in a 2 sec on/4 sec off pattern
0000 0010	Intercept tone on	Alternating 440 Hz and 620 Hz tones, each for 250 ms (not ordinarily employed in North America)
0000 0011	Network congestion tone on	480 Hz tone added to a 620 Hz tone, repeated in a 250 ms on/250 ms off pattern
0000 0100	Busy tone on	480 Hz tone added to a 620 Hz tone, repeated in a 500 ms on/500 ms off pattern
0000 0101	Confirm tone on	350 Hz tone added to a 440 Hz tone, repeated three times in a 100 ms on/100 ms off pattern
0000 0110	Answer tone on	Not supported in North America
0000 0111	Call waiting tone on	300 ms burst of a 440 Hz tone
0000 1000	Off-hook warning tone on	Sum of four frequencies (1400 Hz, 2060 Hz, 2450 Hz, 2600 Hz) repeated in a 100 ms on/100 ms off pattern
0011 1111	Tones off	
0100 0000	Alerting on - pattern 0 (note)	
0100 0001	Alerting on - pattern 1 (note)	
0100 0010	Alerting on - pattern 2 (note)	
0100 0011	Alerting on - pattern 3 (note)	
0100 0100	Alerting on - pattern 4 (note)	
0100 0101	Alerting on - pattern 5 (note)	
0100 0110	Alerting on - pattern 6 (note)	
0100 0111	Alerting on - pattern 7 (note)	
0100 1111	Alerting off	

Note: The use of alerting signals is network-dependent. For example, alerting code 0100 0000 (64) is normal alerting.

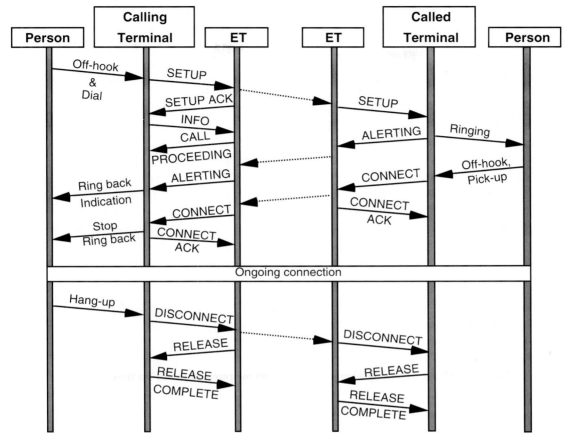

Figure 5–5   Example of an ISDN connection establishment and termination.

EXAMPLES OF Q.931 OPERATIONS

Figure 5–5 provides an example of how a call is set up with the Q.931 messages. The two persons involved in this connection are using conventional telephone handsets that are attached to ISDN terminals, shown in this figure as the calling terminal and the called terminal. The exchange terminations (ETs) are located at the central offices.

The calling party goes off-hook and dials the telephone number of the called party. This information is used by the calling terminal to create an ISDN SETUP message, which is sent across the ISDN line to the local ET. This ET acknowledges the message with the SETUP ACK message, and initiates actions to set up a circuit to the next ET, which is shown in the figure with the dashed arrow. The SETUP ACK and INFORMATION messages are optional and were described in the previous section. The local ET sends a CALL PROCEEDING message to the calling terminal to indicate that the call is being processed.

At the called end, the SETUP message is forwarded to the called terminal by the terminating ET. This terminal examines the contents of the message to determine who is being called and what services are being requested. It checks the called party's line to see if it is idle, and if so, places the ringing signal on the line. When the ringing signal is placed on the line, the called terminal transmits an ALERTING message in the backwards direction, which is passed all the way to the calling terminal. This message indicates to the calling terminal that the called party has been signaled, which allows a ring back signal to be placed on the line to the calling party.

When the called party answers the call (picking up the phone and going off-hook), the called terminal sends a CONNECT message in the backwards direction, which is passed to the calling terminal. Upon receiving this message, ring back is removed from the line, and the connection is cut through to the calling party. To complete the connection set up procedures, the CONNECT messages are acknowledged with CONNECT ACK messages.

Of course, either party can terminate the call by hanging up the telephone handset. This on-hook action initiates the ISDN connection termination operations shown in the bottom part of Figure 5–5. The DISCONNECT messages are used to indicate that the connection is to be terminated. The RELEASE and RELEASE COMPLETE messages follow the DISCONNECT messages. Afterwards, the resources that were seized for this connection are now available for another call.

The Keypad Protocol

Figure 5–6 shows an example of how the ISDN keypad protocol is used to hold an ongoing call while establishing a second one (new). The keypad facility and display information elements are used during these operations. The first call is active between users A and B. User A wishes to place this call on hold and sends an INFORMATION message with the keypad information element coded to "HOLD." Party B receives this information in a display information element. After call progress tones and

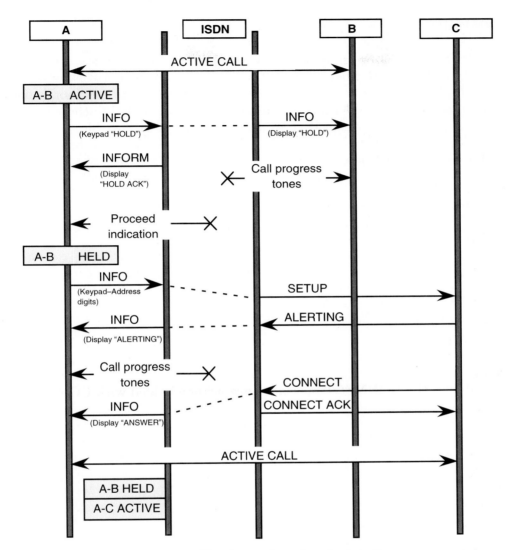

Figure 5–6 The keypad protocol operation.

proceed indication signals are exchanged by ISDN with parties B and A, respectively; the A–B connection is placed on hold.

The next set of operations sets up the second new call between A and C, with the result that the A–B call is on hold while the A–C call is active. Once again, the key pad and display information elements are used for these operations.

SUMMARY

ISDN layer 3 is implemented with Q.931, which is responsible for setting up connections between the user station and the network and terminating the connection when one of the parties in the connection issues a disconnect request. With most implementations of ISDN, the connections are mapped into the B channels, although it is possible to send a limited amount of data traffic in the D channel when it is not being used for signaling operations.

6

National ISDN, Internet Access, and Other Services

INTRODUCTION

This chapter examines the subject of National ISDN, a term coined by the BOCs and Bellcore to describe a nationwide plan to bring ISDN into most of the large and medium-sized cities. The features of National ISDN are explained, and the progress of the plan is tracked from its inception in 1991.

At the end of this chapter, we explore how ISDN is being used to provide Internet access and examine some of the other services (and products) available in the ISDN marketplace.

GENESIS OF NATIONAL ISDN

In the early 1990s, the Regional Bell Operating Companies (RBOCs) launched what is called National ISDN. It is a U.S. plan for a nationwide, standardized implementation in the United States of ISDN technology. It places strict requirements on the vendors and manufacturers who build the ISDN equipment and on the ISDN service providers.

As part of the plan, each RBOC set up deployment goals for 1991, 1992, 1993, 1994 for: (1) the number of access lines that support ISDN, (2) the number of wire centers to have ISDN presence, (3) the total number of switches to have ISDN capabilities, and (4) the total number of

Table 6–1   National ISDN

- In the U.S., a nationwide, standardized implementation of ISDN technology with strict requirements levied on vendors, manufacturers, and service providers.
- Each RBOC set up deployment goals for 1991, 1992, 1993, 1994 for:
  > Number of access lines
  > Number of wire centers to have ISDN presence
  > Total number of switches to have ISDN capabilities
  > Total number of switches to have SS7 capabilities
- *National ISDN-1 (1992):*
  Basic installations, consisting of basic services and protocols for seven capabilities (now called ISDN ordering codes ([IOCs])
- *National ISDN-2 (1992–1993):*
  Builds on ISDN-1, and expands the seven capabilities
- *National ISDN-3 (1994–1995):*
  Builds on ISDN-2 and expands the seven capabilities
- *National ISDN 1995 and 1996:*
  Bellcore document SR-3476: Summarizes National ISDN features, phases, and capabilities that are available in 1996 (in some areas).

switches to have SS7 capabilities. These goals were tracked each year with each RBOC publishing its progress report.

National ISDN was divided into three phases. National ISDN-1 (begun in 1992) specified basic ISDN installations and described services and protocols for seven capabilities (now called ISDN ordering codes ([IOCs]). National ISDN-2 (1992–1993) builds on ISDN-1 and expands the seven capabilities, as does National ISDN-3 (1994–1995). For more information on the National ISDN services, Bellcore document SR-3476 summarizes all the National ISDN features and capabilities that are to be available by 1996. Table 6–1 provides a summary of the milestones of National ISDN.

EXAMPLE OF A DEPLOYMENT PLAN

Table 6–2 reflects one example of the initial deployment plans for ISDN. The example chosen is for Southwestern Bell. Other RBOCs plans are similar, although some were not as aggressive as Southwestern Bell in the ISDN deployment in the earlier years. The columns, listed by date in the table, show that plans were established to deploy ISDN in an incremental manner; by the year 1994, the lines and switches were to be ISDN-compliant. In addition to the plans to deploy ISDN, all RBOCs es-

Table 6–2   Example of a Initial Deployment Plans for National ISDN (Southwestern Bell)

ISDN Capability	Year 1	Year 2	Year 3	Year 4
Total access lines	12.4	12.8	13.2	13.5
Total number of wire centers planned for ISDN presence	57	80	92	101
Total number of lines in wire centers planned for ISDN presence	1.6 m	2.0 m	2.1 m	2.2 m
% of lines in wire centers planned to have ISDN presence	12.9%	15.6%	15.9%	16.3%
Total number of switches planned to be equipped with ISDN	65	96	108	117
Total number of switches planned to have SS7	—	62	91	106
% of switches planned to incorporate SS7	—	65%	84%	91%

tablished goals for the deployment of SS7 in their switches, as well. The last entry of Table 6–2 shows Southwestern Bell's SS7 deployment plans.

SEVEN BASIC CAPABILITIES

The seven basic capabilities were introduced in National ISDN-1. They stipulate the requirements that must be satisfied for a product to be in conformance with the National ISDN standards. These capabilities have been expanded significantly in National ISDN-2 and National ISDN-3. They are summarized in Table 6–3 and explained in more detail in the following material.

Access, Call Control, and Signaling

This capability involves the following services:

- Circuit-mode voice (speech/3.1 kHz audio) call control
- Circuit-mode data (56/64 kbit/s) call control
- Packet-mode data (provisioned B-channel) call control
- Multiple DS1 facilities controlled by a single D-channel
- D-channel backup
- Access to selected PRI services on a per-call basis

Table 6–3   National ISDN Capabilities

1. *Access, Call Control, and Signaling*
   Definition of a uniform BRI protocol, as well as a uniform SS7 interoffice interface

2. *Uniform Interface Configurations for BRI*
   Definition of two interfaces for the BRI: (a) single user of a BRI, (b) two users using same BRI

3. *Uniformity of BRI Services*
   Definition of a minimum set of BRI services from all suppliers

4. *Primary Rate Interface Capabilities*
   Definition of a minimum set of PRI capabilities

5. *Data Capabilities*
   Definition of circuit-switched and packet-switched data interfaces

6. *Operations Support Capabilities*
   Definition of operations capabilities that allow service providers to provision and maintain their offerings

7. *Billing Capabilities*
   Definition of standardized methods for generating records for accounting and billing purposes

This capability also provides for SS7 procedures to establish and clear interoffice calls that originate from or terminate to a PRI.

Uniform Interface Configurations for Basic Rate Interfaces

For National ISDN-1 (NI-1), a switching system is required to support two interface configurations for BRI: (1) a single user with multiple applications on a single BRI, and (2) two users sharing the same BRI where each user may have access to the same applications. National ISDN-2 (NI-2) relaxes the NI-1 interface restrictions by requiring switching systems to provide the capabilities described below.

The support of more than two B-channel terminals on a BRI capability allows the user to place more than two B-channel terminals on a BRI. Since there are only two B-channels on a BRI, only two terminals can use the B-channels at the same time, although the maximum number of terminals is eight per BRI. These terminals can use the B-channels, the D-channel, or a combination of the two.

Uniformity of Basic Rate Interface Services

In NI-1, a switching system is required to support the uniform BRI protocols for service invocation, as defined in the Bellcore requirements. Since the protocol is uniform, ISDN end-user equipment will be able to operate on any NI-1 BRI. This capability includes the following.

Electronic Key Telephone Service (EKTS). The requirements for EKTS are as follows:

- Multiple DNs per terminal
- Multiple directory number appearances/call appearance call handling
- Hold/retrieve
- Intercom calling
- Membership in a multiline hunt group
- Abbreviated ringing and delayed ringing
- Automatic and/or manual bridged call exclusion

ISDN Call Forwarding. The requirements for ISDN call forwarding are as follows:

- Call forwarding variable
- Call forwarding interface busy
- Call forwarding don't answer

ISDN Call Hold. The requirements for the call hold feature are as follows:

- Hold and retrieve
- B-channel reservation (excluding release)

Additional Call Offering. The requirements for additional call offering (ACO) include procedures for both circuit-mode and packet-mode calls. NI-2 only requires a switching system to provide ACO for circuit-mode calls (i.e., speech and circuit-switched data call types). ACO for packet-mode requires that the switch support unconditional notification, which is not part of NI-2; therefore, ACO for packet-mode is not part of NI-2.

Flexible Calling. The requirements for flexible calling contain these subfeatures:

- Conference calling (three-port and six-port)
- Consultation hold
- Implicit call transfer
- Explicit call transfer
- Drop last call on conference

Calling Number ID Services. The calling number ID services (CNIS) requirements include:

- Delivery of network-provided calling number
- Privacy of calling number
- Delivery of redirecting number
- Privacy of redirecting number
- Delivery of redirecting reason

Primary Rate Interface Capabilities

NI-1 provides a minimum set of PRI capabilities. In the absence of the appropriate TAs and TRs, supplier-specific offerings are the only ones possible. NI-2 begins to define uniform PRI call control, as well as additional PRI capabilities, as described below.

Call-by-Call Service Selection. The following requirements for the call-by-call service selection feature are to be provided in a uniform manner in NI-2:

- Access to and termination from non-ISDN foreign exchange (FX) facilities
- Access to and termination from non-ISDN tie trunks
- Inward wide area telecommunications service (INWATS)
- Outward wide area telecommunications service (OUTWATS)

Calling Identification Services (CNIS) for PRI. The following features for the CNIS for PRI feature will be provided in a uniform manner in NI-2:

- Delivery of network-provided calling number
- Privacy of calling number
- Delivery of redirecting number
- Privacy of redirecting number
- Delivery of redirecting reason
- Screening functions

Switched DS1/Switched Fractional DS1 Service (SWF-DS1) Capability. The SWF-DS1 allows the user to establish and clear calls to and from a PRI at N times 64 kbit/s rates, where N ranges from 2 through 24.

Interworking with Private Networks. The interworking with private networks capability allows a PRI to be used within a private network as a tie trunk. A tie trunk is one that is leased by a user for exclusive utilization by that user. Access to a tie trunk can be via dial access codes or a private network routing feature such as automatic route selection (ARS).

Data Capabilities

This capability allows a user to request that a connection be established over that user's BRI via a B-channel to the ISDN packet-handling function (PHF). Once connected to the PHF, the user can originate and receive packet-switched data calls over the B-channel. When the B-channel is no longer required, the user can clear the B-channel connection. When not being used for packet-switched data, the B-channel can be used for speech and circuit-switched data.

NI-2 provides improvements over the packet-switched data features in NI-1. These packet switched data features are to be provided in a uniform manner in NI-2, unless otherwise noted:

- Clearing subnetwork identification for X.75'
- Transit subnetwork count for X.75'
- Multilink procedures on X.75/X.75' (supplier specific alternative acceptable in NI2)
- Support of X.75 end office connections

The ISDN X.25 local charging prevention feature provides ISDN users with a way of restricting their DN from being charged for any packet-switched data calls, whether incoming or outgoing. The ISDN local charging prevention feature will be provided in a uniform manner in NI-2.

Operations Support Capabilities

Parameter Downloading. Parameter downloading is a capability where the switch will send certain service parameters (e.g., directory numbers, feature activators/indicators) to the terminal. It is intended to minimize the need for end users to manually enter these parameters into their terminals and therefore eliminates the potential for human errors that can occur with manual entry.

Billing Capabilities

This last set capabilities is a set of conventions and procedures established by the ROBCs to use common billing and accounting operations.

INTERNET ACCESS

One of the widely used implementations of the ISDN UNI is to access a public Internet or private Internet. The main attraction is the 64 kbit/s transfer rate offered by ISDN; and, in some offerings, two B channels are available at 128 kbit/s. This rate is considerably more attractive that conventional dial-up modems, especially the lower-speed V.32, V.32 bis, and V.33 modems that offer speeds only up to 19.2 kbit/s (and in some installations, 9.6–14.4 kbit/s). The B or B+B channel rates, when coupled with compression, can give the user throughput at three times (conservatively) the raw channel rate.

As browsing tools increase their capabilities, and as Internets provide more voice and video services, the lower-speed modems will not be up to the task of handling large transfer rates. But, on the other side of the coin, a V.34 modem operating at 28.8 kbit/s channel rate is quite satisfactory for many users, especially when this rate is coupled with data compression. Nonetheless, as the ISDN prices drop, and as Internet Service Providers (ISPs) deploy ISDN-based services, we can expect the user of ISDN to continue to increase.[1]

To gain an idea of the differences in throughput between a V.34 modem and one ISDN B-channel, consider that the V.34 modem requires approximately 30 to 45 seconds to establish a connection with the network provider's modem. A connection with an ISDN interface consumes about 10 seconds. The differences in connect time have two important consequences:

1. The end user is sitting at the terminal for a relatively long period of time with nothing happening
2. With an ISDN connection, approximately 200 to 400 kbit/s of information can be transferred during this 30 to 45 second period. This latter consequence is important for calls that are being metered on time.

---

[1]Many people in the industry believe that the 64 or 64+64 kbit/s rate is not sufficient for real-time, interactive browsing with multimedia applications. My prediction is that during the next few years, cable modems, other physical layer transmission schemes, cable/fiber hybrid media, and increased wireless capabilities will (a) slow the growth of ISDN, (b) foster its alteration at the physical layer, or (c) both a and b (which is more likely).

ISDN Packages for the Internet

A wide variety of Internet offerings are available to users in the United States. The offerings usually come in two packages. One package is intended for an individual user (perhaps working from home) in which the ISP offers dynamic IP address assignment. The second package is designed for small or medium-sized businesses in which the subscribers are first attached to the company's LAN and then connected to the Internet through a dial-up LAN bridge/router. For this package, the customer can be assigned (although it is not required) a permanent IP address.

For both packages, the interfaces can take the form of an external unit or a network interface card that resides inside the user equipment. Regardless of which package is used, part of the interface houses the ISDN terminal adapter, which is described in Chapter 3 and Appendix C.

With some exceptions, the first category of service entails a standard V.120 rate adaptation scheme with asynchronous point-to-point (PPP) to synchronous PPP service. Speeds of up to 128 kbit/s are available in some cities.

The second category involves a similar architecture as in the first category and almost all of the dial-up bridges and routers have migrated to PPP. The main difference is that the second category offers primary rate interfaces (PRI) as well.

Ordering ISDN for Internet Services

I explained earlier in this chapter that the National ISDN program provides standard ISDN ordering codes (IOC). For Internet access, IOCs are available to define two types of services: (a) the single B channel service offers circuit mode operations at speeds up to 64 kbit/s and (b) the dual B channel service offers circuit mode operations at speeds up to 128 kbit/s.

The IOC convention that closely fits single B channel access procedure is now called capability B. Although the reader is encouraged to check with the provider in your service area, because capability C may be more attractive, because it supports voice and circuit-mode calling on one B-channel.

Dual B-channel access is now called capability I and provides two B-channels with circuit mode and calling number identification. For some service providers, capability M may be more attractive, because it provides two B-channels with alternate voice and circuit mode data as well as calling number identification services.

Table 6–4   Telephone Company Contact Numbers for ISDN Internet Access

Company	Contact	Telephone Number
Ameritech	National ISDN hotline	1 (800) TEAMDATA
Bell Atlantic	ISDN Sales & Tech Ctr	1 (800) 570–ISDN In NJ call your local telephone office
BellSouth	ISDN HotLine	1 (800) 428–4736
Cincinnati Bell	ISDN Service Center	1 (513) 566–DATA
Nevada Bell	Small business	1 (702) 333–4811
	Large business	1 (702) 688–7100
Nynex	ISDN Sales Hotline	1 (800) GET–ISDN
Pacific Bell	24-hour automated ISDN/ available hotline	1 (800) 995–0346
Rochester Telephone	ISDN Information	1 (716) 777–1234
SNET	Donovan Dillon	1 (203) 553–2369
Stentor (Canada)	ISDN "Facts by FAX"	1 (800) 578–ISDN
Southwestern Bell	ISDN HotLine	1 (800) 992–ISDN
U.S. West	Denver, CO	1 (800) 246–5226

Table 6–4 provides a list of telephone numbers furnished by the telephone companies for information about ISDN/Internet access services.

SUMMARY

The success of ISDN in the United States should be attributed to the RBOCs and Bellcore. Without a national plan, ISDN would not have succeeded in the United States. In addition, the need for greater bandwidth on the local loop has spurred the use of ISDN, especially as prices have dropped for this service.

However, ISDN will need to change at the physical layer if it is to continue to compete in the local loop. Layer 3's Q.931 is likely to endure (as well as layer 2's LAPD for a while) by running on a higher-speed carrier technology.

7

Signaling System Number 7 (SS7) Architecture

INTRODUCTION

This chapter introduces the Signaling System Number 7 network, abbreviated hereafter as SS7. The concepts behind the SS7 design are explained and the SS7 nodes are examined. The relationship of SS7 and the OSI Model is clarified, as well as the SS7 topologies and link (communications channel) types. SS7 addresses are explained, and we show some examples of these addresses. The chapter concludes with a discussion on internetworking and international SS7 networks.

EARLY SIGNALING

As discussed in Chapter 1, early signaling systems used a technique called per-trunk, in-band signaling. With this approach, the call control path is the same physical circuit as the speech path. This is not an efficient technique, since the traffic of the telephone calls and the traffic of the control signals are competing with each other. Supervisory functions, such as on-hook and off-hook; call information, such as dial tone and busy signals; and addressing information, such as the called number, must be interspersed with the voice traffic.

COMMON CHANNEL SIGNALING (CCS)

In contrast to per-trunk signaling, CCS separates the call control path from the speech path, as shown in Figure 7–1. As a consequence, call control does not compete with voice traffic for use of the channel. Moreover, this approach reduces call setup time and provides the opportunity to build redundant signaling links between offices, which improves reliability. Another advantage of CCS is the ability to look ahead when setting up a connection. Therefore, resources do not have to be reserved until it is determined that a connection can be made. Thus, the high reliability of CCS, coupled with faster operations and increased capabilities, provides both local exchange carriers and interexchange carriers with a powerful tool for enhancing telephone operations.

Figure 7–2 illustrates two types of communications employed in CCS: associated signaling and quasi-associated signaling. With associated signaling, common-channel signaling messages pertaining to a particular operation are conveyed over communication links that are connected directly between the network nodes (Figure 7–2a). With quasi-associated signaling, the messages are transferred indirectly through at least one tandem point, usually known as the signaling transfer point (STP) (see Figure 7–2b). Even though intermediate nodes are involved in the transfer of the messages, the messages take a fixed, predetermined path between the two communicating entities.

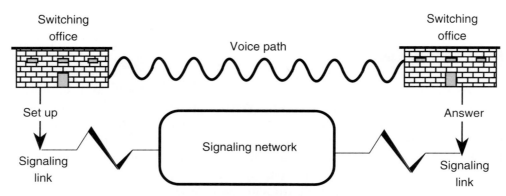

Figure 7–1   Common channel signaling (CCS).

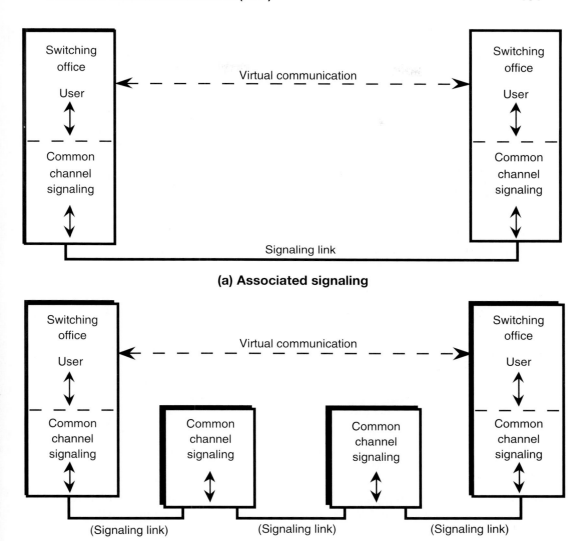

(a) Associated signaling

(b) Quasi-associated signaling

Figure 7–2   Associated and quasi-associated signaling.

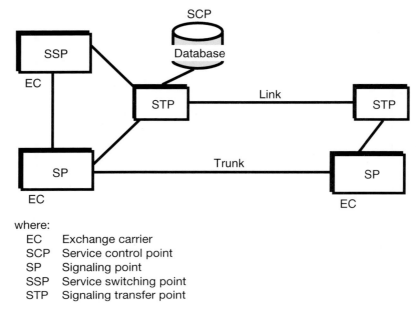

where:

EC	Exchange carrier
SCP	Service control point
SP	Signaling point
SSP	Service switching point
STP	Signaling transfer point

Figure 7–3   CCS and SS7 components.

CCS ARCHITECTURE

As stated earlier, the common channel signaling (CCS) system is a separate network from the voice network. Terms used to describe this aspect of CCS are an overlay network or an out-of-band network. The CCS network is used to convey signaling messages between CCS nodes. The purpose of the CCS message exchange is to set up, manage, and release connections in the network. To introduce some of the major CCS terms used in an SS7 network, Figure 7–3 shows that a CCS network consists of the following components, which are introduced in a general manner in this part of the chapter and discussed in more detail later:[1]

- DB: Databases
- EC: Exchange carrier
      SP: Signaling point, or SEP: Signaling end point
      SSP: Service switching point

---

[1]Some of these terms are used in the United States by the telephone companies and Bellcore, and not in other countries.

- STP: Signaling transfer point
- SCP: Service control point

CCS nodes that are able to communicate with each other are network nodes called signaling points (SPs). An SP that originates or terminates SS7 messages may also be called a signaling end point (SEP). The SPs are connected to each other by point-to-point signaling links. Multiple links between two SPs can be organized as a link set, and the common practice is for the switch to load-balance the traffic across all the links that belong to the link set. Link sets can be associated with each other, in what is called a combined link set. Traffic can also be load-balanced across combined link sets.

The SP/SEP switch can switch voice or data calls, and can support the following capabilities:

- *CCS switching office (CCSSO)*. This component is a digital switch that runs the ISDN user part (ISUP) of SS7. The CCSSO can run in end offices, tandems, or access tandems.

- *Service switching point (SSP)*. An SSP is a SP/SEP that runs the SS7 transaction capabilities application part (TCAP). It is capable of supporting SCP database operations, halting call progress, and other operations. The SSP can run in end offices, tandems, or access tandems. The SSP and CCSSO complement each other and are usually co-located in the same network node.

- *Operator service system (OSS)*. The OSS is a SP/SEP that is configured to provide operator services to end users. Increasingly, OSS is automated and is discussed in more detail in Chapter 2.

- *Signaling transfer point (STP)*. SP is configured for routing traffic. It is responsible for relaying messages between SPs, and therefore plays an important role in the network. Later discussions explain that STPs are deployed in pairs for backup purposes. The STP runs SS7's message transfer part (MTP) and the signaling connection control part (SCCP). The STP only interfaces with SS7 links and does not interface with voice or data links. In the United States, the approach taken by the RBOCs is to concentrate the STP functions in a relatively small number of nodes, with the nodes dedicated to STP functions only.

- *Service control point (SCP)*. The SCP is also an SP/SEP that provides database support operations to another SCP or SSP. For example, 800 services are provided through the SCP.

EVOLUTION TO SS7

CCS systems were designed in the 1950s and 1960s for analog networks and were later adapted for digital telephone switches. In 1976, AT&T implemented the Common Channel Interoffice Signaling (CCIS) into its toll network. This system is referred to as CCS6 and was based on the CCITT Signaling System No. 6 Recommendation. SS6 and CCS6 were slow and designed to work on low bit-rate channels. Moreover, these architectures were not layered, which made changing the code a complex and expensive task.

Consequently, the CCITT began work in the mid-1970s on a new generation signaling system. These efforts resulted in the publication of SS7 in 1980, with extensive improvements published in 1984 and again in 1988. Today, SS7 and variations are implemented throughout the world. Indeed, SS7 has found its way into other communications architectures, such as personal communications services (PCS) and global systems for mobile communications (GSM). Table 7–1 lists some of the major milestones and names for SS7.

OVERVIEW OF SS7 OPERATIONS

SS7 defines the procedures for the set up, ongoing management, and clearing of a call between telephone users. It performs these functions by exchanging telephone control messages between the SS7 components that support the end users' connection.

The SS7 signaling data link is a full-duplex, digital transmission channel operating at 64 kbit/s. Optionally, an analog link can be used

Table 7–1   Signaling System No. 7 (SS7) Milestones

- In 1976, AT&T introduced Common Channel Interoffice Signaling (CCIS), based on CCITT Signaling System No. 6 (SS6).
- In 1980, enhancements were made with datagram mode of operation and 800 services.
- SS6 had low-speed links and limited routing capabilities—in mid-1970s, CCITT began work on SS7 for a signaling system for digital trunks.
- SS7 was first published in 1984 and revised in 1988 as the Q.700 Recommendations.
- In Canada, CCS7 is based on the ITU-T Recommendations.
- In United States and other countries systems are identified as SS7, SS No 7, or SS#7

with either 4 or 3 kHz spacing. The SS7 link operates on both terrestrial and satellite links. The actual digital signals on the link are derived from pulse code modulation multiplexing equipment or from equipment that employs a frame structure. The link must be dedicated to SS7. In accordance with the idea of clear channel signaling, no other transmission can be transferred with these signaling messages and extraneous equipment must be disabled or removed from an SS7 link. Table 7–2 provides a brief and partial summary of some of the SS7 functions. We shall examine the SP functions in subsequent chapters.

Table 7–2   Examples of the SS7 Functions

Setup and clear down a telephone call

Provide the called party's number (caller id)

Indication that a called party's line is out of service

Indication of national, international, or other subscriber

Indication that called party has cleared

Nature of circuit (satellite/terrestrial)

Indication that called party cleared, then went off-hook again

Use of echo-suppression

Notification to reset a faulty circuit

Language of assistance operators

Status identifiers (calling line identity incomplete; all addresses complete; use of coin station; network congestion; no digital path available; number not in use; blocking signals for certain conditions

Circuit continuity check

Call forwarding (and previous routes of the call)

Provision for an all-digital path

Security access calls (called closed user group [CUG])

Malicious call identification

Request to hold the connection

Charging information

Indication that a called party's line is free

Call setup failure

Subscriber busy signal

Identifiers of circuit signaling points, called and calling parties, incoming trunks, and transit exchanges

EXAMPLE OF AN SS7 TOPOLOGY

Figure 7–4 depicts a typical SS7 topology. The subscriber lines are connected to the SS7 network through the service switching points (SSPs). The SSPs receive the signals from the CPE and perform call processing on behalf of the user. SSPs are implemented at end offices or access tandem devices. They serve as the source and destination for SS7 messages. In so doing, SSP initiates SS7 messages either to another SSP or to a STP.

The STP is tasked with the translation of the SS7 messages and the routing of those messages between network nodes and databases. The STPs are switches that relay messages between SSPs, STPs, and service control points (SCPs). Their principal functions are similar to the layer 3 (network layer) operations of the OSI Model.

The SCPs contain software and databases for the management of the call. For example, 800 services and routing are provided by the SCP. SCPs receive traffic (typically requests for information) from SSPs via STPs and return responses (via STPs) based on the query.

Although Figure 7–4 shows the SS7 components as discrete entities, they are often implemented in an integrated fashion by a vendor's equipment. For example, a central office can be configured with a SSP, a STP, and a SCP or any combination of these elements. These SS7 components are explained in more detail later in this chapter.

FUNCTIONS OF THE SS7 NODES

We continue our analysis of SS7 here with a more detailed view of the SSP, STP, and SCP. In this section, the major functions of these signaling points (SPs) are described.

The Service Switching Point (SSP)

The SSP is the local exchange to the subscriber and the interface to the telephone network. It can be configured as a voice switch, an SS7 switch, or a computer connected to switch.

The SSP creates SS7 signal units at the sending SSP and translates them at the receiving SSP. Therefore, it converts voice signaling into the SS7 signal units, and vice versa. It also supports database access queries for 800/900 numbers.

The SSP uses the dialed telephone numbers to access a routing table to determine a final exchange and the outgoing trunk to reach this ex-

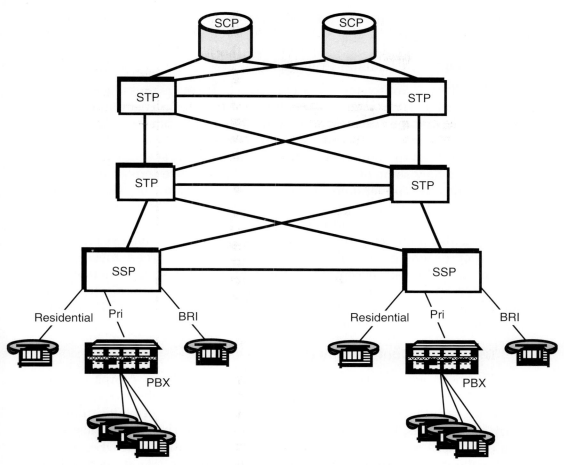

Note: Another node called the signaling point (SP) may exist between user and SSP
where:

BRI	Basic rate interface
PBX	Private branch exchange
PRI	Primary rate interface
SCP	Service control point
SSP	Service switching point
STP	Signaling transfer point

Figure 7–4   Example of an SS7 topology.

change. The SS7 connection request message is then sent to the final exchange.

The Signaling Transfer Point (STP)

The STP is a router for the SS7 network. It relays messages through the network but it does not originate them. It is usually an adjunct to a voice switch, and may or may not stand alone as a separate machine.

The STP is installed as a national STP, an international STP, or a gateway STP. Even though SS7 is an international standard, countries may vary in how some of the features and options are implemented. The STP provides the conversions of the messages that flow between dissimilar systems. For example, in the United States, the STP provides conversions between ANSI SS7 and ITU-T SS7.

STPs also offer screening services, such as security checks on incoming and/or outgoing messages. The STP can also screen messages to make certain they are acceptable (conformant) to the specific network.

Other STP functions include the acquisition and storage of traffic and usage statistics for OAM and billing. If necessary, the STP provides an originating SCP with the address of the destination SCP.

The Service Control Point (SCP)

The SCP acts as the interface into the telephone company databases. These databases contain information on the subscriber, 800/900 numbers, calling cards, fraud data, and so on. Bellcore provides guidance on SCP databases, but BOCs vary in how they use them. The most common databases used are: (a) business services database (BSDB), (b) call management service database (CMSDB), (c) line information database (LIDB), (d) home location register (HLR), and (e) visitor location register (VLR).

The contents of the databases that are made available through SCP vary among SS7 service providers. Figure 7–5 lists some of the contents of the databases as defined by Bellcore. Be aware that the exact contents of these databases vary from service provider to service provider.

The SS7 Levels (Layers)

Figure 7–6 shows the levels (layers) of SS7. The right part of the figure shows the approximate mapping of these layers to the OSI Model. Beginning from the lowest layers, the message transfer part (MTP) layer 1 defines the procedures for the signaling data link. It specifies the functional characteristics of the signaling links, the electrical attributes, and

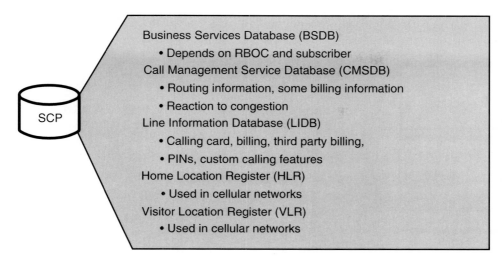

Business Services Database (BSDB)
- Depends on RBOC and subscriber

Call Management Service Database (CMSDB)
- Routing information, some billing information
- Reaction to congestion

Line Information Database (LIDB)
- Calling card, billing, third party billing,
- PINs, custom calling features

Home Location Register (HLR)
- Used in cellular networks

Visitor Location Register (VLR)
- Used in cellular networks

SCP

Figure 7–5   Contents of the databases.

the connectors. Layer 1 provides for both digital and analog links although the vast majority of SS7 physical layers are digital. The second layer is labeled MTP layer 2. It is responsible for the transfer of traffic (frames or signaling units) between SS7 components. The SU is quite similar to an HDLC-type frame and indeed was derived from the HDLC specification.

The MTP layer 3 provides the functions for network management and the establishment of message routing as well as the provisions for passing the traffic to the SS7 components within the SS7 network. Many of the operations at this layer pertain to routing, such as route discovery (and routing around problem areas in an SS7 network). The signaling connection control part (SCCP) is also part of the MTP-3 layer, and provides for both connectionless and connection-oriented services.[2] The main function of SCCP is to provide for translation of addresses, such as ISDN and telephone numbers to SS7 identifiers and addresses.

The ISDN user part (ISUP) is responsible for transmitting signaling information between SS7 network nodes. In essence, this is the call control protocol, in that ISUP sets up, coordinates, and takes down connections. It also provides features such as call status checking, trunk management, trunk release, calling party number information, privacy

---

[2]Some literature describes SCCP as a layer 3 protocol. While it provides support function for MTP 3, it also contains many features of the OSI layer 4.

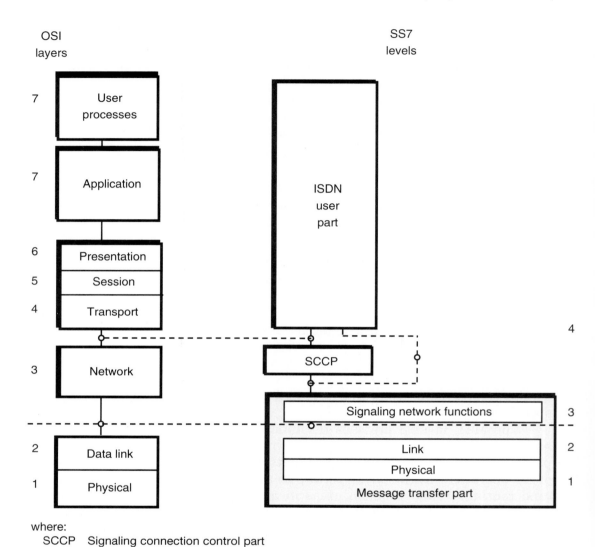

Figure 7–6   SS7 levels (layers).

indicators, and detection of application of tones for busy conditions. ISUP works in conjunction with ISDN Q.931. Thus, ISUP translates Q.931 messages and maps them into appropriate ISUP messages for use in the SS7 network.

Figure 7–7 provides another view of the SS7 levels and will serve as an introduction to subsequent material. We just learned about the functions of MTP. One more thought is important. The three MTP levels

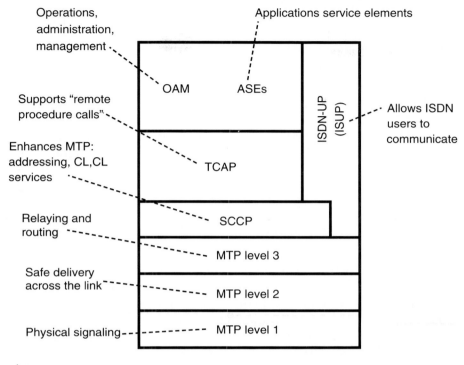

Figure 7–7   The SS7 levels in more detail.

serve as a connectionless transport system. With this approach, each SS7 message is routed separately from other messages, and there is no connection set up for the message transport.

We also learned that SCCP corresponds to several of the operations associated with OSI layers 3 and 4. Some of its principal jobs are: (1) supporting the MTP levels with address translation, (2) providing connectionless or connection-oriented services, and (3) providing sequencing and flow-control operations between any two (or more) signaling points.

The transaction capabilities application part (TCAP) corresponds to several of the functions of the OSI layer 7. It embeds the remote operations service element (ROSE) in its architecture. As such, it performs connectionless, remote procedure calls on behalf of an "application" running on top of it.

Finally, the ISDN user part (ISDN-UP or ISUP) provides circuit-related services needed to support applications running in an ISDN environment. However, non-ISDN originated calls are also supported by ISUP.

LINK TYPES

The architecture of North American SS7 signaling and its associated link types are shown in Figure 7–8(a). To begin the discussion, A links are also known as access links. They are used to connect SSPs, and SCPs to STPs, usually to an STP pair, which is considered to be its home STP pair.

B links are also known as bridge links. They are used to join mated STP pairs to other mated STP pairs. The result of this association and connection is known as a quad structure. The connection is on the same hierarchical level, such as between two local STPs (LSTPs).

C links are also known as cross links. They connect STPs together to form mated pairs. The purpose of this association is, once again, to create redundancy by forming a fully meshed topology among the four STPs. This topology provides 100 percent redundancy. Any single point of failure does not bring down the system, because the traffic can be diverted around the failure. However, to take advantage of this configuration, Figure 7–8(b) shows how the physical links between these pairs should be on diverse paths[3] (AB,AC), (BD,BE), (CD,CE). Either pair (BD,CE) or (CD,BE) should also be on a diverse path.

Larger systems employ a two-level hierarchy. As Figure 7–9 illustrates, the hierarchy is an extension of the mesh architecture, described previously. This architecture also provides a convenient boundary between operating companies. The two levels are known as the primary level and the secondary level. The rules for the association require that secondary level STP pairs must always be "homed" to specific primary pairs.

Primary STP pairs are connected through B links, forming the B-link quad, and secondary STP pairs are connected with their primary STP pairs through D links (diagonal links), forming a D-link quad. The D links connect STP pairs at two different hierarchical levels; for example, from a local STP (LSTP) to a regional STP (RSTP).

---

[3]Diverse paths mean two (or more) links between SPs should not be in the same conduit or cable sheath. It does little good to have two links if both of them are cut with a back hoe.

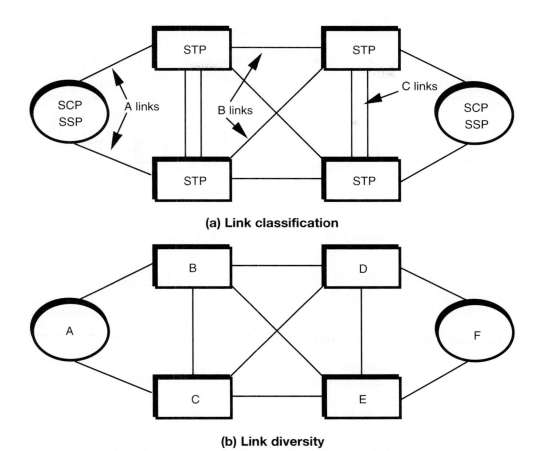

(a) Link classification

(b) Link diversity

(AB,AC), (BD,BE), (CD,CE) on diverse paths
Either pair (BD, CE) or (CD,BE) on diverse paths
where:

MTP	Message transfer part
SCCP	Signaling connection control part
SCP	Service control point
SSP	Service switching point
STP	Signaling transfer point
TCAP	Transaction capabilities application part

Figure 7–8   SS7 link types.

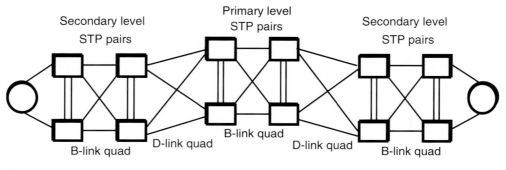

where:
  STP   Signaling transfer point

Figure 7–9   STP levels and link types.

The term quad link (or quad-link sets) is used because the STPs are paired nodes and the B or D links are used to connect them.

Two other types of links are employed in SS7. E links also known as extended links—they connect SSPs or SCPs to a mated STP pair. The distinction of this connection is that the mated STP pair is not the "home" STP pair of the SSPs or SCPs. In Figure 7–10, the connection through the E link refers to the STP pair as the remote pair. In BOC terminology, E links connect an SP/SEP to an STP pair other than the home STP pair.

Finally, F links, or fully associated links, refer to the links in which the SCPs and SSPs are connected directly to each other. These links do not connect any STP nodes and (as we shall see later) are used by associated routes. This approach is also called associated signaling and is used when SPs have high interest in each other; that is, they communicate with each other frequently.

The terms and concepts listed in Table 7–3 summarize CCS links. The link designator is listed with the link name and the corresponding function of the link.

Figure 7–11 provides a full view of all the link types and their interfaces into SCPs, SSPs, and STPs. All these links may be of the same physical type and may use the same physical interface card at each machine. Their designations as A, B, and so on simply reflect the roles they play and their location in the SS7 topology.

The topology in Figure 7–11 is organized and classified as (1) the regional signaling network, (2) the local signaling network, and (3) the trunk network. This arrangement is illustrated in Figure 7–12, and is implemented within the LEC CCS network. The STPs are called either local STPs (LSTPs) or regional STPs (RSTPs). The LSTPs support local

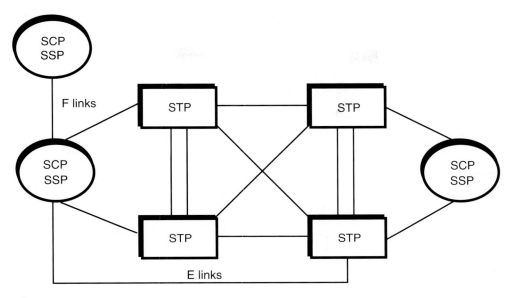

where:
    SCP   Service control point
    SSP   Service switching point
    STP   Signaling transfer point

Figure 7–10   Link types E and F.

call setup and immediate message routing for the SEPs. The routing support can extend to other local networks, higher levels within the same network, or to another LEC through an IC.

The following points apply to the LEC CCS network in relation to the LSTPs and RSTPs:

- A links connect local SEPs to the LSTP pair
- C links cross-connect the LSTP pair

Table 7–3   CCS Links

Designator	Name	Function
A links	Access links	Connect SCP/SSPs to home STP
B links	Bridge links	Connect two STPs at the same level
C links	Cross links	Connect mated STPs to each other
D links	Diagonal links	Connect STPs at different levels
E links	Extended links	Connect SCP/SSPs to non-home STP
F links	Fully associated links	Connect (directly) SCP/SSPs

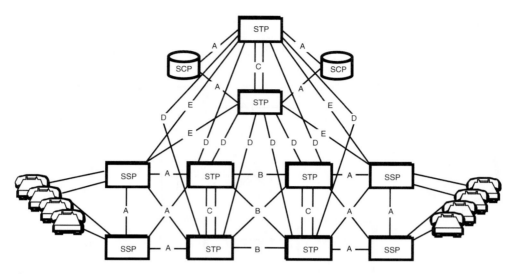

where:
  SCP   Service control point
  SSP   Service switching point
  STP   Signaling transfer point

Figure 7–11   The complete view of the signaling links.

- B links connect LSTP pairs
- D links connect an LSTP pair to the RSTP

Figure 7–12 depicts several other terms that are used in the LEC CCS network topology. The LSTPs provide several functions: (1) interface to another LEC; (2) interface to an IC; (3) interface to a cellular provider; (4) interface to a private CCS network; (5) interface out of the local trunk network within the same LEC network.

The RSTPs are used to interface higher level network signaling for SCPs that provide services such as 800.

SS7 IDENTIFIERS AND NUMBERING SCHEME

SS7 signaling points (nodes) are identified with an address, and each node must have a unique address. The SS7 addresses are called point codes (PCs) or signaling point codes. The point code is kept transparent to entities operating outside the SS7 network; no direct correlation is made between the point code and a telephone number or an ISDN

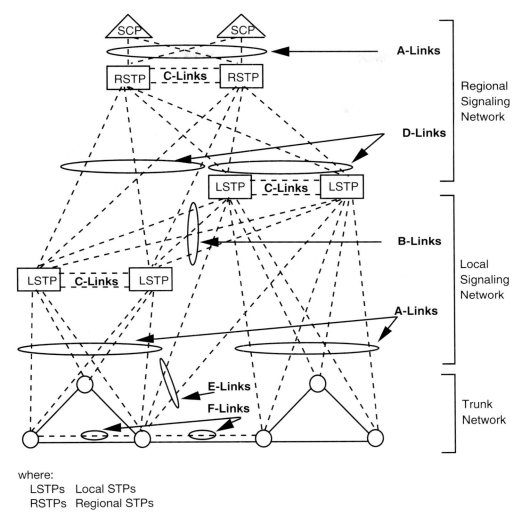

Figure 7–12   Another view of the SS7 architecture.

address. The correlation between these identifiers is made by each net-work. The point code (PC) is placed inside the MTP 3 message and used to route the message to the appropriate signaling point.

The PC is a hierarchical address consisting of (1) a network identi-fier, (2) a network cluster, and (3) a network cluster member. The net-work identifier, as its name implies, identifies a signaling network. The network cluster identifies a cluster of nodes that belong to that network. Typically, a cluster of signaling nodes consists of a group that home in on a mated pair of STPs. They can be addressed as a group. The network cluster member code identifies a single member (signaling point [SP]) operating within a cluster. The structure of the PC and its relationship to signaling points is depicted in Figure 7–13.

The structure of the point code fields is different in the United States, ITU-T, and other national specifications. Each country may implement its own point code structure, but is expected to support an ITU-T structure at the international gateway between two countries.

In addition to the point code (PC) used by MTP for routing to an SP in the network, SS7 also utilizes a subsystem number (SSN). This number does not pertain to a node but to entities within a node, such as an application or some other software entity. As examples, it could identify enhanced 800 (E800) services running in a node, an automated calling card service (ACCS) module operating in the node, ISUP, and so on.

SS7 also supports the global title (GT) identifier, which could be the dialed digits of a telephone number. The best way to view the GT is that it is mapped to an SS7 network address of PC + SSN.

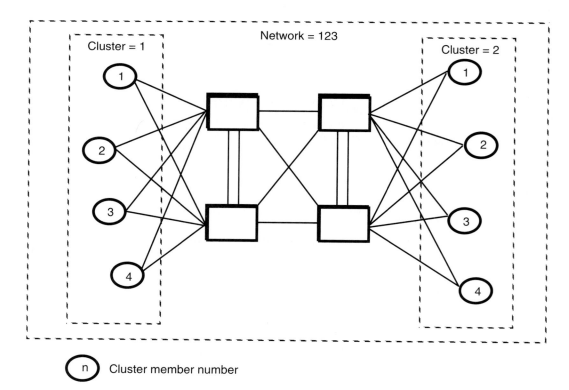

Figure 7–13   SS7 numbering plan.

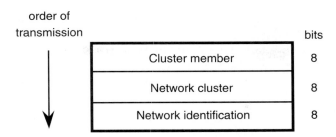

Figure 7–14   Format of signaling PC.

As we shall see later, an SS7 subsystem operates as a user to SCCP. Therefore, SCCP "routes" traffic to and from the proper subsystem operating on top of SCCP.

Format of the Signaling PC

The PC consists of three 8-bit fields, as shown in Figure 7–14. The cluster member field is transmitted first, then the network cluster field, followed by the network identification field.

Code Assignments

The assignment of the codes is governed by each country's telecommunications administrations. In the United States, the network code is set up according to the conventions shown in Table 7–4. The assignment scheme provides for three types of registration: (a) network code, (b) network code and cluster code, and (c) network code, cluster code, and cluster member codes.

For large networks, registration type (a) is used. Logically enough, large networks are classified by their size. Large networks must have

Table 7–4   Signaling PC Assignments

Network Code	Assignment
7–255	Large network
6	Unassigned
5	Signaling point code block
1–4	Small network
0	Not used

more than 75 signaling points and 5 STPs in the first years of operation, and then several other requirements must be met in the following years.

For small networks, registration type (b) is used. Registration type (c) is used for a group of signaling points that are not part of a network and have no STP. Some examples of the registration types are provided in Table 7–5.

Table 7–5   Examples of Signaling Point Code Assignments

Large Networks:			
Network Code	*Network*		
254	AT&T		
245	Stentor (Canada)		
246	Bell Atlantic		
241	Defense Communications Agency		
240	GTE		
233	Rochester Telephone		
235	Contel		
227	North American Cellular Network		
220	Southwestern Bell		
Small Networks:			
Network Code	*Cluster*	*Network*	
1	1	Puerto Rico Telephone Co.	
1	26	LDDS	
1	44	Teleglobe Canada	
1	120	Bell Mobility Cellular	
1	98	Central Texas Telephone Cooperative	
1	131	Ameritech Cellular Services, Inc.	
Signaling Code Point Block:			
Network Code	*Cluster*	*Members*	*Network*
5	1	7–11	Phone America
5	1	127–131	Roanoke Telco
5	1	216–219	Rochester Telephone Company
5	6	112–115	Colorado Valley Telephone Cooperative
5	7	136–139	Call America

Global Title Addressing and Translation

Obviously, the telephone user should not be concerned with SS7 addresses. This customer need only enter a called party telephone number, and SS7 will set up the call. To the SS7 network, the telephone number is a global title and, as such, does not contain sufficient information for routing in the signaling network. Furthermore, a user may not always dial a conventional telephone number as a called party address. Other identifiers may be used; as examples, 911 number, a mobile phone number, a telex number, or an 800 number.

SS7 is adaptable enough to accept these logical addresses, and translate them to a routing address in order to support the call. Typically, an SS7 network contains sites that are responsible for these translations, and most systems place these operations at designated STPs. As we shall see in later discussions, SCCP is the SS7 entity that provides for global title translations.

CONNECTING NETWORKS

To facilitate worldwide connections of SS7 networks, the standards organizations have set up an internetworking model, depicted in Figure 7–15. The model operates as two functionally independent levels, one at the national level and one at the international level. This separation permits the clear division of responsibilities between service providers in different countries and allows these networks to operate independently of one another, with each country implementing the features of SS7 that it deems appropriate. All SS7 networks must adhere to the conventions defined in the internetworking standards, if worldwide communication is to take place.

This model is also set up to permit the SS7 addresses (point codes) and their administration to be independent of one another. Not all countries use the same addressing scheme that was introduced earlier in this chapter. Indeed, the ITU-T (Q.700) defines point codes differently than the U.S. Standards groups. Each country is free to choose its own addressing scheme, just as long as the address is the same length as the international standard.

For the internetworking operations, a signaling transfer point is assigned to one of three categories. The first category is a national signaling point (NSP). This STP belongs to a national network and uses point codes according to the national numbering plan of that country. The second category is an international signaling point (ISP), which belongs only to the international signaling network, and is identified by the interna-

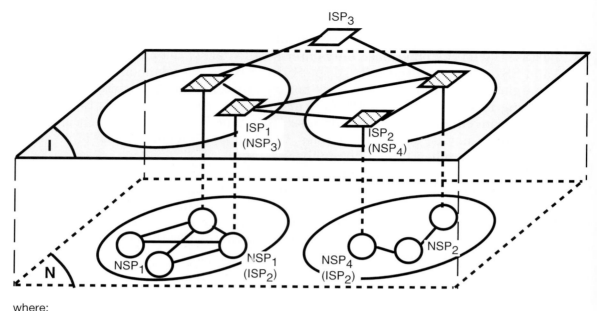

where:
ISP   International signaling point
NSP   National signaling point

Figure 7–15   Internetworking architecture.

tional point code. The third category is an STP that operates as both an ISP and an NSP, which is identified by two point codes. The latter two categories of STPs are responsible for providing gateways between the national networks to support address conversion and protocol mapping, if the national networks' implementations of SS7 differ.

SUMMARY

SS7 is the international standard for out-of-band signaling systems. Most systems in the world are quite similar with some minor variations on a national or regional basis. Initially, employed for use by the telephone network, SS7 is now used in mobile, wireless networks, and asynchronous transfer mode (ATM) networks.

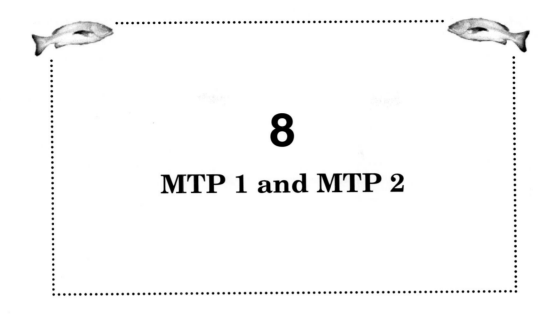

8

MTP 1 and MTP 2

INTRODUCTION

This chapter examines the lower two layers of SS7, MTP 1 and MTP 2. The emphasis in this chapter is on MTP 2. MTP 1 is covered in a general discussion. A companion book in this series, *T1 and SONET: Foundation for Digital Transport Systems,* has more detailed information on MTP 1, and other physical layers.

MESSAGE TRANSFER PART (MTP) LEVEL 1

The SS7 MTP 1 signaling data link is a full-duplex, digital transmission channel operating at 56 or 64 kbit/s. Optionally, an analog link can be used with either 4 or 3 kHz spacing, and a minimum signaling rate of 4.8 kbit/s. The SS7 link operates on both terrestrial and satellite links. The actual digital signals on the link are derived from pulse code modulation (PCM) multiplexing equipment or from equipment that employs a frame structure. MTP 1 resides at the physical layer (layer one) of the OSI Model, as depicted in Figure 8–1.

The MTP link must be dedicated to SS7. In accordance with the idea of clear channel signaling, no other transmission can be transferred with the signaling messages. Extraneous equipment must be disabled or re-

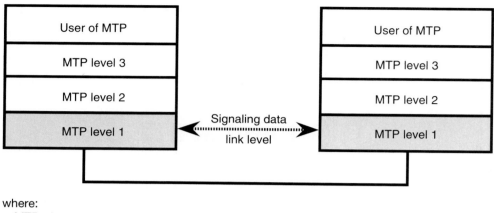

where:
   MTP   Message transfer part

Figure 8–1   Physical level (MTP 1).

moved from the SS7 link. For example, the A and μ law conversions must be removed. Also, equipment such as echo suppressers must be disabled.

SS7 permits data transfer rates greater or less than the 64 kbit/s rate. The standard 2.048 Mbit/s, and 8.448 Mbit/s (in North America 1.544 Mbit/s) rates are all permitted if used within the appropriate ITU-T recommendations.

The use of analog signals is supported through several of the V Series recommendations. While SS7 provides leeway in the bit transfer rates for an analog connection, it stipulates the use of V.27 or V.27 bis for a 4.8 kbit/s link.

MESSAGE TRANSFER PART (MTP) LEVEL 2

ITU-T Recommendation Q.703 of SS7 and ANSI T1.111 describe the procedures for transferring SS7 signaling messages across one link (in SS7 terms, the signaling link) with MTP 2. The link connects any two signaling points (SPs), and MTP2 is responsible for the reliable transfer of signaling messages between these points. In essence, it transfers all upper layer traffic (MTP3, SCCP, TCAP, ISUP, etc.) safely across the link. The messages that are delivered by MTP 2 are placed into the MTP 2

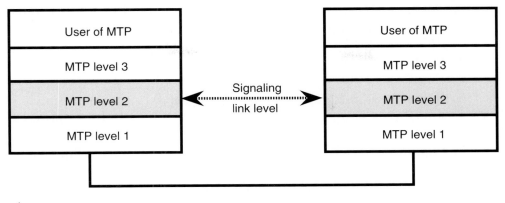

where:
  MTP   Message transfer part

Figure 8–2   Data link level (MTP 2).

"signal unit" for transport across the link. MTP 2 resides at the data link layer (layer two) of the OSI Model, as depicted in Figure 8–2.

As explained in the remainder of this chapter, MTP 2 performs the operations that are typical of layer two protocols. It has many similarities to the well-known High Level Data Link Control (HDLC) protocol. For example, both protocols use flags, error checks, and sending/receiving sequence members. MTP 2 uses the term signal unit (SU) in place of frame, which is used in most layer 2 protocols.

RESPONSIBILITIES OF MTP 2

MTP 2 is responsible for seven major link operations. They are summarized briefly here and described in more detail in the following material:

1. *Signal unit delimitation.* Uses flags to detect the beginning and ending of the SU.
2. *Signal unit alignment.* Insures the SU length is valid and that any bits between the two legitimate flags are not misinterpreted as flags.

3. *Signal unit error detection.* Uses the FCS field in the SU to detect any bits that were damaged during transmission across the link.

4. *Signal unit error correction.* Provides methods for correcting an error.

5. *Signal unit initial alignment.* Provides services to initialize a link (bring it up) and restore it (upon a failure) by a "proving" process.

6. *Signal unit error monitoring.* Determines if an active link should or should not stay in service and, if the proving process for a new or restored link warrants, makes the link active.

7. *Signal unit flow control.* Controls the flow of SUs between the two signaling points.

THE SIGNAL UNITS (SUs)

Level two messages are transferred in variable length SUs, and the primary task of MTP 2 is to ensure their error-free delivery. The SUs are one of three types: message signal unit (MSU), link status signal unit (LSSU), and fill-in signal unit (FISU). These signal units are described in a general way in this section and in more detail in the remainder of this chapter. Refer to Figure 8–3 during this discussion.

The Message Signal Unit (MSU)

The MSU carries the signaling message, which is an MTP 3 message (Figure 8–3a). It also carries messages of the other upper layers (user parts [UPs]), such as SCCP. The system transfers the MSU across the link and determines if the message is uncorrupted. If the message is damaged during the transfer, it is retransmitted.

The Link Status Signal Unit (LSSU)

The LSSU is used to bring up a link, verify that it is operating correctly, and if necessary, take a link down (see Figure 8–3b). One of its responsibilities is link alignment, which entails operations that ensure the traffic on the channel is of the correct length, and that the two signaling points at the end of the link are receiving the signal units without problems (receiving the flags properly, which is discussed in the next section). In the event of problems, MTP 2 will work with MTP 3 to take a link out of service, and make efforts to correct the problems.

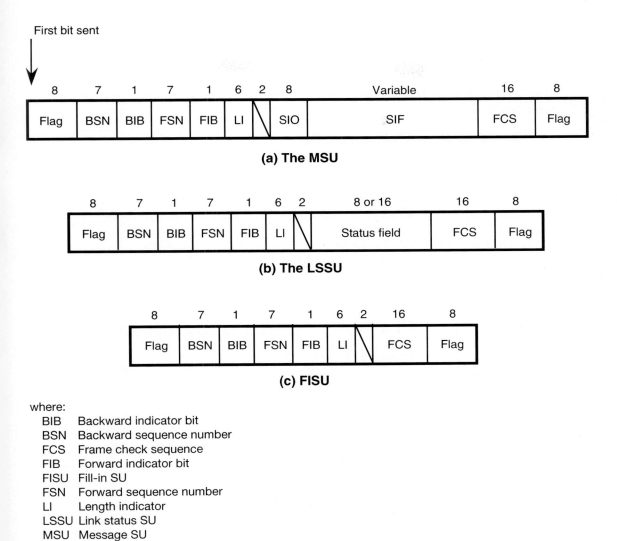

First bit sent

(a) The MSU

(b) The LSSU

(c) FISU

where:

BIB   Backward indicator bit
BSN Backward sequence number
FCS Frame check sequence
FIB   Forward indicator bit
FISU Fill-in SU
FSN Forward sequence number
LI   Length indicator
LSSU Link status SU
MSU Message SU
SIO   Service indicator octet
SU   Signal unit

Figure 8–3   SS7 level 2 PDUs.

The Fill-in Status Unit (FISU)

The FISU occupies the link when there is no traffic from MTP 3 and the upper layers (see Figure 8–3c). It performs functions similar to HDLC-type protocols, which send continuous flags during periods of link inactivity. However, MTP 2 sends flags and several other fields during this idle condition. One that we highlight in this introductory section is the frame check sequence field (FCS). It is used by the receiver to determine if the signal unit has any errored bits. This approach determines how many signal units are being damaged during transmission on the link and is a good tool to determine if the link is of sufficient quality for continued use.

Contents of the Fields in the SUs

As shown in Figure 8–3, all SUs begin and end with the 8-bit flag. The flags are coded as a specific and constant sequence of bits that are not allowed to exist within the SU; that is, between two valid flags. The sending machine checks all the bits that are bounded by the flags before these bits are sent and places a 0 in the bit stream when it encounters a value that would be interpreted as a flag at the receiver. This process is called bit stuffing. The receiving machine performs a complementary operation to remove these stuffed bits. With this approach, MTP 2 ensures that the link is "in alignment", and that the flags are being used correctly to "frame" the traffic at the receiver.

All SUs use a $X^{16} + X^{12} + X^5 + 1$ cyclic redundancy check (CRC) operation for the frame check sequence field. The FCS field is created at the sending signaling point and checked at the receiving signaling point to determine if the SU was damaged (corrupted) during its transmission.

Two sequence numbers are used to provide flow control and user message accountability. The backward sequence number (BSN) acknowledges messages and the forward sequence number (FSN) identifies and sequences the SU in which it resides. The BSN and FSN perform the same functions as the N(R) and N(S) fields that are used in many other layer two protocols (HDLC, SDLC, LAPB, etc.). However, the manner in which the BSN is incremented is different from these other layer 2 protocols. The BSN is set to the same value as the FSN that it is acknowledging. In contrast, for the HDLC-type protocols, the N(R) is set to one greater than the N(S) that it is acknowledging.

The BSN and the FSN are used with the forward indicator bit (FIB) and the backward indicator bit (BIB), respectively, to perform sequencing and acknowledging functions. The FSN/FIB are associated with the BSN/BIB in one direction on the link (to use a phrase, the east direction). They are independent of the FSN/FIB and BSN/BIB in the other direction (the west direction). This concept permits independent flow across both directions of the full duplex link.

Therefore, using the terms east and west to indicate the two directions of SU flow across the link, if the operations across the link are correct, the FIB in the east direction will equal the BIB in the west direction. If an error occurs, the BIB is toggled (flipped to a 1 if it were a 0, and to a 0 if it were a 1) in the next SU sent. When the receiving machine detects this new value in the BIB, it knows that this SU conveys a negative acknowledgment (NAK) and that the BSN in this SU represents the value of the FSN that was received in error. This convention informs the machine that it must resend the identified SU.

For example, assume signaling point A has sent a SU with FSN = 4, and FIB = 1. If this traffic is accepted by signaling point B, it will respond with BSN = 4, and BIB = 1. But if this traffic were corrupted during transmission and is not accepted by signaling point B, it will respond with BSN = 4, and BIB = 0. Consequently, signaling point A knows to resend the SU that is sequenced and identified by FSN = 4. I show more examples of the use of the these fields later in this chapter.

The length indicator (LI) field specifies the number of octets that follow it, up to the FCS field. The number of octets vary, depending upon the type of SU. For the FISU, it is 0. For the LSSU, it defines the length of the status field (one or two octets). For the MSU, it defines the combined length of the service indicator octet (SIO) and the signaling information field (SIF). The SIF is one octet, and the SIF can be as small as two octets and as large as 272 octets.

The SIO is divided into two fields: the service indicator field and the subservice field. The service indicator field is used by level 3 to perform message distribution and routing functions. The values identify the type of message. For example, the user parts (UPs) are identified, such as ISDN user part (ISUP) or telephone user part (TUP). The *subservice field* is used by signaling message handling functions to distinguish between international and national messages.

The service indicator field consists of 4 bits and is coded for U.S. networks as shown in Table 8–1. These codes are similar to the codes assigned by the ITU-T, except that in the ITU-T Recommendation, codes 0010, 1101, and 1110 are spare.

The subservice field also contains 4 bits and is coded as shown in Table 8–2. Bits D and C are used to allow a signaling point to discriminate between national and international messages. The two spare bits (A and B) are available for national use if bits D and C are set to 10 or 11. In the United States, priority 3 is assigned to MTP and SCCP messages that are important to the operations of SS7.

The status field (SF) is an 8-bit field, in which three bits are used to activate and restore the link and to ensure link alignment; that is, proper recognition and delineation of the flags and the SU's contents. It

Table 8–1   Service Indicator Codes

Bits				
D	**C**	**B**	**A**	**Meaning**
0	0	0	0	Management messages
0	0	0	1	Testing and maintenance regular messages
0	0	1	0	Testing and maintenance special messages
0	0	1	1	SCCP
0	1	0	0	Telephone user part (TUP)
0	1	0	1	ISDN user part (ISUP)
0	1	1	1	Data user part
1	0	0	0	MTP testing user part
1	0	0	1	Spare
1	0	1	0	Spare
1	0	1	1	Spare
1	1	0	0	Spare
1	1	0	1	Reserved for individual network use
1	1	1	0	Reserved for individual network user
1	1	1	1	Spare

Table 8–2   Subservice Field

Bits		
D	**C**	**Meaning**
0	0	International message
0	1	Spare (international use only)
1	0	National network
1	1	Reserved for network use
B	**A**	
0	0	Priority 0
0	1	Priority 1
1	0	Priority 2
1	1	Priority 3

is also coded to indicate if a node is busy in order to institute flow control measures.

Signal Unit Delineation and Alignment

All SUs must start and end with the flag (F) fields. The signaling points on to the data link are required to continuously monitor the link for the flag sequence. The flag sequence consists of 01111110. Flags are transmitted on the link between SUs to keep the link in an active condition. A end flag of one SU can be the begin flag of the next SU, or if no message SUs are being sent, continuous fill-in SUs (FISUs) are transmitted.

On occasion, a flag-like field, 01111110, may be inserted into the SIF by an upper layer (MTP 3, for example). To prevent "phony" flags from being inserted into the frame, the transmitter inserts a zero bit after it encounters five continuous 1s anywhere between the opening and closing flag of the frame. As the frame is stuffed, it is transmitted across the link to the receiver.

The procedure to recover the frame at the receiving signaling point can be summarized as follows: The receiver continuously monitors the bit stream. After it receives a zero bit with five consecutive 1 bits, it inspects the next bit. If it is a zero bit, it pulls this bit out; in other words, it unstuffs the bit. Then, the receiver checks the SU length to determine if the length of the SU is valid. If so, it stores the SU for further processing.

Signal Unit Error Detection

The implementation of the MTP 2 FCS is accomplished with a *shift register*. The transmitter initializes the register to all 1s and then changes the register contents by the division of the generator polynomial on all fields between the flags. The 1s complement of the resulting remainder is then transmitted as the FCS field. At the receiver, the register is also set to all 1s, and the fields are subjected to the calculation and checked for errors.

MTP 2 uses a convention, in which the calculation by the generator polynomial $x^{16} + x^{12} + x^5 + 1$ is always 0001110100001111 (7439 decimal), if no bits in the two calculations have been damaged during the transmission between the transmitter and receiver.

Signal Unit Support by MTP 2

Levels 3 and above of SS7 depend on level 2 to ensure the safe transmission and reception of all SUs across the link. Level 2 accomplishes this service through the use of two types of error correction operations: the basic method and the preventive cyclic retransmission (PCR) method. The basic method assumes the use of terrestrial links and the PCR method assumes the use of satellite links. Table 8–3 provides a summary of these two operations. FISUs and LSSUs are not part of these operations.

Some writers use the following terms: The basic method is referred to as a non-compelled positive/negative acknowledgment retransmission error correction system and the PCR method is referred to as a non-compelled positive acknowledgment cyclic retransmission, forward error correction system. Also, during this discussion, the term SU refers only to a message SU (MSU).

Basic Method.   The basic method uses a conventional link control operation known as "go-back-N." The transmitting machine retains copies of all message signal units (MSUs) until the receiver returns either a positive or negative acknowledgment (ACK or NAK). If a NAK is received, the machine retransmits the errored MSU and all succeeding MSUs that were transmitted subsequent to the NAK'd MSU.

Example of an Error-free Operation.   Figure 8–4 shows an example of the basic method with no errors occurring. The first rule to remember as you analyze this figure is that the forward indicator bits (FIB) in the transmitted SUs (east direction) are equal to the backward indicator bits (BIB) in the received SUs (west direction) if the link is operating without errors. The station (i.e., east station) that detects an error inverts its BIB and sends it to the receiving (west) station, which notes the bit is not

Table 8–3   Dealing with Errors on the Link

Error correction: Basic method

- Also known as non-compelled positive/negative acknowledgment retransmission error correction system.
- Transmitter retains SU and awaits positive or negative ACK from receiver.

Error correction: Preventive cyclic retransmission (PCR) method

- Also known as non-compelled positive acknowledgment cyclic retransmission, forward error correction system.
- Transmitter retains SU and awaits positive ACK from receiver.
- During periods of inactivity, unacknowledged SUs are retransmitted cyclically.
- Transmission of new SUs can be interrupted if excessive SUs remain unacknowledged.

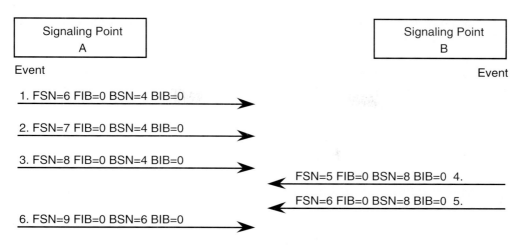

Figure 8–4   Basic operations, no errors.

equal to its FIB in its outgoing SUs. In this manner, the west station knows it has received a NAK.

The second rule to remember is that the BSN value in the NAK indicates the value of the FSN that was coded in the last correctly-received SU.

Figure 8–4 is explained with six events. In events 1 through 3, signaling point A sends 3 MSUs to signaling point B. The FSN value in the first SU = 6 and is incremented by 1 with each transmission. The reason FSN does not begin with 0 is because the proving period (explained later) used some of the FSN and BSN values. The transmission of the MSUs continues the ongoing numbering that was performed with the FISUs during proving.

The FIB and BIB are set to 0 initially. The BSN in these SUs is set to 4 to indicate to B that A is expecting the next SU from B to contain an FSN = 5. From previous transmissions, B has already sent SUs 0–4, and A's BSN = 4 simply continues to tell B that they have indeed been acknowledged and A is still "looking for" the next SU of FSN = 5.

In event 4, B acknowledges A's SUs by sending the value of 8 to its BSN. It keeps its BIB set to 0 (the same value as A's FIB). Also, in event 4, B sends a message as well, so its FSN = 5 is the next send sequence number in this direction. Notice that the SU in event 4 with BSN = 8 inclusively acknowledged all of A's outstanding SUs (6, 7, and 8).

In event 5, B sends its second MSU, and so indicates with FSN = 6. It keeps its BSN = 8 because it has not received any additional SUs from A.

In event 6, A acknowledges B's SUs by sending back BSN = 6, which acknowledges B's 5 and 6 SUs.

Example of Error Handling.   Figure 8–5 shows what happens in the event an error occurs with the basic method. Events 1-3 are the same as in Figure 8–4. In event 4, B inverts its BIB, sets the BSN to the last accepted SUs and sends this SU to A. (In events 4 and 5, B is still allowed to send its own traffic). A notices that the received BIB value is different from its ongoing FIB value; therefore, it knows it has received a negative acknowledgment. Recovery occurs in events 6 and 7 by A inverting its FIB, and resending SUs FSN = 7 and FSN = 8, that were transmitted originally in events 2 and 3. In event 8, A continues to send traffic. In event 9, B indicates that all SUs have been received correctly from A, and this event completes the recovery operations for A's SUs 7 and 8.

Notice that the NAK in event 4 requires that the retransmission beginning with the SU that has an FSN of one more than the BSN associated with the BIB inverted bit.

During the operations just described, both nodes turn on a timer designated as T7, which is called the *excessive delay of acknowledgment timer*.

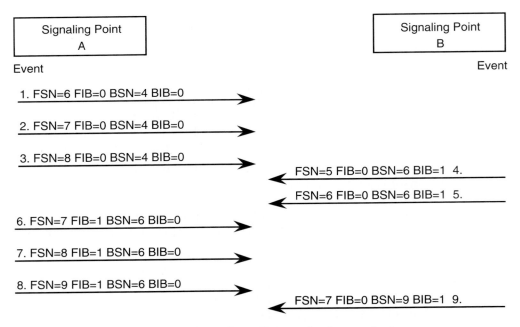

Figure 8–5   Error detection and retransmission.

The timer is turned on when the first MSU is sent onto the channel. It is turned off upon receiving ACKs for the outstanding MSUs. If T7 expires and at least one SU is outstanding, level 3 is informed of a link failure.

One T7 timer is used for all SUs. Referring to Figure 8–4, the timer is started in event 1 only, and not events 2 and 3. As a general practice, if an acknowledgment is received but the BSN does not acknowledge all the outstanding SUs, T7 is reset to await the subsequent acknowledgments.

PCR Method. Like the basic method, the PCR method maintains copies of the SUs at the transmitter until positive acknowledgments are received. Unlike the basic method, during periods of inactivity on the channel, the transmitting machine simply resends unacknowledged SUs to the receiver. If the receiver does not return ACKs, the transmitter will cease sending new SUs and force retransmission of the unacknowledged SUs.

PCR utilizes logic states that will keep forced retransmission in operation if the link becomes unstable or error-prone. PCR is also designed for use on links that have long propagation delays. These links do not work well with the go-back-N technique, because excessive retransmissions may result even though only one SU may have been damaged.

Figure 8–6 shows how the PCR operates. In event 1, A sends B an SU. Note that the FIB and BIB are set to 1 and are not used. As long as no new SUs are available for retransmission, those SUs available for retransmission are resent, subject to the following rules. The sending node maintains two counters: number of SUs available for retransmission (N1), and number of SU bytes available for retransmission (N2). The counters are incremented each time a new SU is sent onto the link and then checked to determine if either has reached a set limit (as in event 2). If the answer is no (as in event 3), new SUs are sent. In event 4, if one of the counters reaches a set limit, no new SUs are introduced onto the link, and the outstanding units are retransmitted, as shown in events 5 and 6.

Signal Unit Initial Alignment

This procedure is used to activate and restore a link. Two proving periods are available (which are chosen by MTP 3): normal proving period or emergency proving period. Four alignment status indicators are used during this operation. They are coded in the status field of the LSSU:

1. O = Out of alignment
2. N = Normal alignment status

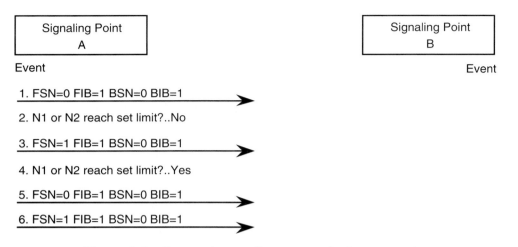

Figure 8–6   Preventive cyclic retransmission procedure.

3. E = Emergency alignment status

4. OS = Out of service

Figure 8–7 provides an example of how an SS7 link is initialized. A link is considered "not aligned" when it is first put into service or when it is being restored (as in event 1). To set up the link, the two machines correctly receive a status indication out of alignment (SI = O) message, shown as event 2. This operation is controlled by the T2 timer. If an SIO message has not been received upon timer T2 expiring, then the link must remain in a not aligned state. If the SIO message is received within the T2 timer limit, the link is set to aligned, and the T2 timer is turned off.

Once the link has been aligned (event 3), the machines can send either a status indicator normal (SI = N) signal or a status indicator emergency (SI = E) signal, which is shown in event 4. These signals determine the type of "proving" that is to be performed on the link. Timer T3 governs this part of the operation. If timer T3 expires with the machine having received no S = Ns or S = Es, then the link must return to a not aligned state. Otherwise (in event 5), the proving state is entered, and timer T4 is turned on and timer T3 is turned off.

With normal proving, a link must prove itself (determine it is reliable) for a proving period known as Pn before it is allowed to transmit live signals. Normal proving is used if there is any other link in the route set available to handle signaling. Pn is defined as 2^{14} octet transmission

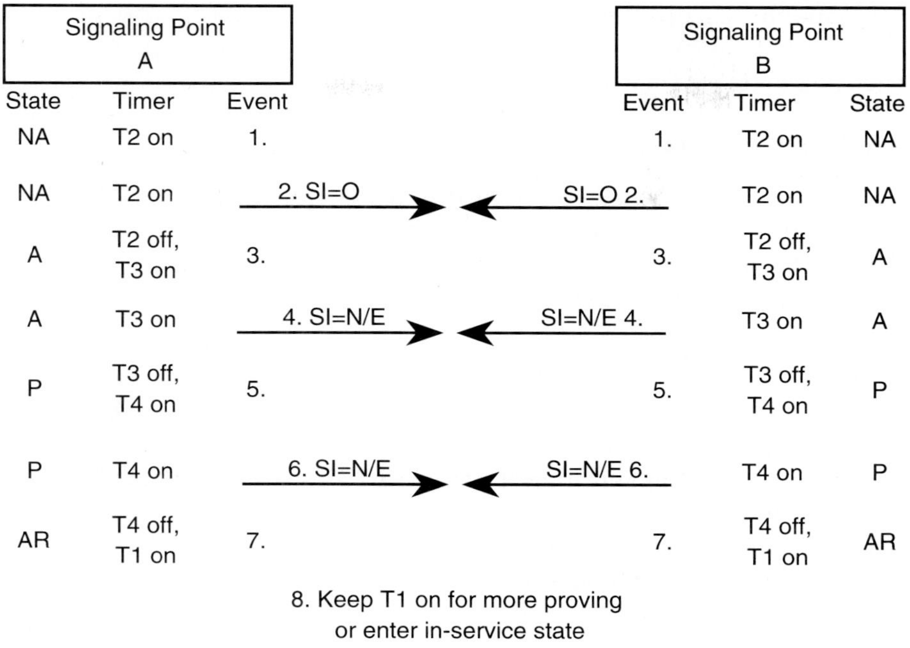

Signaling Point A				Signaling Point B		
State	Timer	Event		Event	Timer	State
NA	T2 on	1.		1.	T2 on	NA
NA	T2 on	2. SI=O $\longrightarrow$	$\longleftarrow$ SI=O 2.		T2 on	NA
A	T2 off, T3 on	3.		3.	T2 off, T3 on	A
A	T3 on	4. SI=N/E $\longrightarrow$	$\longleftarrow$ SI=N/E 4.		T3 on	A
P	T3 off, T4 on	5.		5.	T3 off, T4 on	P
P	T4 on	6. SI=N/E $\longrightarrow$	$\longleftarrow$ SI=N/E 6.		T4 on	P
AR	T4 off, T1 on	7.		7.	T4 off, T1 on	AR

8. Keep T1 on for more proving
or enter in-service state

where:
SI = O   Status indication set to out of alignment
SI = N/E Status indication set to normal or emergency alignment
NA   Not aligned state
P   Proving state
AR   Aligned/ready state

Figure 8–7   Initial alignment/restoration.

time, which equals 2.3 seconds for 56 kbit/s link and 2.0 seconds for a 64 kbit/s link.

With emergency proving, a link must prove itself for a period defined as Pe before carrying live traffic. Emergency proving is used if there are no available links in an entire route set to handle signaling. Pe is defined as 2^{12} octet transmission time, which translates to 0.6 seconds for a 56 kbit/s link and 0.5 seconds for a 64 kbit/s link.

After proving has been completed (events 6 and 7), the link moves to an "aligned ready" state and the machines can begin sending FISUs. At this point, timer T1 is once again initiated and, if it fails, the link returns to "out-of-alignment" state. If FISUs are exchanged successfully, the link enters the "in service" state and MSUs can then be exchanged.

If the machines on the link have trouble completing the proving process (for example, if proving fails 5 times) then the link must return to the "not aligned" state.

Signal Unit Error Monitoring

A procedure is also used to monitor an active link. Statistics are kept on the number of SUs that were rejected due to errors, as well as a ratio of the SUs received in error to total SUs received. Level 3 is informed when the ongoing monitoring detects excessive errors.

Signal Unit Flow Control

In the event of congestion at either signaling point, an LSSU is sent to the other node with a link status field set to B (busy). The receiving node must then cease the sending of MSUs (FISUs can be sent). This operation also turns off timer T7.

Normal operations are resumed when the congested node sends an LSSU with the link status field set to N (normal).

SUMMARY

SS7 defines several options for the interfaces and protocols operating at the physical level, known as MTP 1. MTP 1 defines the signaling rate, synchronization requirements, cabling, and physical connectors for the signaling link.

In contrast, the data link level MTP 2 stipulates the use of only one set of procedures on the link. MTP 2 is responsible for the safe delivery of messages across the signaling link between two signaling points.

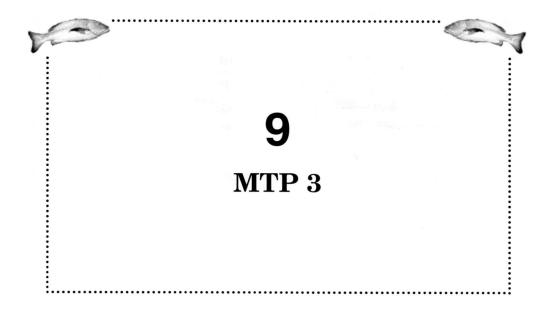

9
MTP 3

INTRODUCTION

This chapter examines the SS7 MTP level 3 functions. The focus in the first part of the chapter is to examine the two major sets of MTP 3: the signaling message handling functions and the signaling network management functions. After this discussion, SS7 routing tables are explained, as well as how the MTP 3 functions are used to divert traffic around problem nodes and links in the network. We then learn how the SS7 network uses its mesh topology to recover from problems.

LOCATION OF MTP 3 IN THE PROTOCOL STACK

Figure 9–1 shows the placement of MTP 3 in the layers of SS7. Since MTP 2 is a service provider to MTP 3 (and performs error checks with possible retransmissions), MTP 3 assumes the traffic given to it from MTP 2 is error-free. Other than performing edits on the fields of the received messages, it relies on MTP 2 for reliable link transfers.

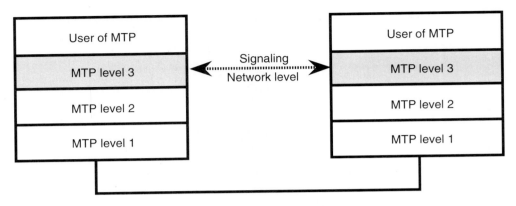

Figure 9–1   Network level (MTP 3).

USE OF THE ROUTING LABEL

The STPs use fields in the SU to determine the SU routing destination (see Figure 9–2). A routing label contains the identification of the originating and destination SPs. A code in the label is also used to manage load sharing within the network. The routing label is used by the STP in combination with a routing table to make the routing decisions. The route is fixed unless failures occur in the network. In this situation, the routing is modified by MTP 3 functions. The load-sharing logic and a code in the label permit the distribution of the traffic to a particular destination to be distributed to two or more output signaling links.

Figure 9–2 shows the organization and structure of the routing label within the message signal unit (MSU). The label is coded in every MSU message type and consists of the three fields: the signaling link selection (SLS), the origination point code (OPC), and the destination point code (DPC). The OPC and DPC are explained in Chapter 7. The SLS is used to select the signaling link within a given link set. Figure 9–2 shows the breakout of the OPC; the DPC is not shown, but it contains the same fields as the OPC.

MTP 3 ORGANIZATION

MTP 3 is organized around two major functions: signaling message handling and signaling network management. In turn, these functions are each separated into three major operations (see Figure 9–3).

Signaling message handling insures that the messages generated by a specific user part at the originating point are delivered to the same

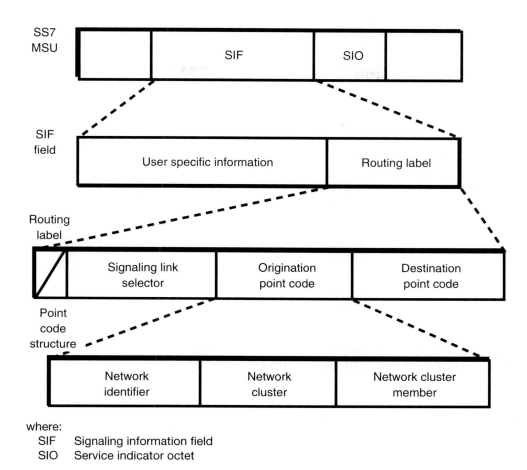

where:
SIF   Signaling information field
SIO   Service indicator octet

Figure 9–2   Routing label.

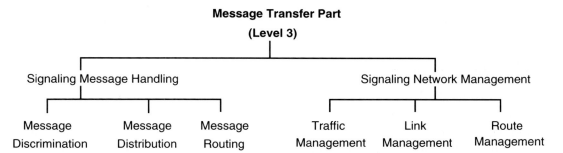

Figure 9–3   The MTP level 3 architecture.

user part at the destination point. The routing label is used by the signaling message handling operations for this delivery operation. The signaling message handling functions are divided into three parts:

- *Message discrimination*. Determines at each signaling point if the message is to be forwarded to message routing or message distribution. In effect, it determines if the message is destined for another node or to the node in which message discrimination resides.
- *Message distribution*. Selects the user part at the destination point by checking the service indicator code.
- *Message routing*. Selects the link to be used for each message by examining the point code of the address.

Signaling network management handles reconfiguration operations in the event of a failure. It also controls the flow of traffic in the event of congestion. It is divided into three functions:

- *Signaling traffic management*. Controls the message routing functions of flow control, rerouting, changeover to a less faulty link, and recovery from link failure.
- *Signaling link management*. Manages the activity of the MTP 2 function. Provides a logical interface between MTP 2 and MTP 3.
- *Signaling route management*. Transfers status information about signaling routes to remote signaling points.

SIGNALING MESSAGE HANDLING

With the exception of message routing, signaling message handling is quite simple. The other two functions, message discrimination and message distribution, act as simple internal MTP 3 routers, directing traffic between MTP 2, MTP 3, and the upper layers (the users of MTP 3).

Message Discrimination

Figure 9–4 shows the relationships of the three signaling message handling operations. Message discrimination handles all incoming messages. Using the routing label's destination point code, it determines if the incoming message is destined for this node or for another node. If the message is destined for another node, it is passed directly to message

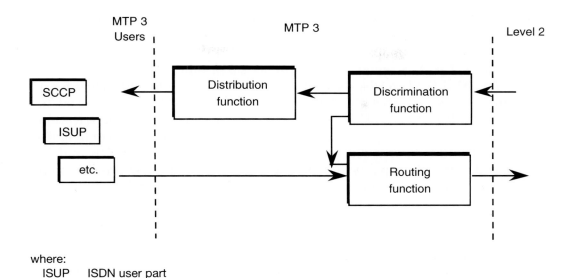

where:
  ISUP   ISDN user part
  SCCP   Signaling connection control part

Figure 9–4   Signaling message handling.

routing. If it is destined for this local node, it is passed to message distribution.

Message Distribution

Message distribution passes the SU to the appropriate application (the MTP 3 users) in the local node. The identification to determine the recipient of the message is provided in the service indicator octet (SIO) field (discussed in Chapter 8). As examples, the message is passed to ISUP, SCCP, a network management module.

Message Routing

Message routing passes the SUs it receives to the appropriate link by examining the destination point code in the routing label, which we learned earlier includes: the network identifier, the cluster identifier, and the member number. It also uses the signaling link selection field (SLS) to determine which link within a link set is to be used. This function also performs load sharing in order to distribute traffic evenly over the links of a link set. In addition, it can load share between links that are not members of the same link set.

Signaling Link Selection.   One of the functions of message routing is to perform load sharing operations by selecting links within a link set or link sets not belonging to the same link set. A five-bit SLS field is coded as $X_4X_3X_2X_1X_0$, where X_i represents a 1 or 0 bit.

The SLS field can be used in a variety of ways. One approach for a combined link set uses the format of $Y_0X_3X_2X_1X_0$, where X_0 is used to choose the link set, and the other four bits are used for link selection within the chosen link set. With this approach, an X is a uniform distribution of 0s and 1s, and the Y is also a uniform distribution of 0s and 1s only if the signaling point is generating the SLS codes for the outgoing message. If a single link set is used, the format of $Y_0X_3X_2X_1X_0$ is employed, but Y_0 is not examined.

The idea behind bit rotation is that it permits load sharing so that each subsequent signaling point will have a uniform distribution of bits in the SLS code for sharing. A subsequent signaling point's load sharing is independent of the previous signaling point.

Routing in the SS7 Network.   Routing in the SS7 network is based on the destination point code (DPC) in the MTP 3 message. The DPC is used in one of two ways by MTP. The first method examines the entire DPC to determine the route for the message, and the second method examines only part of the DPC. The most efficient approach is the second method because it allows some signaling points to reduce the size of their routing tables. For example, if a signaling point does not need to know the cluster number or cluster member number in order to route the traffic, then it need not store these values in its routing table. Indeed, for the majority of cases, the complete DPC does not need to be stored at each SP.

The partial DPC approach is similar to the approach used in switching offices for a call setup. For example, some switching offices examine only the area code of the dialed number; others examine only the central office code; whereas the terminating switching office need only examine the 4-digit station number.

Figure 9–5 shows a simple SS7 network topology consisting of STPs, clusters, and cluster members. Each node in the figure is identified with a point code, with the network number arbitrarily chosen as 3 (0000 0011). Each link set at each node is associated with an outgoing route from the node. For purposes of simplicity, only signaling points F and I are depicted with these numbers: routes 1, 2, 3, 4, 5, 6, and 7 at F and routes 9 and 10 at I.

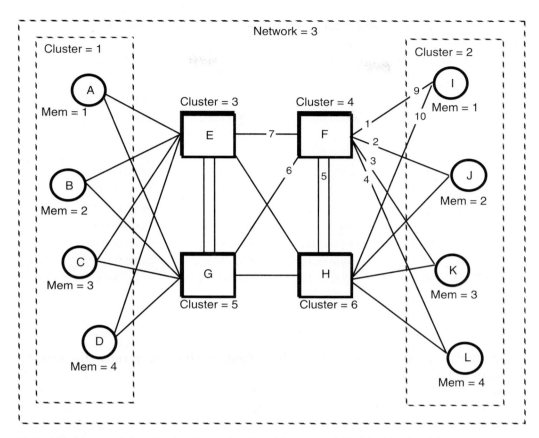

Note: Numbers on links attached to nodes F and I represent physical port numbers.

Figure 9–5   Addressing of the signaling points.

An address table reflecting the topology, addresses, and links of the signaling points in Figure 9–5 would appear as shown in Table 9–1. The table is self-explanatory, with the note that each STP is assigned a cluster number, but not a cluster member number.

The specific organization and contents of the SS7 routing tables are not defined in the standards. As discussed earlier, a common approach is to design the tables and software to examine the relevant parts of the destination point code (DPC). For example, using a full point code, as a first step, the switch examines the network ID of the DPC. If more information is needed (no route exists in the table), the second step is to examine the cluster code. If no route exists in the table, the member code is

Table 9–1   Address Table for the Topology in Figure 9–5

Signaling Point	Signaling Point Code		
	Network	*Cluster*	*Member*
A	0000 0011	0000 0001	0000 0001
B	0000 0011	0000 0001	0000 0010
C	0000 0011	0000 0001	0000 0011
D	0000 0011	0000 0001	0000 0100
E	0000 0011	0000 0011	0000 0000
F	0000 0011	0000 0100	0000 0000
G	0000 0011	0000 0101	0000 0000
H	0000 0011	0000 0110	0000 0000
I	0000 0011	0000 0010	0000 0001
J	0000 0011	0000 0010	0000 0010
K	0000 0011	0000 0010	0000 0011
L	0000 0011	0000 0010	0000 0100

examined. The cluster and cluster member tables are accessed through pointers. This approach permits an efficient, hierarchical routing operation.

This approach is facilitated by designing the tables in a modular fashion, with pointers from a network table to a cluster table, which points to a member table. Tables 9–2 and 9–3 show two examples of rout-

Table 9–2   Routing Tables for Signaling Point I

Network Table		
Network Code	*Route*	*Alternate Route*
0000 0011	Pointer to cluster table	—
Others	9	10

Cluster Table		
Cluster Code	*Route*	*Alternate Route*
0000 0100	9	10
0000 0110	10	9

Table 9–3   Routing Tables for Signaling Point F

Network Table

Network Code	Route	Alternate Route
0000 0011	Pointer to cluster table	—
Others	To other quad pairs, not shown	—

Cluster Table

Cluster Code	Route	Alternate Route
0000 0011	7	6
0000 0101	6	5
0000 0110	5	6
0000 0010	Pointer to member table	—

Member Table

Member Code	Route	Alternate Route
0000 0001	1	5
0000 0010	2	5
0000 0011	3	5
0000 0100	4	5

ing tables. The first set of tables in Table 9–2 illustrates how the routing tables might be constructed to signaling point I. Table 9–3 depicts a configuration for signaling point F. As Tables 9–2 and 9–3 reveal, the MTP 3 routing tables also contain information on alternate routes. In the event of problems on the primary route, the alternate route is used.

Using Table 9–2, if an SU at signaling point I contains DPC = 3, the cluster table is examined. This table contains information that determines if the SU is to be sent to cluster 4 or cluster 6 through routes 9 and 10 respectively.

Table 9–3 shows the routing table stored at SP F. All SUs that arrive at F with a DPC = 3 are routed with first, the cluster table, and next, the cluster member table. The cluster table directs the SU to the next cluster within network 3. If the SU is destined for cluster 2, the cluster member table is accessed to determine the route to the cluster x member signaling point.

SIGNALING NETWORK MANAGEMENT

My approach in explaining SS7 signaling network management is to provide a detailed description of the key functions, supplemented with a general portrait of others. This approach is necessary because each function is documented in great detail in the standards, and it does little good to merely parrot these documents. It is my intent to give you a sound understanding of the MTP 3 services, without a lengthy digression into each protocol rule for each function. Following this description, I show several examples of signaling network management operations.

The second major part of MTP 3 is signaling network management, which provides services to ensure recovery from disruptions in a signaling point or a link. These disruptions may result from physical failures, congestion, ongoing maintenance activity, changes in the status of a link, or operations within the signaling point. As depicted in Figure 9–6, the signaling network management function is organized around three complimentary operations described in the following material.

Relationships of Signaling Message Handling and Signaling Network Management

Figure 9–7 shows the relationships of signaling message handling and signaling network management. The solid lines in the figure represent the message flow between the entities. Even though messages are exchanged between the entities or the two major functions, signaling network management does not send any traffic onto the link; all signal units go through the message routing function.

The dashed lines indicate the flow of control signals between the functions. Most of these signals are OSI-type primitives, which define what signals (and parameters) are passed internally between these functions; that is, how they coordinate their activities. These primitives are used by programmers to code function or system calls between the software modules that execute the functions of MTP 3.

Signaling Traffic Management

Signaling traffic management diverts signals on one link or route to one or more alternate links or routes. Additionally, it reduces traffic flow in the event of congestion. Signaling traffic management consists of the following procedures.

Changeover. In the event of link problems, signaling traffic is changed (transferred) from an unavailable signaling link to an alternative signaling link. Changeover is designed to avoid any loss of traffic

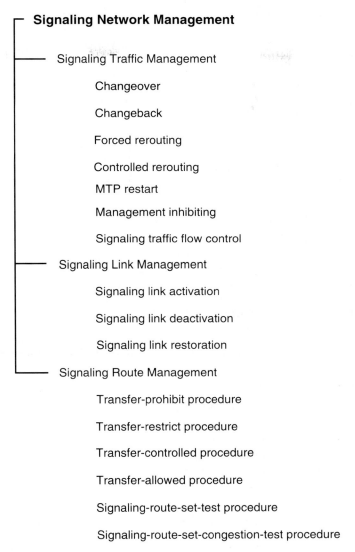

Figure 9–6   **Signaling network management.**

and to prevent the duplication or mis-sequencing of traffic. As a result of a changeover, the new link will match one of three cases. Figure 9–8 is used for this discussion.

1. The new link is parallel to the old link. In the figure, the diversion of traffic is from one link on link set AF to another link.

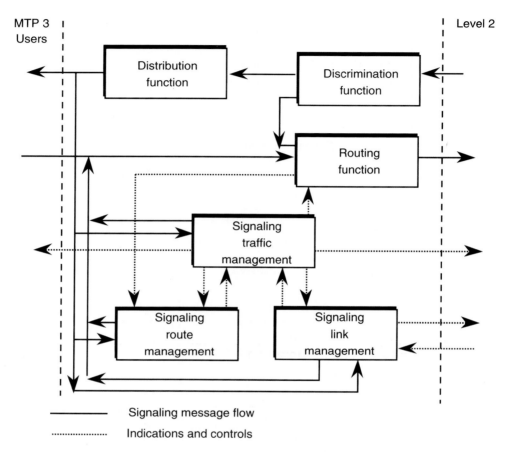

Figure 9–7   Relationships of signaling message handling and signaling network management.

2. The new link is through another signaling route, but the route passes through the signaling point at the far end of the old link (signaling point B). The diversion of traffic is from link set AF, to link set AC, then link set CF.

3. The new link is through another signaling route, and the route does not pass through the far end signaling point of the old link. The diversion of traffic is from link set AB, BF, to link set AC, then link set CF.

Figure 9–9 provides as example of changeover operations pertaining to cases 1 and 2. (I exclude the BIB and FIB fields in this example; the

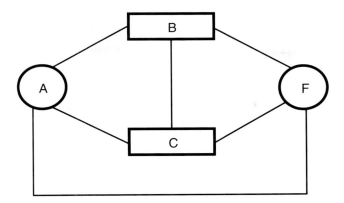

Figure 9–8   Changeover and changeback cases.

reader can refer to Chapter 8 for an explanation of their use.) In events 1 through 3, signaling point A sends SUs across link set AB to signaling point B, and B acknowledges these units. In event 4, A sends its third SU, but before it is delivered to B, the link fails (in event 5). Therefore, SU with FSN = 8 is still outstanding and has not been acknowledged. Both A and B must divert traffic to an alternative link (event 6).

In event 7, A sends an MTP 3 changeover order message to B. This message contains the label (with the destination and originating signaling points), the SLC (indicating the identity of the unavailable link), and the FSN of the last SU accepted from the unavailable link. Since the FSN in this message is 5, B knows that its signal unit sent in event 3 is safe at A. Consequently (event 8), it is not necessary to transfer any signal units awaiting transmission from the BA link set buffer to the BC link set buffer.

In event 9, B sends a changeover ACK to A with the FSN of the last signal unit accepted from the unavailable link from A, which is the last FSN = 7. Upon receiving this signal unit, A recognizes that the signal unit sent in event 4 did not arrive correctly. Consequently, in event 10, it transfers from its AB link set buffer to its AC link set buffer all outstanding signal units that are one greater than the FSN value in event 9—which is only one signal unit (FSN = 8). In event 11, A resends this signal unit, and in event 12, B acknowledges it.

Changeback. Changeback accomplishes the same operation as changeover but switches traffic from the alternative signaling link to the signaling link. It is the opposite operation of the changeover and diverts traffic to a link that is uninhibited, restored, or unblocked.

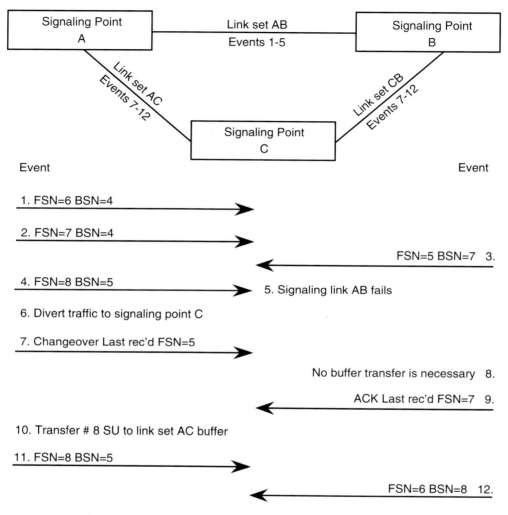

Figure 9–9   The changeover operation for cases 1 and 2.

Changeback provides a procedure to insure that traffic remains in sequence and is not lost or duplicated during the changeback operations. It also supports the case 3 situation with a sequence control procedure.

Forced Rerouting.   Forced rerouting is employed when a signaling route become unavailable. Forced rerouting restores, as soon as possible, the signaling capability between two signaling nodes that are operating in the direction towards a specific destination point. The objective of forced rerouting is to minimize the impact of a failure. Nonetheless, forced rerouting may result in the loss of messages.

This procedure is rather simple. It is activated when a signaling point discovers a route and/or signaling link is unavailable. Outstanding traffic on the route is immediately stored in a forced rerouting buffer. A routing table is examined (discussed later in this chapter) to determine an alternative route. The traffic is moved to the outgoing alternate link set buffer that pertains to the new link, and then sent to the next signaling point.

Controlled Rerouting. Controlled rerouting is designed to restore the best (optimal) signaling route(s) and is used for maintenance purposes as well as the recovery of route(s) that failed previously. The idea is to keep the network traffic flowing through the optimal routes by the reliance on link restoration and routing tables to continually seek out these routes. The actions for this procedure are supported by changeback operations.

MTP Restart. The MTP restart procedure allows an MTP at a signaling point to recover and also bring enough signaling links to the available state to handle all expected traffic.

Management Inhibiting. Management inhibiting is ordinarily implemented for ongoing maintenance and testing operations. Its purpose is to pull a link out of service in order to make it unavailable to end user traffic. The procedure can be initiated by a management function at either end of the link.

When a signaling point receives a link inhibit request message, it must determine (as best as it can) if the inhibiting will result in a destination becoming inaccessible. If so, it must deny the request. If the link request is granted, the link is taken out of operation by the changeover procedures described earlier.

Signaling Traffic Flow Control. Signaling traffic flow control reduces the amount of traffic at a source node in the event of congestion or failure problems in the network. Many of the signaling traffic flow control operations are described in Chapter 8, dealing with MTP 2.

Signaling Link Management

Signaling link management restores failed links, activates idle links, and deactivates aligned links. These activities are described in more detail shortly, and are listed here to give the reader a complete view of this part of MTP 3. Signaling link management consists of the following procedures.

Signaling Link Activation. Signaling link activation activates a signaling link and, as part of this procedure, starts the initial alignment procedure for the link.

Signaling Link Deactivation. Signaling link deactivation deactivates a link (assuming no active traffic is running on the link).

Signaling Link Restoration. Signaling link restoration returns a previously failed link to service.

Signaling Route Management

Signaling route management disseminates information between signaling nodes in order to block or unblock signaling routes. Signaling route management consists of the following procedures.

Transfer-prohibit. The transfer-prohibit procedure is performed by an STP with its neighbor signaling nodes. The procedure informs these nodes that they *must* no longer route certain messages via that STP to a given destination.

Transfer-restrict. The transfer-restrict procedure is quite similar to the previous procedure except this procedure informs the adjacent nodes that they *should* no longer route certain messages via that STP to a given destination. An example of transfer-restrict is explained later in this chapter.

Transfer-control. The transfer-control procedure is performed by an STP with its neighbor signaling nodes. The procedure informs these nodes that they *must* no longer route certain messages of a given priority or lower via that STP to a given destination.

Transfer-allowed. The transfer-allowed procedure is performed by an STP with its neighbor signaling nodes. The procedure informs these nodes that they *may* start to route certain messages via that STP to a given destination.

Signaling-route-set-test. This procedure determines if traffic towards a certain destination may be routed through an adjacent STP.

Signaling-route-set-congestion-test. This procedure is used by a signaling node to update congestion information associated with a certain destination and its associated route set.

EXAMPLES OF RECOVERY FROM FAILURES

SS7's use of multiple links between nodes and the mesh topology of STP mated pairs make for a very reliable network. We will use Figure 9–10 to show how MTP 3 uses this topology to recover from link or signaling point failures. This discussion is based on the ANSI model; it does not show all possible failure recovery operations, but will give you a good idea of SS7's robustness. For more details and more examples, refer to ANSI T1.111.

To provide a more robust topology for our examples, E and F links are employed in addition to the conventional links. The E links connect A to a non-home STP pair (D and E). The F links connect directly between signaling points (A and F) to form associated signaling. The E and F links may not be implemented in some systems; they provide for a very robust architecture, but they are expensive due to the many interconnections that must be supported.

As discussed earlier in this chapter, each signaling point is configured with a routing table. The routing table contains the preferred link set for normal routing and an alternative link set (or sets) in the event of failure on the normal link set. Table 9–4 shows a example of an alternate

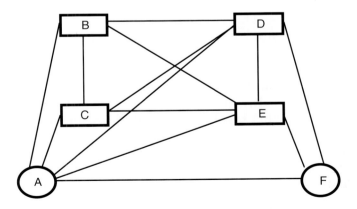

Figure 9–10   ANSI T.111.7 model for alternate link sets.

Table 9–4   Normal and Alternative Link Set Table

Signaling Point	Normal Link Set	Alternative Link Set	Priority
A	AF	AD	2
		AE	2
	AC	AB	1
	AB	AC	1
	AE	AD	1
	AD	AE	1
B	BD	BE	1
		BC	2
	BE	BD	1
		BC	2
	BA	BC	2
	BC	None	—

link set table for the ANSI model in Figure 9–10. The alternative link sets are used based on their priorities. If the priorities are the same for two alternative link sets, SS7 uses the load sharing procedure to distribute traffic across the link sets.

Please refer to Figure 9–10 during this discussion. For normal operations, routing traffic goes through the most direct route. For STP-to-STP mated traffic, the signal units are sent across C links (at B, the BD link set). If a failure occurs between an STP pair (B and C), no routing change occurs. The reasons are that A can still reach its two STPs (B and C). Also, under most conditions, upon receiving traffic from its attached signaling points (in this example, A) B would not send this traffic to C, but to a more direct route of BD or BE. Therefore, if link set BC fails, only STPs B and C are aware of the failure. As shown in Table 9–4, the BC link set is always a lower priority than its alternatives.

It is possible for this topology to break down to such an extent that traffic is not routable for a particular STP. For example, at STP B, if link sets BD, BE, and BC are unavailable, B cannot relay traffic. But, as explained in Chapter 7, this topology provides 100 percent redundancy. Any single point of failure does not bring down the system, because the traffic can be diverted around the failure. So, even if B's links are down (or for that matter if B is down), traffic is diverted, and the network remains fully operational. Anyway, multiple link failures are rare; such an event would mean that all link sets and links within each link set have failed.

Failure of Access Links and/or Switches

The entries in Table 9–4 do not tell the whole story. Some examples will illustrate how effectively SS7 handles link and switch failures. Figure 9–11(a) shows the recovery operations when an F link fails between nodes A and F. Traffic is diverted across the shortest path (the fewest number of hops) by A and F based on the routing table (Table 9–4). For A, it diverts traffic to alternate links sets AD and AE. For F (not shown in the table), it diverts traffic to alternate link sets FD and FE. Two link sets are used by A and F for the purpose of load sharing. Although not entered in the routing table, link sets AC and AB could have been used by A, say as priority 3 if necessary. Node F does not have this option, because it is not as fully connected as is node A.

In Figure 9–11(b), a link set failure occurs between A and E on an E link and traffic is diverted to link AD. In Figure 9–11(c), failure of both E links at node A creates a problem because both links to an STP pair are lost, and the routing table provides for no other alternate links. This situation blocks traffic in both directions; node A cannot reach F, and node F cannot reach A. This situation can be corrected by adding two entries in the routing table, as shown in Table 9–5. Alternative link sets AC and AB have been added with a priority of 2.

Table 9–5   Alternative Link Set Table Modification (Modifications are underscored)

Signaling Point	Normal Link Set	Alternative Link Set	Priority
A	AF	AD	2
		AE	2
	AC	AB	1
	AB	AC	1
	AE	AD	1
		AC	*2*
	AD	AE	1
		AB	*2*

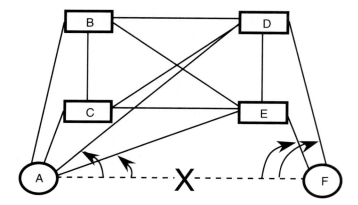

(a) Failure of a link set between two signaling points

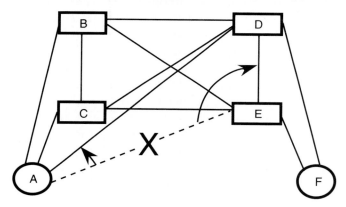

(b) Failure of an E link on a signaling point and an STP pair

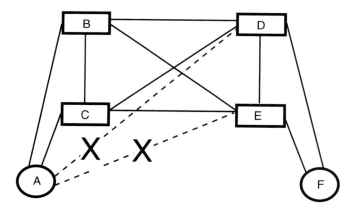

(c) Failure of an A link between an SP and STP pair

Figure 9–11   Failure of nonbackbone links.

Example of Initial and Final Traffic Diversion

The next examples do not include link sets types A and F, since not all networks use these types. In Figure 9–12(a), traffic is routed between signaling points F and A through link sets FD-DB-BA. In Figure 9–12(b), a failure occurs on the link (or link set) between B and A. These nodes take this link set out of operation and B diverts the traffic to C on link set BC. However, a better route exists between F and A. If the BA failure persists for greater than a set period, B will send messages to D and E to inform them that traffic for A should be sent on link sets DC and EC respectively. This operation is part of the transfer restricted operation sig-

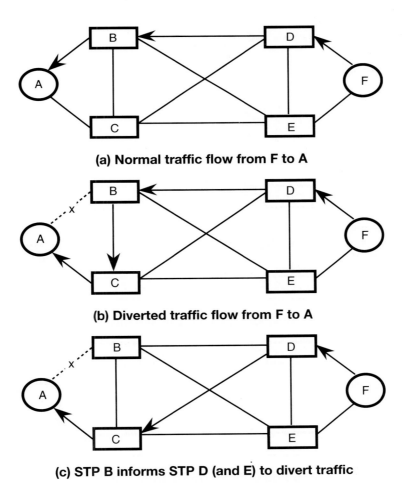

(a) Normal traffic flow from F to A

(b) Diverted traffic flow from F to A

(c) STP B informs STP D (and E) to divert traffic

Figure 9–12   Failure of an access link.

naling route management, which was introduced briefly earlier in this chapter. The new configuration is shown in Figure 9–12(c).

The Transfer-prohibit Procedure

Earlier in this chapter, we introduced the transfer-prohibit procedure. Figure 9–13 shows an example of its operations. In Figure 9–13(a), traffic is flowing smoothly from F to A, through D and B. In Figure 9–13(b), D notes link failures between it and nodes F and E, so it sends transfer-prohibit messages to B and C. These nodes adjust their routing, and in Figure 9–13(c) divert the traffic away from D and toward E, in order to stay in contact with F.

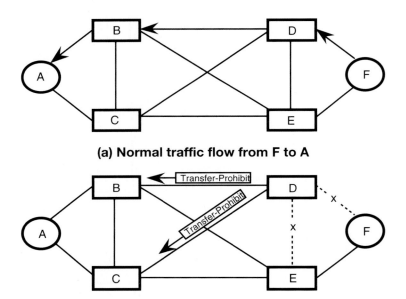

(a) Normal traffic flow from F to A

(b) D notes loss of links and send transfer-prohibit messages

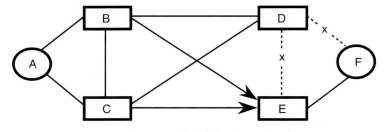

(c) B and C divert traffic from D to E.

Figure 9–13   Transfer-prohibit procedure.

It is instructive to note that the transfer prohibit message tells signaling points B and C how to divert traffic. Its purpose is not to inform signaling point F, which has no choice but to use alternative routing on link set FE.

The Transfer-allowed and Controlled Rerouting Procedures

This next example (see Figure 9–14) shows the transfer-allowed and controlled rerouting procedures, which were introduced earlier in this chapter. We pick up the discussion from Figure 9–13, where traffic had

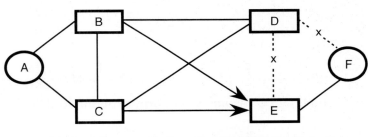

(a) B and C are still diverting traffic from D to E

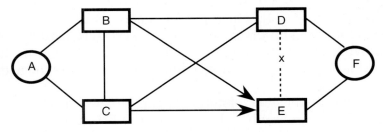

(b) The link between D and F is restored

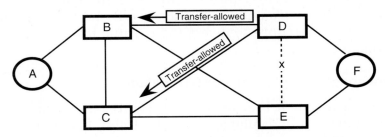

(c) D informs B and C about the link DF availability

Figure 9–14   Transfer prohibited and controlled rerouting procedures.

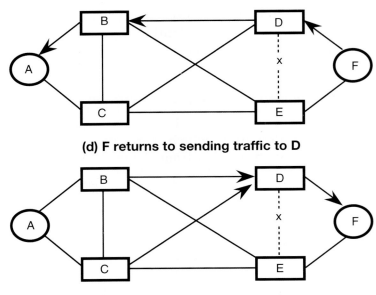

(d) F returns to sending traffic to D

(e) B and C resume their normal routing to D

Figure 9–14 (*Continued*).

been diverted from D to E, which is shown once again in Figure 9–14(a). In Figure 9–14(b), the link between D and F is restored, after undergoing the link proving process (Chapter 8). Once D has confidence in the link to F, it sends to B and C the transfer allowed message, shown in Figure 9–14(c).

The results of the link restoration can be seen in Figures 9–14(d) and 9–14(e). In Figure 9–14(d), F now uses the F-D link. During the failure, it had diverted all its traffic to E. Although not shown in this figure, it may now load share across links F-D and F-E. In Figure 9–14(e), if D is the primary route for B's and C's traffic to D, B and C undertake a controlled rerouting procedure to divert their traffic back to their primary route (through D)

Recovery of Multiple Links or STP Failure

For this example, it is assumed that STP D goes down, and/or all of D's link sets become unavailable. If the routing tables are set up properly, this major failure does not block traffic. In Figure 9–15(a), under normal conditions, traffic is moving from F to A through link sets FD-DB-BA. In Figure 9–15(b), STP D goes down and any links that inter-

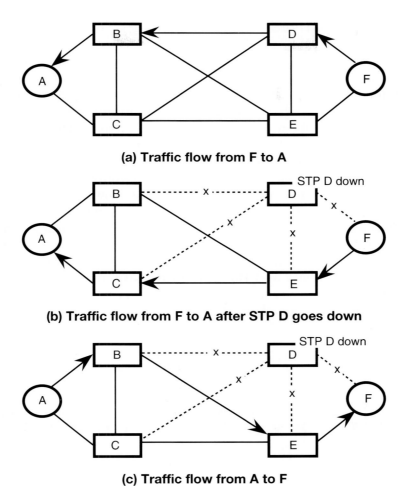

(a) Traffic flow from F to A

(b) Traffic flow from F to A after STP D goes down

(c) Traffic flow from A to F

Figure 9–15   Failure of multiple links or STP failure.

face into D are unavailable. Traffic flowing from F to A is diverted to E, through C, and then to A. In Figure 9–15(c), traffic flowing from A to F that was going through B is now diverted to B, to E, and then to F.

Once again, it is obvious how the SS7 meshed backbone topology provides for 100 percent recovery from any single point failure. And some multiple points of failure are also recoverable. For example, assume that nodes B and E are declared unavailable. Traffic from A to F is diverted through link sets AC-CD-DF, and traffic from F to A is diverted through link sets FD-DC-CA.

DOWNTIME OBJECTIVES

The point was made earlier in this book that failures in an SS7 network can have severe consequences if traffic is blocked or delayed. In a national network, such as the common channel signaling systems in the United States, the failure of SS7 would affect millions of users, resulting in the loss of enormous sums of money, not to mention the psychological toll it would take on some individuals during a personal crisis.

Given the inherent robustness of the SS7 architecture, what are reasonable and realistic objectives for a network administrator to set for the signaling network? Bellcore and ANSI publish downtime objectives for the message transfer part (MTP) of SS7.[1] The objectives are high: In a SS7 mesh topology, the total downtime between two signaling end points (SEPs) should not exceed 10 minutes per year. This value is based on topology depicted in Figure 9–16 in which the architecture has two-way diversity for A link sets and three-way diversity for B and D link sets. For the SS7 backbone, downtime is 0 minutes per year! So, the slogan for SS7 is, "Whatever it takes, keep it up."

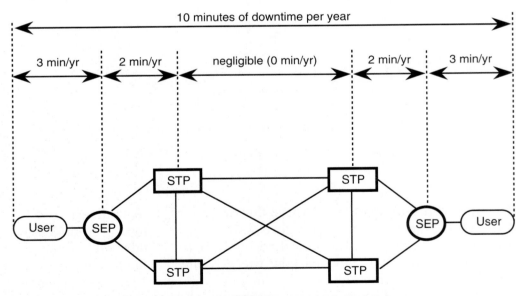

Figure 9–16   MTP downtime objectives.

---

[1]For more information, refer to ANSI T1.111, Section 5.1.2, and Bellcore's SR-TSV-002275, Issue 2, April, 1994.

SUMMARY

MTP 3 is responsible for the routing of signal units between all signaling points. It uses the destination point code and the SLS fields in the routing label to make its routing decisions. MTP 3 provides a wide array of functions for the purpose of keeping the SS7 network operational. Extensive backup and recovery operations take advantage of the mesh topology of the SS7 backbone to keep most failures transparent to users and user applications.

10

Signaling Connection
Control Part (SCCP)

INTRODUCTION

This chapter examines the Signaling Connection Control Part (SCCP) of SS7. We learn how SCCP enhances the operations of MTP 3 by assisting MTP 3 in address translation and routing. The SCCP protocol classes are examined and the connection-oriented and connectionless operations are compared and contrasted. Examples are provided of address translation, routing, and end-to-end traffic acknowledgment.

LOCATION OF SCCP IN THE PROTOCOL STACK

In keeping with our layered approach, Figure 10–1 shows the position of SCCP in relation to the other SS7 layers. It rests on top of MTP 3 and thus uses the services of MTP 3. The user layers rest on top of SCCP and rely on SCCP for a wide variety of services. Of course, as with all the SS7 layers, peer entities (in this case, SCCP entities) communicate with each other to coordinate functions between different signaling points.

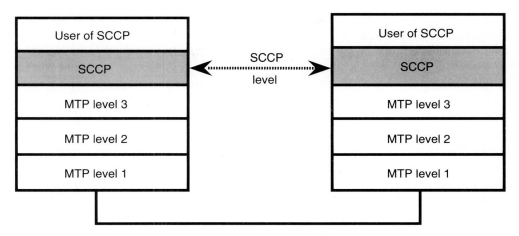

Figure 10–1   SCCP and the SS7 layers.

MAJOR FUNCTIONS OF SCCP

SCCP provides additional functions to the MTP to support both connectionless and connection-oriented network services between SS7 nodes. Connection-oriented services require a session to be set up end-to-end and the transmitted messages associated with each connection can be kept in sequence and related to each other. Connectionless services use no setup and data units are treated as independent entities.[1]

SSCP messages are used to support non-circuit-related information between the applications in the SS7 network nodes. The messages can be used by the applications to access databases at a remote node without having to set up a call to that node.

The combination of the MTP and SCCP is called the "Network Services Part" and adheres to the OSI Reference Model X.200. For example, primitives, protocol data units, connectionless and connection-oriented services, and service access points (SAPs) are defined.

Another major function of SCCP is address translation. For example, it can receive an address, such as dialed digits from a user, and translate

---

[1]Connectionless implementations of SCCP are more common than connection-oriented implementations.

the digits into a destination point code, which is then used by MTP 3 for routing between signaling points. In SS7 these dialed digits (or other forms of identification, such as an X.121 address) are called Global Titles (GT).

While SCCP performs some routing operations, these capabilities are somewhat limited. SCCP receives messages from MTP 3 and determines which upper layer protocol is to receive the traffic. In this regard, this function is like MTP 3's message discrimination and message distribution functions. Additionally, upon receiving traffic from the upper layer protocol, it "routes" the traffic to the MTP 3 layer, to another entity in SCCP, or to another upper layer protocol. But, once again, its global title translation function is one of its most important operations.

ARCHITECTURE OF THE SCCP LAYER

Figure 10–2 depicts the architecture of the SCCP layer. It sits between the upper layer, which may consist of a wide variety or applications—such as ISUP, MAP, and so on—and the lower layer, MTP 3.

SCCP is made up of four entities: (1) SSCP routing control (SCRC), (2) SCCP connection-oriented control (SCOC), (3) SSCP connectionless control (SCLC), and (4) SCCP management (SCMG).

SCRC is responsible for two major operations: routing and addressing. Routing is done internally by relaying the traffic to another user entity or to one of the three other SCCP entities. Addressing is actually address translation. SCRC can translate different types of addresses, such as a global title to a destination point code.

SCOC is responsible for setting up a connection between two users of SCCP, transferring traffic between these users, and tearing down the connection. It supports several features, such as segmentation, sequencing, and flow control, explained later.

SCLC is responsible for transferring traffic between two users of SCCP but it does not create a connection. In addition, unlike SCOC, it has limited features.

SCMG is used for management and status operations. Some of its primary functions are: (a) coordinating the withdrawal of a subsystem (SSN), (b) informing SCCP management about the status of an originating user or the status of a connection, and (c) providing information about the type of traffic pattern a user is receiving.

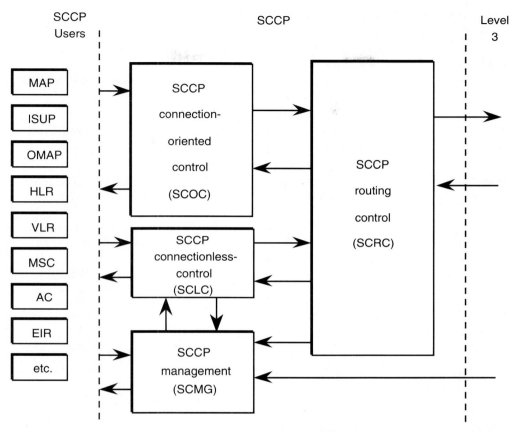

Figure 10–2   Architecture of the SCCP layer.

ADDRESSES AND OTHER IDENTIFIERS

As stated earlier, one of the more important tasks of SCCP is the addressing and address translation services performed for the user layers and MTP 3. In order to understand these services, the various addresses and identifiers used in SS7 should be reviewed. Table 10–1 shows the calling/called addresses and other identifiers that can be carried in the SCCP messages. A later section in this chapter shows the coding rules for several of the SCCP addressing and identifier fields.

The address indicator field is used by SCCP to determine what type of translation it needs to perform; for example, whether an SSN or a

Table 10–1   SCCP Addresses and Other Identifiers

Field	Contents in SCCP Message Field
Address Indicator	Flag to indicate if address has a SSN
	Flag to indicate if address has an originating point code (OPC) and/or destination point code (DPC)
	Flags to indicate if address has Global Title (GT)
	Flag (routing indicator flag) to indicate which part(s) of address is to be used for routing: GT, SSN, DPC
	Flag to indicate a national or international address
Subsystem Number (SSN)	One of these entries: Reserved, ISDN user part (ISUP), SCCP management, MAP, HLR, VLR, EIR, AC, spares, or not used (don't pass to user application)
Addresses (called and calling)	Subsystem number (SSN), originating point code (OPC: network, cluster, cluster member), but usually not destination point code (DPC), Global Title (GT) [see next])
Global Title	One of these entries: Reserved, ISDN/telephony plan (E.164/E.163), X.121 address, Telex address (XF.69), maritime numbering plan (E.210, E.211), land mobile numbering plan (E.212), ISDN/mobile numbering plan (E.214), see next.
Digits	Digits of the Global Title plan.

global title is to be used for routing, or (in some situations) if the global title is supplied only for information purposes and is not to be used for routing. Also, keep in mind that point codes (PCs) may be in the MTP 3 message routing label, as well as in the SCCP message address field. The reasons for these distinctions are described in the next section.

Values for the Subsystem Number (SSN)

Most of the fields (see Table 10–1) have been explained in previous parts of this book, but a brief word about the SSN is helpful. Remember that the SSN identifies the user application layer that resides above SCCP in the protocol stack, as shown in Figures 10–1 and 10–2.

Several of the SSN values are reserved as a one-octet field for "well known" operational entities. Table 10–2 lists the values as defined in ANSI T1.112-1992. Later discussions in this chapter show more examples of the SCCP addresses and identifiers.

Table 10–2   Subsystem Numbers (SSNs)

SSN Value (one octet)	Meaning
00000000	SSN not known or not used
00000001	SCCP management
00000010	Reserved
00000011	ISDN User Part
00000100	OMAP
00000101	Mobile Application Part (MAP)
00000110	Home Location Register (HLR)
00000111	Visitor Location Register (VLR)
00001000	Mobile Switching Center (MSC)
00001001	Equipment Identity Register (EIR)
00001010	Authentication Center (AC)
00001011 to 11111110	spare
11111111	Reserved

PROCESSING MESSAGES AND TRANSLATING ADDRESSES

To begin this discussion, let us examine the called and calling SCCP addresses that reside in the SCCP message header. As shown in Table 10–1, the destination point code (DPC) is usually not included in the SCCP called-party address field, because it duplicates information found in the MTP 3 message routing label. As a general practice, even if the DPC is present in the called-party address field, it is ignored.[2]

However, the SCCP calling-party address is used, and reveals the origination of the SCCP message. This field is important, because it is used to identify the signaling point that is to receive a response (if one is returned), or to return undeliverable messages. Address translation at an intermediate node results in the OPC of the MTP 3 routing label being changed to the point code of the intermediate node. So, without the use of

---

[2]An exception to this practice is found when using the Intermediate Signaling Network Identification (ISNI), which is described in Chapter 11.

Table 10–3   Common SCCP Translations

Performed by	Called SCCP Address	Translation Operation	New Called SCCP Address
STP	GT	GT → PC+SSN	SSN & PC used in routing label
STP	GT+SSN	GT → PC	SSN & PC used in routing label
STP	GT	GT → PC+GT	GT PC used in routing label
Endpoint	GT	GT → SSN	Nothing, message terminates

the SCCP calling-party address, information about the originator of the message is lost.[3]

The SCCP address may contain a point code, an SSN or global title, or some combination of these addresses and identifiers. Two basic types of addresses are discerned by SCRC: a global title (GT) and a point code (PC) and the subsystem number (SSN).

Later, we examine some examples of SCCP address translations, but to conclude this introductory discussion, remember that SCCP can perform a translation of any combination of a point code, a subsystem number, or global title. The combinations are determined by the SS7 network administrator, and several possibilities, derived from Bellcore SR-TSV-002275, Issue 2, April 1994, are shown in Table 10–3.

The SCRC performs address translation for its upper layer user application (an entity internal to the node) or its lower layer MTP 3. In the former case, the application need not know routing numbers but is concerned with an address or a telephone number. In the latter case, MTP 3 has received a signal unit from a remote signaling point and needs SCRC to perform a translation. These two situations are now described in more detail.

Receiving a Message from an Entity Internal to the Node

If SCRC receives traffic from a user layer within the node (through SCOC or SCLC), it will receive one of the following forms: (1) destination point code (DPC), (2) DPC + (SSN and/or GT), (3) GT, or (4) GT + SSN. If SCRC does not receive a DPC from the user layer, it must derive one from (typically) the GT passed to it by the application. The derivation is

---

[3]Use of the SCCP calling-party address does not solve the entire problem of identifying the originator of traffic. For example, at the MTP 3 level, any congestion information is sent to the translator node instead of the source node.

usually through a mapping table that has been created by the SS7 network craftspeople.

If the DPC is present in the message, and it does not identify this node, then SCCP must pass the message to MTP 3 for relaying to another node. If the DPC is the node itself, SCCP must pass the traffic to an entity (through SCOC or SCLC) based on a supplied SSN.

Receiving a Message from MTP 3

If the SCRC receives traffic from its MTP 3 layer, this means the DPC in the MTP 3 routing label is the signaling point of this SCRC. It also means that the originator of the traffic may want an address translation. The SCRC examines the address indicator field in the incoming signal unit (see Table 10–1). One of the bits in this field, called the routing indicator field, is set to indicate that routing is to be performed based on the GT in the SSCP called party address field, or that routing is to be performed based on the DPC in the MTP 3 routing label and the subsystem number in the SSCP called party address.

If the first case is to be carried out, SCRC must use the GT value in the called address to find the new DPC, possibly a new SSN or GT, and possibly a new address routing indicator in a mapping table. It passes the DPC to MTP 3, which places this value in the DPC field of the routing label. The signal unit is then relayed to the next signaling point. For the second case, it means the message has arrived at the terminating SCCP, and further routing must be done on the SSN.

ROUTING

The SS7 routing functions can be performed entirely by MTP 3 without any assistance from SCCP. If the DPC in the routing label of a received signal unit is complete and is coded to identify a non-local signaling point, MTP 3 need not pass the signal unit to SCCP. It uses routing tables and MTP 3 to relay the traffic.

As depicted in Figure 10–3, SCCP is invoked when the signal unit needs address translation, or it is to be passed (through SCCP) to a user application.[4] In event 1, MTP 3 has passed the signal unit to SSCP's

---

[4] I have simplified this discussion and have not included several principles that govern how connection request messages are handled. The reader should study the specifications if more detailed information is needed. With this caveat, these explanations reflect the major operations of SCCP routing for ongoing traffic.

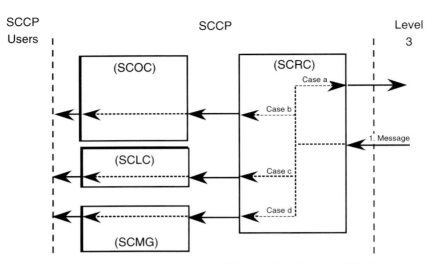

Figure 10–3   Processing traffic received from MTP 3.

SCRC, because the DPC in the routing label is this local signaling point. That means the signal unit must be processed by SCCP.

SCRC examines the address indicator field in the SCCP header (see Table 10–1). If the routing indicator bit in this field indicates that the routing is to be performed on the global title, an address translation will be performed to determine both the DPC and the SSN. If the DPC is the node itself, and the SSN is correct (and available), the message is passed to either SCOC or SCLC, which are labeled cases b and c respectively in the figure.

If the DPC is not the node itself, the message is passed back to MTP 3 (case a). One exception to the previous statement should be explained. If the message is associated with an end-to-end connection (between three or more signaling points), it is passed to SCOC for some housekeeping operations, then back to SCRC, and to MTP 3 for further relaying.

If the message is non-user traffic, such as status messages, diagnostics, and so on, it is passed to SCMG for further processing. This situation is shown as case d in Figure 10–3.

Figure 10–4 shows the flow of traffic through SCCP when it emanates from the user application. The operations are more straightforward than when the messages come from MTP 3, and I have labeled all traffic flows as case a to reflect this simplicity. However, before event 1 occurs, SCRC must make several decisions when it receives traffic from the user. Briefly, they are as follows:

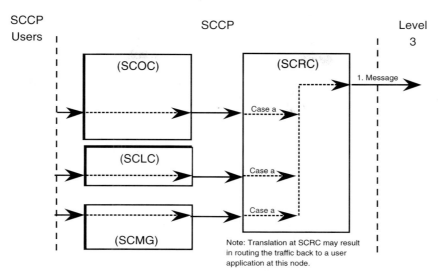

Figure 10–4   Processing traffic received from user.

- If the message contains a valid DPC, it is forwarded to MTP 3
- If the message contains a valid destination global title and SSN (and the routing indicator indicates "route on global title"), a translation occurs and the message is passed to MTP 3, or back to a local user application (see note in Figure 10–4).
- In all situations, if the user does not provide sufficient information to SCCP, it cannot process the message and will discard the traffic (and issue an error message).

EXAMPLES OF ADDRESSING AND ROUTING

To tie together the concepts of SCCP addressing and routing, this section provides three examples of these operations. The first example, in Figure 10–5, shows a successful operation with one translation. The second example, in Figure 10–6, shows an unsuccessful operation. The third example, in Figure 10–7, shows a successful operation with two translations.

Successful Operation with One Translation

Figure 10–5 is an example of a successful operation, where the translations take place at signaling point B. Three nodes are involved, A, B, and C. For simplicity, they are identified as point codes (PC) A, B, and

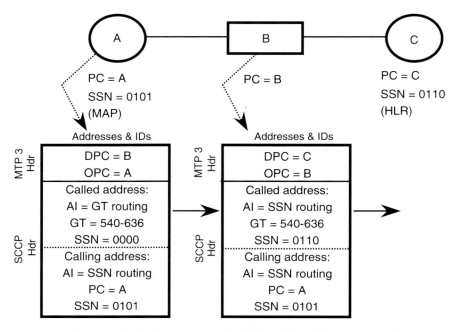

Figure 10–5   Example of address/identifier translations.

C respectively. A is sending traffic from its mobile access part (MAP) user application, which must be identified with the SSN = 0101 (a reserved number for MAP).

A places its originating point code (OPC) A and the destination point code (DPC) B in the MTP 3 header. In the SCCP header, it codes the called address and calling address fields. For the called address, a bit in the address indicator (AI) field connotes that routing is to be performed on the global title (GT), which is 540-636. The subsystem number (SSN) is set to 0000, which is a reserved number stipulating that the SSN is not used (or not known).

For the calling address, the AI bit is set by A, but is not used (in this example). The PC is A (originating point code), and the SSN is set to the reserved number of 0101, which identifies the originator of the message as the mobile application part (MAP) of a mobile, wireless application.[5]

---

[5]This example shows how SS7 supports a mobile, wireless network, such as the GSM (Global System for Mobile Communications) or PCS (Personal Communications System). As explained earlier in this book, SS7 is used in many types of networks.

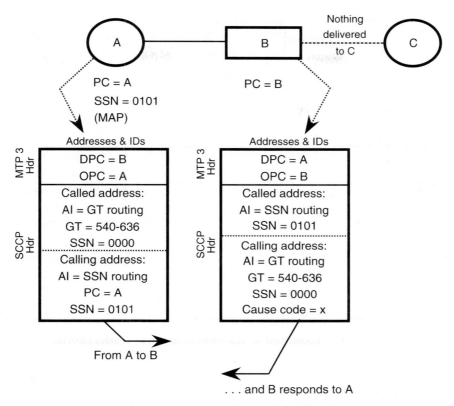

Figure 10–6   Example of a routing or translation problem.

This message is routed to signaling point B (for example, an STP). MTP 3 passes the message to SCCP, which examines the SCCP header. Based on the fields in the header, SCCP creates/modifies these fields, changes the DPC and OPC values, and passes this information to its MTP 3 layer for relaying to signaling point C.

SCCP has changed the DPC to C, and the OPC to B. In effect, SCCP translated the GT of 540-636 to PC = B; it also changed the SSN to 0101, the home location register (HLR) application at C.

MTP 3 uses these values to relay the signal unit to the next node, which in this example is C. Notice that the calling address in the SCCP header remains as PC = A. Notice also that the AI bit is set to indicate SSN-based routing, which is used at C to determine what part of the SCCP address is used. As we know from Table 10–1, the SSN identifies the application that originates and receives the traffic.

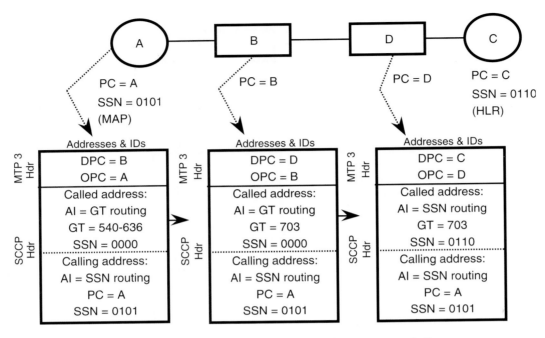

Figure 10–7   Successful operations with two translations.

Unsuccessful Operation

Figure 10–6 shows an example of an unsuccessful routing/translation operation. The message sent from A to B is the same as in Figure 10–5. Node B cannot process the message, so nothing is delivered to C, and B returns a message to A with a cause code that explains why the operation was not successful. The cause code value (depicted as "x" in the figure) may indicate that node B does not have a translation available for the SCCP called address party, or that some type of failure occurred that has nothing to do with translation. Whatever the case may be, the message from B has the SCCP called address coded as: SSN routing, with A's SSN of 0101 filled into the SSN value. This allows node A to give this response to the application that originated it, in this example, MAP. The SCCP calling address field is coded as GT routing, with GT set to the same value that was in A's SCCP called address field. The presence of this value allows A to know GT 540-636 cannot be processed by B. Typically, this type of message will invoke troubleshooting procedures between A and B, some of which are described in Chapter 13.

Although not shown in this example, the terminating node (node C) may also experience a problem. If it does, it returns a message to A, through B, but B will process the message only up to the MTP 3 layer. SCCP will not participate in the operation at B, since it processed the request successfully. It is up to nodes A and C to resolve the problem, although the actual troubleshooting operations can bring B back into the picture. But once again, this actual playing-out of the resolution of the problem is dependent upon the particular SS7 network implementation.

Successful Operation with Two Translations

The last example shows a successful operation in which translations occur at two STPs, STP B and STP D in Figure 10–7. The message from A to B is the same as in the previous two examples. At node B, GT 540-636 is translated into DPC D and GT 703; at this node, no SSN is determined since the message has not arrived at the final node. Upon node D receiving this message from B, it translates the GT of 703 to DPC = C and SSN = 0110. This message is then sent to node C, which delivers it to the home location register (HLR) application.

SCCP CONNECTION-ORIENTED OPERATIONS

The connections between SCCP entities are not physical connections; rather the connections are logical, in that the SCCP entity creates entries in a database or memory that allow it to know about the ongoing interactions with another SCCP entity. Furthermore, each SCCP in the signaling points that rest between (say) two other SCCP entities do not have to participate in the connection. This idea is shown in Figure 10–8(a). SCCP A and F are participants in the connection, whereas SCCP B and D are not participants. In these circumstances, A and F do not need the services of the SCCP modules in signaling points B and D, so it is not necessary for B and D to be part of the connection.

Figure 10–8(b) reveals another type of connection. All SCCPs at the four signaling points participate in the connection. This scenario is used if the services of all SCCPs in all signaling points are needed. Figure 10–8(c) shows another possibility wherein A, B, and F participate in the connection, and D does not. This situation is not uncommon. For example, SCCP B might perform destination global title to destination signal point conversion; thereafter, this conversion is not needed. At signaling

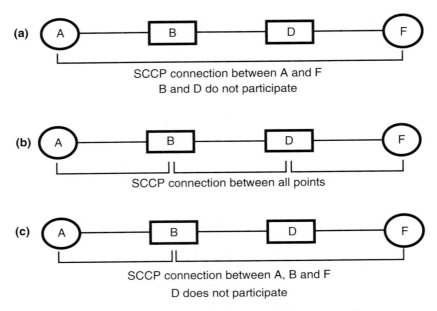

Figure 10–8   Participants in the SCCP connection.

point D, SCCP is not invoked, and D's MTP 3 relays the traffic without any assistance from SCCP.

Reference Numbers

SCCP must have a mechanism to keep track of the connections to the SCCPs in other signaling points. Two fields in the SCCP message are used for this purpose: the source local reference (SLR) and the (DLR) destination local reference. Figure 10–9 shows an example of how these fields are used between two SCCP modules. The connection is identified by local reference numbers 6 and 20. In event 1, SCCP A accesses a reference number table and selects a number that is not being used (in this example, 6). It places this value in the SLR field of the SSCP connection request message (CR), which is relayed to SCCP F in event 2.

In event 3, SCCP F stores SLR 6, selects a number that is not being used at its end (in this example, 20). It stores information that matches (correlates) 6 and 20. Then, in event 4, it responds to SCCP with a connection confirm (CC) message. In this message are the reference numbers

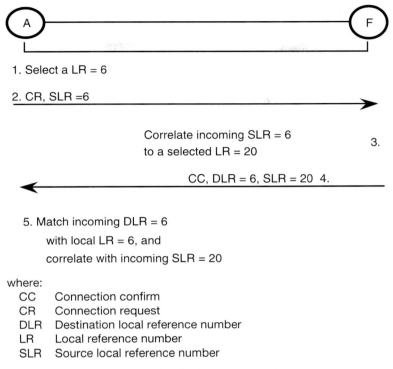

Figure 10–9   Reference numbers.

6 and 20, with SLR = 20 and DLR = 6 (from the perspective of SCCP F, of course).

In event 5, this message reaches SCCP A, which stores information about the correlation of 6 and 20. Thereafter, the ongoing exchange of messages between SCCP A and F use these reference numbers for this individual connection. Other reference numbers are used for other connections.

Notice that A does not choose F's reference number, nor does F choose the reference number for A. Hence, these reference numbers are managed locally; the only requirement is for the SCCPs to make certain they identify, unambiguously, each connection.

The advantage to using reference numbers is that they are relatively small (three bytes). During the connection setup, the SCCPs correlate these reference numbers with the more lengthy calling and called-address fields in the messages. Thereafter, only the reference numbers are needed to identify the connection.

SCCP CONNECTIONLESS OPERATIONS

Connectionless operations do not set up a connection before the transfer of traffic. Consequently, reference numbers are not present in the messages. In order to identify each message, it must contain the complete calling and called-party address fields. The result is a very simple procedure, resulting in less processing overhead (no state diagrams, etc.).

SCCP CLASSES OF SERVICE

The ANSI SCCP provides four classes of network service, which are categorized as protocol classes. Some vendors and other standards support a fifth class as well. The classes and their functions are:

- *Protocol class 0, Basic Connectionless Service.* Data units are passed to SCCP from upper layers without prior connection setup and are transported independently of each other. They may be delivered out-of-sequence. This protocol class is a connectionless service.
- *Protocol class 1, Sequenced (MTP) Connectionless Service.* Enhances class 0 by performing sequencing of the data units. Basically, class 1 is a sequenced connectionless service. The upper layer protocol can indicate to SCCP that it wishes the traffic to be delivered in sequential order.
- *Protocol class 2, Basic Connection-oriented Class.* Supports a temporary or permanent signaling connection between nodes. It also supports the multiplexing of a number of SS7 connections onto one MTP network connection. Flow control and sequencing are not provided. It is a simple connection-oriented service.
- *Protocol class 3, Flow Control Connection-oriented Class.* Supports class 2 and provides enhanced features: expedited data transfer, message loss detection, and sequence checks. This class is connection-oriented with flow control. Message loss detection does not ensure the integrity of traffic. In such a situation, the connection is reset (and traffic may be lost).

Table 10–4 provides a summary of the classes and the message types that are exchanged for each protocol class. Notice that some of the messages are used for connection-oriented services only. It should be evident

Table 10–4 SCCP Message Types and Protocol Classes

SCCP Message	Classes of Protocol			
	0	1	2	3
CR connection request			X	X
CC connection confirm			X	X
CREF connection refused			X	X
RLSD released			X	X
RLC release complete			X	X
DT1 data form 1			X	
DT2 data form 2				X
AK data acknowledgment				X
UDT unitdata	X	X		
XUDT extended unitdata	X	X		
UDTS unitdata service	X	X		
XUDTS extended unitdata service	X	X		
ED expedited data				X
EA expedited data acknowledgment				X
RSR reset request				X
RSC reset confirmation				X
ERR error			X	X
IT inactivity test			X	X

from an examination of Table 10–4 that SCCP is quite flexible in how it can be configured by the network designer. However, this flexibility must be controlled carefully and communicating machines must implement the same features of SCCP if the machines are going to interact without extensive conversion routines.

SERVICE DEFINITIONS (PRIMITIVES)

Figure 10–10 shows the service definitions (also known as primitives) that operate between MTP, SCCP, and the layers above SCCP, such as TCAP. In accordance with the OSI Model, these primitives are

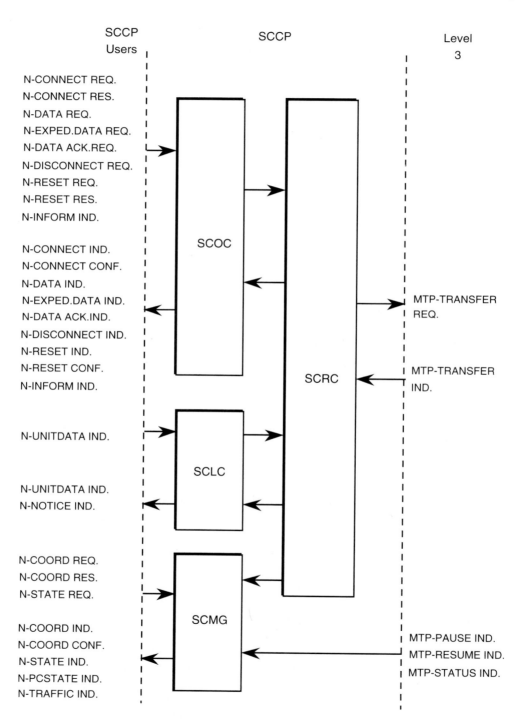

Figure 10–10   SCCP service definitions.

concatenated with some or all of the following primitive calls: (a) request, (b) indication, (c) response, and (d) confirm.

The functions of the primitives can be summarized as follows:

- *N-UNITDATA, MTP-TRANSFER, N-DATA N-EXPED.DATA.* These service definitions transfer ongoing user traffic between the layers.
- *N-NOTICE*. This service definition is used for SCLC and the upper layers to notify each other about various activities.
- *N-COORD*. This service definition is used to coordinate the withdrawal of some systems from active operations through SCMG.
- *N-STATE*. This service definition is used to inform entities about various states of an entity within a layer.
- *N-TRAFFIC*. This service definition is used for the distribution of traffic-type information.
- *MTP-PAUSE and MTP-RESUME*. These service definitions temporarily stop and resume the sending of traffic.
- *MTP-STATUS*. This service definition is used to inform layer entities about the availability or nonavailability of a destination address.
- *N-CONNECT*. This service definition is used to set up connections through SCOC.
- *N-DATA ACK*. This service definition is used to request and receive end-to-end acknowledgments of traffic.
- *N-DISCONNECT*. This service definition is used to tear down connections.
- *N-RESET*. This service definition is used to reset connections.
- *N-STATE*. This service definition is used to inform SCCP management about the status of the originating user.
- *N-PCSTATE*. This service definition is used to inform a user about the status of a signaling point.

Figure 10–11 provides an example of how several of the primitives operate between MTP, SCCP, and the user layer. As suggested in the figure, the primitives themselves are a means to an end. The end goal is to accomplish peer-to-peer communications between adjacent protocol entities in the same layers of the different machines.

With few exceptions, the request primitive is sent from an upper layer to its lower layer to invoke a service. The indication primitive is sent from a lower layer to an upper layer to inform that layer about some

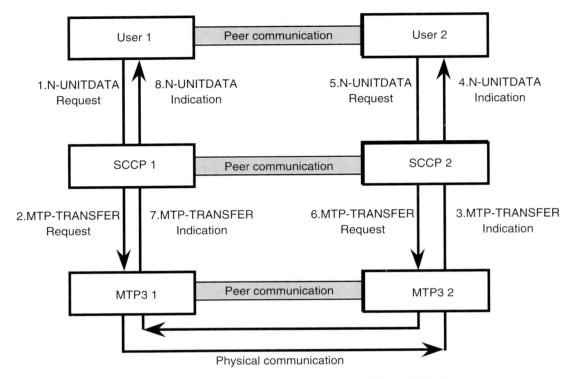

Figure 10–11   Example of primitives to/from SCCP.

aspect of an operation. The response primitive is then returned to the lower layer that issued the indication primitive. Finally, the confirmation primitive is usually invoked as a result of a request primitive. As a general rule, the invocation of a request primitive in a local machine results in an invocation of an indication primitive in a remote machine. This indication primitive results in an invocation of a response primitive at that remote machine and this primitive results in an invocation of a confirm primitive at the local machine.

SEQUENCING, FLOW CONTROL, AND SEGMENTATION/REASSEMBLY OPERATIONS

SCCP protocol class 3 permits the use of sequencing, flow control, and segmentation/reassembly operations. Sequencing may be needed in some situations if more than one message, pertaining to a transaction, is exchanged between two SCCP modules, and these messages must be kept in order. The operation is also useful if a message must be segmented into smaller pieces (due to MTP 2 signal unit size restrictions or the receiving SCCP buffer limitations). Through the use of the "more data" (M) bit, and the sequence numbers, the sender and receiver can coordinate their segmentation and reassembly operations.

Flow control may also be needed to prevent a sending SCCP module from sending excessive traffic to its peer receiving SCCP module. Flow control allows each module to make the best use of its receive buffers in relation to how fast these buffers are serviced (with the traffic removed and passed to other modules).

Figure 10–12 shows an example of how operations are set up and performed by SCCP. The terms P(S) and P(R) describe the sending sequence number and receiving sequence number, respectively. First, in event 1 SCCP sends a connection request message to SCCP B. The figure does not show all the fields in the message, which contains a code to identify the connection request (CR) message, the called- and calling-party addresses, the source local reference number, the suggested protocol class (in this example, class 3), an optional data field (if data are to be exchanged in this initial handshake), and a hop counter. This last field is used to insure the message does not transit too many intermediate signaling points. It is usually set to 15, and if this limit is exceeded, an error

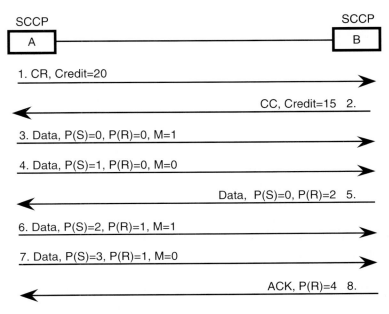

Figure 10–12   Operations.

message is returned to the originator of the message from the signaling point that recognized the excessive (sixteenth) hop.

The credit field in the connection request is set to 20. This is interpreted at SCCP B to mean that A will accept twenty successive messages from B. In other words, B has a window to A of twenty messages, and B need not exercise any flow control restrictions within this window limit. Stated another way, B cannot send more than twenty messages to A until A has returned a message to B that renews (or opens) the window. In event 2, B returns a connection confirm (CC) message. In this message is a credit of 15. This sets the window in the other direction, from A to B.

Thereafter, traffic is exchanged between the two SCCP modules. In events 3 and 4, SCCP A sends two signal units; they are two segments from a larger unit. SCCP indicates that these units are related with the M bit set to 1 in the first segment (more data follows), and to 0 in the second segment (no more data follows).

In event 5, SCCP B acknowledges A's traffic by returning $P(R) = 2$. This procedure is called an inclusive acknowledgment in that it acknowledges more than one message (in this case 0 and 1). In event 5, B also sends a message, and so indicates with its $P(S) = 0$.

In events 6 and 7, SCCP A sends two more segments and acknowledges B's only message with the $P(R) = 1$. In event 8, SCCP B has no traffic to send to A, so it returns an acknowledgment message (with no data) of $P(R) = 4$. Since no data resides in the message, the acknowledgment has no $P(S)$ field.

With the completion of event 8, all traffic between SCCP A and SCCP B has been received correctly and acknowledged.

SS7 SCCP MESSAGE FORMAT

The SS7 messages are carried within the signal units (SUs) in the signaling information field (SIF) of MTP 3. Their purpose is to provide a peer-to-peer session between two SCCPs. The messages are created by SCCP as a result of receiving OSI primitives from an upper layer. In turn, SCCP exchanges primitives with MTP with the goal of transferring the message unit to the remote SCCP.

The format of the SCCP message is shown in Figure 10–13. It contains five major fields:

- *Routing Label.* This field is the standard routing label explained in previous chapters.

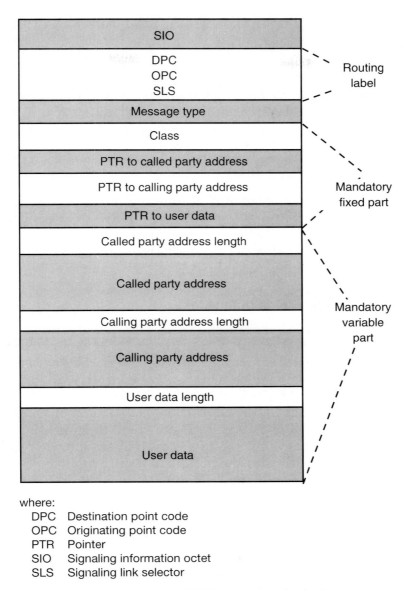

Figure 10–13   SSCP message format.

where:
    DPC   Destination point code
    OPC   Originating point code
    PTR   Pointer
    SIO   Signaling information octet
    SLS   Signaling link selector

- *Message Type.* This field identifies the types of SCCP messages (e.g., connection request [CR], data form 1 [DT1]).
- *Mandatory Fixed Part.* This field contains the mandatory parameters for a particular message type (addresses, cause codes, etc.)
- *Mandatory Variable Part.* Some messages use a variable number of parameters. They are contained in this field.
- *Optional Part.* Certain messages are used only with specific protocol classes.

The optional part contains a variety of optional parameters. One of interest is a parameter that identifies information pertaining to the Intermediate Signaling Network Identification (ISNI) protocol. This information is used by SS7 for dictating a route through a signaling network (networks), and for recording the network(s) that the message transited. ISNI is described in Chapter 11.

Examples of Key Fields in the Message

It is not practical to examine all the fields in the SCCP message, but certain key fields warrant our attention. Figure 10–14 depicts the address and identifier fields and their formats. Figure 10–14(a) shows the general structure for the calling or called address. The addresses are preceded by the address indicator field. Each address number is coded as a 4-bit binary coded decimal (BCD) digit in the address field. Two digits fit in each octet and length indicators define how many digits are in these fields.

Figure 10–14(b) shows the coding for the address indicator field. The bits in this field are coded according to the following rules:

Bit 1   A value of 1 indicates that the address contains a subsystem number.

Bit 2   A value of 1 indicates that the address contains a signaling point code.

Bits 3-6   These bits contain the global title indicator and are coded as follows:

Bits   *6543* *Meaning:*
            0000 No GT present
            0001 GT includes translation type, numbering plan, and encoding scheme
            0011 GT includes translation type

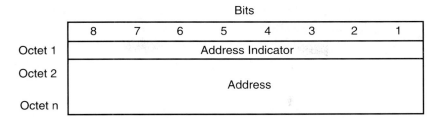

(a) Calling or called-party address

(b) The address indicator

(c) Ordering of addresses and identifiers

Figure 10–14 Address and identifier fields and their formats.

0100
to
1111 Reserved, spare, or not assigned

Bit 7   A value of 1 indicates that routing is to be done with the destination point code in the routing label and the subsystem number in the called party address. A value of 0 indicates that routing is be done with the global title in the address field.

Bit 8   A value of 1 indicates that the address is coded according to national specifications. A value of 0 indicates that the address is coded according to international specifications.

Figure 10–14(c) shows the ordering of the address and identifiers within the address field. The subsystem precedes the point code, which precedes the global title. Remember that these values may be coded twice, one for the calling address and one for the called address.

Within the global title field, additional subfields provide yet more information. The format for this field is shown in Figure 10–15. The field can be coded in one of two formats, depending of the value of the global title indicator that is present in the address indicator field described in the previous figure. If the global title indicator is set to 0001, the format in Figure 10–15(a) is used. If the global title indicator is set to 0010, the format in Figure 10–15(b) is used.

The first subfield in the global title field is the *translation type code*. It is used to pass the message to an appropriate translation function—for example, an 800 number translation, a credit card validation, a cellular roaming service. The format in Figure 10–15(a) is not yet defined (for further study). For the format in Figure 10–15(b), the codes are administered by the T1 Committee. For the reader who wishes more detail or the procedures for requesting a translation type code, Annex B to T1.112.3 has more information. Notice that the format in Figure 10–15(b) does not include the numbering plan or the encoding scheme (which are discussed

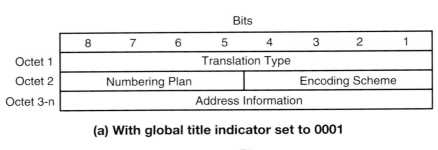

(a) With global title indicator set to 0001

(b) With global title indicator set to 0010

Figure 10–15   The global title field.

next). The translation type code may imply these fields, but it is implementation-specific.

The *numbering plan* is a 4-bit code that is set to one of the following values:

Bits 8765	Meaning:	Pertinent ITU-T Recommendation
0000	Unknown	
0001	ISDN/Telephone numbering plan	(E.164/E.163)
0010	Reserved	
0011	Data numbering plan	(X.121)
0100	Telex numbering plan	(F.69)
0101	Maritime mobile numbering plan	(E.210/E.211)
0110	Land mobile numbering plan	(E.212)
0111	ISDN/mobile numbering plan	(E.214)
1000 to 1110	Spare	
1111	Reserved	

Finally, the *encoding scheme* is the other four bits of the octet and is coded as follows:

Bits 8765	Meaning:
0000	Unknown
0001	BCD, odd number of digits
0010	BCD, even number of digits
0011 to 1111	Spare

PERFORMANCE REQUIREMENTS FOR SCCP

Since many of the SCCP operations are used to support delay-sensitive telephone calls, they must be performed quickly. Excessive delay translates into an unhappy calling party, and well as the consumption of precious network resources. Therefore, in supporting its users

(ISUP, OMAP, and TCAP) SCCP must meet stringent requirements. The ANSI committees investigated the requirements of these SS7 user protocols and developed performance goals for SCCP to support the requirements.

Two types of performance parameters are now defined: quality of service (QOS) parameters that are known to the SCCP user and internal

Table 10–5   SCCP Performance Parameters

Traffic load for the translation function	*Transit time of a UDT message in a relay point (in ms)*	
	Mean	*95%*
Normal	50–155	100–310
+ 15%	100–233	200–465
+ 30%`	250–388	500–775
Traffic load for the relay function	*Transit time of a CR message in a relay point without coupling (in ms)*	
	Mean	*95%*
Normal	50–155	100–310
+ 15%	100–233	200–465
+ 30%`	250–388	500–775
Traffic load for the relay function	*Transit time of a CR message in a relay point with coupling (in ms)*	
	Mean	*95%*
Normal	75–180	150–360
+ 15%	150–270	300–540
+ 30%`	375–450	750–900
Traffic load for the relay function	*Transit time of a CC message in a relay point with coupling (in ms)*	
	Mean	*95%*
Normal	30–120	120–330
+ 30%`	150–275	300–550
Traffic load for the relay function	*Transit time of a DT message in a relay point with coupling (in ms)*	
	Mean	*95%*
Normal	30–110	60–220
+ 15%	60–165	120–330
+ 30%`	150–275	300–550

parameters that are not known to the SCCP user, but which contribute to the overall QOS offered to the user. These two types of parameters are also defined for connectionless classes (0 and 1), and connection-oriented classes (2 and 3).

Before investigating these subjects, several definitions are required in order to understand the performance parameters:

- An SCCP route is an ordered set of nodes where SCCP is invoked.
- An SCCP relation is one in which two SCCP users communicate with each other over the SCCP route.
- A relay point is where SCCP translation functions occur using the connectionless classes.
- A relay point without coupling is where SCCP translation functions occur using connection-oriented classes, but without the coupling of signaling connection sections function.
- A relay point with coupling is where SCCP translation functions occur using connection-oriented classes, and with the coupling of signaling connection sections function.

Transit Time Performance

Given these definitions, Table 10–5 lists the performance parameters for connectionless (user data, or UDT) traffic, connection request (CR) messages, connection confirm (CC) messages, and connection-oriented (DT) data. The values in the table refer to the processing time through the SCCP route between the SCCP users.

There is one other aspect about these tables that we should discuss. The transit times are long, and if several SCCP nodes participate in the SCCP relation, they accumulate. But they were published by the standards groups based on the requirements of the SS7 applications. As processor speeds increase, so too shall the transit delays decrease.

SUMMARY

The Signaling Connection Control Part (SCCP) provides several useful functions to MTP 3. It can be configured to support both connectionless and connection-oriented network services. One of its most widely used services is address translation. Additionally, and as options, it provides segmentation, end-to-end acknowledgments, flow control, and sequencing services for its users.

11

Intermediate Signaling Network Identification (ISNI)

INTRODUCTION

This chapter examines the Intermediate Signaling Network Identification (ISNI), a relative newcomer to the SS7 protocol suite. In this chapter, the rationale for the creation of ISNI is examined, and the major features of the protocol are analyzed. We will learn how an SS7 network uses ISNI to dictate routes through and between signaling networks. The chapter also explores how ISNI can record the signaling points through which an SS7 message travels.

PURPOSE AND PLACEMENT OF ISNI

As the world migrates toward SS7 as the primary signaling technology for the telephone network and other systems such as ATM and mobile networks, it has become apparent that network managers, troubleshooters, financial analysts, security administrators, and others need to know through which networks the SS7 messages travel, and in some situations, dictate the networks through which these message should or must travel. The ISNI protocol is designed to meet these needs. It provides a route recording and route specification capability in the SS7 network.

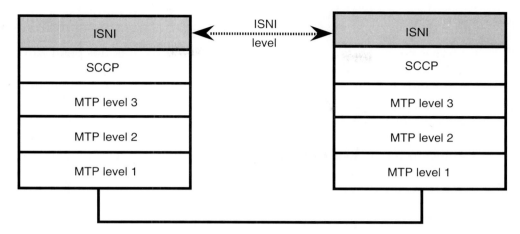

Figure 11–1   Placement of ISNI in the SS7 layers.

As shown in Figure 11–1, ISNI uses the services of SCCP and the MTP layers. ISNI is added to SS7 without the need for any changes at SCCP or MTP. The ISNI traffic is carried as a parameter field in an SCCP extended unit data (XUDT) message and identified with the parameter code value of 11111010. It is not identified with a subsystem number (SSN).

TERMS AND CONCEPTS

Before we analyze the ISNI operations, we need to understand several terms and concepts associated with these operations.

- *Routing Information.* This term describes information in an ISNI message that contains addresses (SS7 point codes) of SS7 networks and signaling points. The information is an ordered set of networks in a list.
- *Constrained Routing Information.* This term describes routing information that indicates one or more networks through which the message will transit. It need not indicate every network in the path but is used by an ISNI-capable STP to direct the message toward a network that is explicitly indicated. The term *constrained* is used because if the routing information is not (or cannot) be followed, then the message is not relayed. This information also con-

tains route recording, because each traversed switching point places its network address into a list in the message.

- *Suggested Routing Information.* This procedure has not been fully defined but should operate in a fashion similar to constrained routing information. The major difference is that with this operation the route is suggested only; it does not have to be followed explicitly.
- *Notification Information.* This term describes the route, recording information in which each transited network places its address into the message. It also contains a list of networks that a network entity wishes to be traversed by the message (this latter function is called anticipation information, discussed in more detail shortly).

    Notification information can serve several purposes: (a) It can notify the terminating signaling point of the networks traversed because the final values contain a list of addresses of the transited networks; (b) it can notify the originating endpoint about the same information if the terminating endpoint returns this message back (and reverses the order in the list) before sending it to the originator; (c) it can be used to dictate the route between endpoints.

- *Identification Information.* This is a form of notification information and contains a sequential list of the networks actually traversed by the message.
- *Anticipation Information.* This is also a form of notification information. It contains a requested list and not a actual list of the networks to be traversed.

ISNI OPERATIONS

ISNI operations begin when the SCCP receives an N-UNITDATA request primitive from the application. This primitive contains the following parameters:

- Routing indicator type: Set to constrained, suggested, or neither.
- Type of ISNI indicator: Set to type 0 ISNI or type 1 ISNI (explained shortly).
- Counter: Uses a pointer into a routing list of network IDs.
- List of network IDs (NIDs): Contains networks that are to be traversed or it may be empty if the route is not defined.

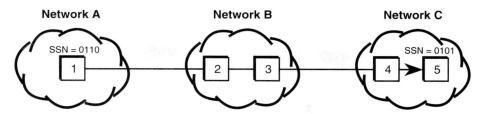

Figure 11–2   Model for ISNI operations examples.

Using this information, the originating SCCP forms a message and sends it to the next node. Each intermediate node examines the contents of the message and reacts accordingly. This means that an intermediate node will follow the constrained routing rules (if stipulated), and/or perform route recording. If the message traverses a node that does not support ISNI, it simply performs routing based on the SCCP called party address.

Figure 11–2 provides an example of the ISNI operations. Three networks are involved and are labeled networks A, B, and C. Five SS7 nodes are involved: node 1 in network A, nodes 2 and 3 in network B, and nodes 4 and 5 in network C. Node 1's subsystem number (SSN) is 0110 and node 5's SSN is 0101. The numbers 1 through 5 are used to identify the SS7 point codes (PCs) of the nodes.

The global title IDs are the same we have used in other examples in this book. The SCCP called global title is 540-636 and the SCCP calling global title is PC = 1, SSN = 0110. Tables 11–1 and 11–2 show the messages that are created by nodes 1 through 4 for constrained routing and identification operations. These tables show partial contents of the MTP-3, SCCP, and ISNI headers. Notice that the SCCP calling address remains the same throughout the process and the SCCP called address is not

Table 11–1   Values of Headers for ISNI Operations (constrained routing)

Message created by node	MTP 3 OPC	MTP 3 DPC	SCCP CdA	SCCP CgA PC, SSN	ISNI Counter	ISNI List
1	1	2	540–636	1,0110	0	B,C
2	2	4	540–636	1,0110	1	B,C
3	3	4	540–363	1,0110	1	B,C
4	4	5	5,0101	1,010	2	B,C

Table 11–2 Values of Headers for ISNI Operations (identification)

Message created by node	MTP 3 OPC	MTP 3 DPC	SCCP CdA	SCCP CgA PC, SSN	ISNI Counter	ISNI List
1	1	2	540–636	1,0110	0	—
2	2	4	540–636	1,0110	1	B
3	3	4	540–363	1,0110	1	B
4	4	5	5,0101	1,0110	2	B,C

translated to a subsystem number until it arrives in the destination network and the ISNI-capable node that supports the termination node (which in this example is node 4).

Two fields in the ISNI header are shown in these tables. The ISNI counter is incremented by 1 as it passes through each network. Notice that this counter is a hop count per network and not per node within a network. The second ISNI field is the list of the networks that are to be traversed. The differences between Table 11–1 and Table 11–2 pertain to the list. In Table 11–1, the list dictates the route, whereas in Table 11–2 the list performs route recording.

These operations should give you a basic understanding of the operations of ISNI. For more detailed information and for some excellent examples, I refer you to ANSI T1.118.1992, Appendix B.

ISNI MESSAGES

In the previous section we examined the ISNI messages in a general way. This section provides a more detailed explanation of the messages. Figure 11–3 shows the format for the type 0 message and Figure 11–4

	Bits							
	8	7	6	5	4	3	2	1
SCCP parameter	1	1	1	1	1	0	1	0
	Length							
Octet 1	Routing Control							
Octets 2-n	Network IDs							

Figure 11–3 The ISNI protocol information (Type 0).

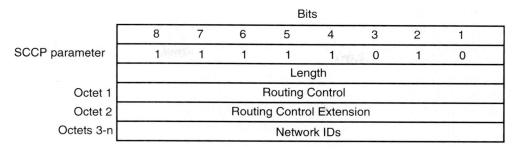

Figure 11–4 The ISNI protocol information (Type 1).

		Bits						
	8	7	6	5	4	3	2	1
	Counter			TI	Res	C/S/N		MI

Figure 11–5 The ISNI routing control indicator.

Table 11–3 Contents of the Routing Control Field

Bit #	Indicator Name	Values	Value Identification
1	Mark for identification	0	Do not identify networks
		1	Identify networks
3 and 2	Type of routing	00	Neither constrained nor suggested ISNI routing
		01	Constrained ISNI routing
		10	Reserved for suggested ISNI routing
		11	Spare
4	Type of ISNI parameter		Reserved for future expansion of the C/S/N field
5		0	Type 0 ISNI
		1	Type 1 ISNI
8, 7, & 6			Counter (maximum number = 7)

shows the format for the type 1 message. The only difference between these two messages is that type 1 has an additional octet, in which bits 1 and 2 are reserved for network specific routing control. The octets labeled network IDs contain the routing information. Each network ID is two octets in length and for large networks, the first octet only is used to identify the SS7 point code and the second octet is coded to 0s. As discussed in Chapter 7, for small networks both octets are coded.

Figure 11–5 shows the formatting contents for the routing control field. It is set to the values as described in Table 11–3.

SUMMARY

The Intermediate Signaling Network Identification (ISNI) is used in the SS7 network to dictate routes through and between signaling networks. ISNI can also record the SPs and networks through which the ISNI message travels.

12

Operations, Maintenance, and Administration Part (OMAP)

INTRODUCTION

This chapter examines the SS7 Operations, Maintenance, and Administration Part (OMAP). The relationship of OMAP to the OSI Model is described and includes OSI-type service definitions, as well as the Common Management Information Protocol (CMIP). But the principal focus in this chapter is on the primary responsibilities of OMAP: routing verification and link verification.

THE SS7 OMAP MANAGEMENT MODEL

OMAP is organized around the upper layers of the OSI Model (see Appendix A for a tutorial on OSI). In OSI, the OMAP functions are called an application entity (AE). An AE is divided into applications service elements (ASEs), as shown in Figure 12–1. In this model, the AE consists of two ASEs: the transaction capabilities applications part (TCAP) ASE and the OMAP ASE. Our concern in this chapter is the OMAP ASE.

The operations above the application layer are shown in this figure as the system management application process (SMAP), which can be considered the user layer. Operations between SMAP and OMAP take place through OM service primitives at the system management service

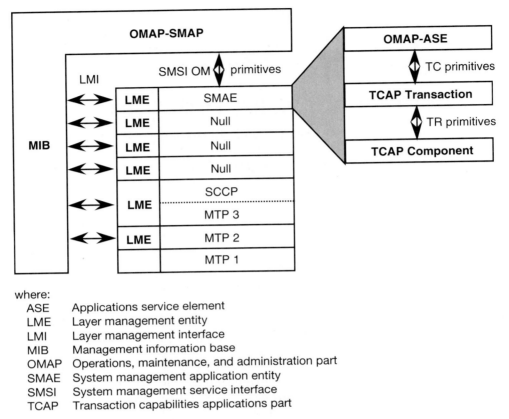

where:

ASE   Applications service element
LME   Layer management entity
LMI   Layer management interface
MIB   Management information base
OMAP   Operations, maintenance, and administration part
SMAE   System management application entity
SMSI   System management service interface
TCAP   Transaction capabilities applications part

Figure 12–1   Layered architecture of OMAP.

interface (SMSI), labeled SMSI primitives in the figure. These primitives are explained later in this chapter.

The layer management interface (LMI) and the management information base (MIB) are not defined in the ANSI OMAP standards. They are left to local implementation.

OMAP Use of OSI Network Management

The OMAP-SMAP is implemented through two OSI network management primitives (at the SMSI OM primitive interface in Figure 12–1, which are defined in detail in the Common Management Information Protocol (CMIP), published by the ITU-T and the ISO. These two primitives (M-ACTION and M-EVENT REPORT) are described here in the generic sense, and later, we show specific examples of how they are used in OMAP. For the reader who has used these primitives in CMIP, be aware that the parameters are different in the OMAP implementation (and are examined in a later section). The term managed object in CMIP means any network element (a switch, a piece of hardware, a link, etc.) that is being managed by network management.

- *M-ACTION*. This primitive is used by the OMAP process (SMAP) to request that another OMAP process perform some type of action. It can be requested in a confirmed or non-confirmed mode. If confirmed, a reply is expected with information about the success or failure of the operation. For OMAP, it is used to initiate an MTP routing verification test for which confirmed is the only support mode.
- *M-EVENT-REPORT*. This primitive is used to report an event to a service user. Since the operations of network entities are a function of the specifications of the managed objects, this event is not defined by the CMIP standard but can be any event about a managed object that the user chooses to report. For OMAP, this service is used to report trace information, which is a list of point codes of a route through the SS7 network. We return to these operations later in this chapter. But before we do, the functions of OMAP must first be described.

PRINCIPAL FUNCTIONS OF SS7 OMAP

OMAP deals with four operations; they are introduced here, and the next four sections of the chapter explain them in more detail.

1. The *MTP routing verification test procedure (MRVT)* operation verifies and maintains the routing information and routing databases.
2. The *SCCP routing verification test procedure (SRVT)* operation verifies and maintains the SCCP global title databases.
3. A *link equipment failure procedure (LEF)* operation detects link failures and notifies concerned parties about them.
4. A *fault sectionalization procedure (LFS)* operation identifies a specific component of a link that has failed.

The first operation is organized into seven functions: creation of routing data; modification of existing data; deletion of existing data; interrogation of databases; activation of specified data (which may already exist); deactivation of specific data; and rearrangement, in a coordinated manner, of routing data in various signaling points (SPs). The second operation is organized into three functions: checking of all SCCP routes; detecting loops in SCCP routing; and verification of global title translations. The LEF and LES operations are simpler and not divided into discrete functions.

The MTP Routing Verification Test (MRVT)

At the heart of SS7 OMAP is the MTP routing verification test (MRVT). Its purpose is to detect (a) loops, (b) excessive length routes, (c) unknown destinations and/or bidirectional reachability between SPs (can they each reach the other?).

Verification is performed by any SP by initiating test messages to a destination SP. The messages will transit all possible routes to the test destination and each intermediate SP on the path will be tracked. If no errors occur, all routing tables in the network are verified. If an intermediate or test SP detects an error, error recovery operations are initiated.

Figure 12–2 provides an example of the verification procedure. Six SPs are involved in the test. SP A is the initiator, SP F is the test destination, and SPs B, C, D, and E are the intermediate points. For this example, SP C receives an MRVT message that originated from SP A (event 1) and was sent through SP B (event 2).

A number of checks are performed at SP C to determine if the verification can be performed (initiator is known, test destination is known, etc.). If the checks are acceptable, SP C accesses its routing tables and constructs a list of routes of adjacent SPs including: (a) STPs that are in the path to the destination SP (excluding the SP that sent the message to SP C [i.e., SP B]); (b) the tested destination, if it is adjacent to SP C.

Each intermediate SP, upon forwarding the MRVT message, places its point code in a parameter in the message. This "route-recording" process (my term) builds a record of the SPs that are crossed (transited) by the message.

SP C then compares its list with the MRVT message fields that contain the list of the transited STPs (the STPs that processed this MRVT message). It checks for the following problems:

- Detected a loop: Is the point code of an signaling point (SP) in the list that is also in the message?
- Detected an excessive length loop: Does the MRVT message exceed a "maximum hop count" (again, my term) value N, which the initi-

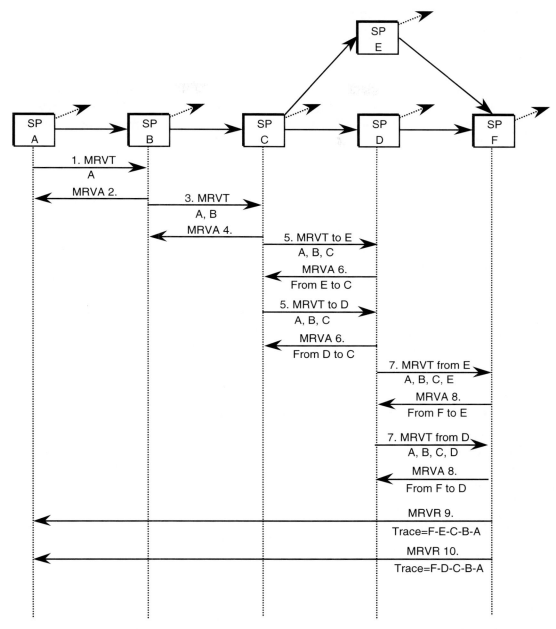

Note: Dotted arrows mean that other paths are explored. For simplicity, the paths for this topology are depicted with solid arrows, along with their associated messages.

where:

   MRVA   MTP routing verification acknowledge message
   MRVR   MTP routing verification result message
   MRVT   MTP routing verification test message

Figure 12–2   An example of the MTP routing verification test procedure.

ating SP (A) sets as a maximum number of STPs that can be crossed by the message? If the point code of an SP in the list is not in the message, SP C knows the route length has been exceeded.

- Detected an inaccessible route: Can the MRVT message be forwarded? Some reasons that prevent a message from being forwarded are: Message must transit a closed network, transit network is non-SS7, and the like.

If no problems are detected, SP C uses its list to send MRVT messages to all remaining SPs that have not processed the message; in this example SP D and SP E. In turn, these SPs send an MRVT message to the test destination (SP F).

As stated earlier, the MRVA messages are acknowledgments and contain no trace information (the list of transited SPs). The MRVA message will contain parameters explaining a problem, if appropriate (detected loop, etc.).

It is the task of the test destination SP to return a trace to the initiator SP in the form of an MTP routing verification result (MRVR) message. This message contains the point codes of all STPs crossed; that is, the point codes in the "route-recording" parameter of the MRVT message that SP F received. In events 9 and 10, SP F sends these messages to SP A.

The SCCP Routing Verification Test (SRVT)

The second major function of SS7 OMAP is the SCCP routing verification test (SRVT). Its purpose is to (1) check all possible SCCP routes, including the translation of global titles and subsystem numbers, (2) detect SCCP routing loops, and (3) detect unknown destinations.

SRVT operates in the same manner as MRVT, but performs consistency checks on the SCCP routing data. SRVT uses the same recursive procedures explained above with MRVT, and the SRVT messages perform the same roles as the MRVT messages. The correlation of these messages is shown in Table 12–1.

Table 12–1   Relationships of MRVT and SRVT Messages

MRVT Messages	SRVT Messages
MRVT	SRVT
MRVA	SRVA
MRVR	SRVA

Link Equipment Failure Procedure (LEF)

The LEF is a very simple procedure used by a SP to inform another SP about a failure on a link interface. The failure is not at the physical layer (which would preclude the SP from sending anything), but at the terminal or link interface equipment.

Two messages are exchanged with this procedure. The link equipment unavailable (LEU) message is sent to indicate that a local terminal or equipment interface has failed. The link equipment available (LEA) message is sent to indicate that the failure is cleared, and the link is ready for the alignment operations.

Link Fault Sectionalization Procedure (LFS)

The LFS is used to identify a defective component on a signaling link. It uses a layer 1 loopback test in the following manner:

- The initiating SP sends a facility test underway (FTU) message to the other SP.
- The initiating SP then sends a layer 1 loopback test for each component on the link (as examples, the DS0 dataport, the data service unit (DSU), the office channel unit (OCU), etc.), until a component fails.
- The initiating SP sends the results of this test to the other SP in a facility test results (FTR) message.
- The initiating SP sends a facility test loopback (FTL) message to initiate a loopback from the other end.
- If the other SP initiates the loopback test, it sends back a facility test acknowledgment (FTA) message.

EXAMPLE OF THE SERVICE DEFINITIONS

Figure 12–3 shows how the user application interacts with the OMAP ASE to invoke the routing verification test operation. In this example, the MTP routing verification test (MRVT) part of the OMAP ASE is invoked.

Two service definitions are used at the system management service interface (SMSI), the OM-CONFIRMED-ACTION, and the OM-EVENT-REPORT. These service definitions conform to the overall OSI-based network management model defined in the ITU-T X.900 recommendations.

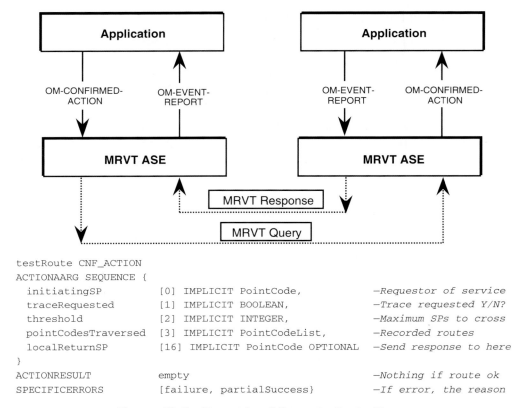

```
testRoute CNF_ACTION
ACTIONAARG SEQUENCE {
  initiatingSP        [0]  IMPLICIT PointCode,           —Requestor of service
  traceRequested      [1]  IMPLICIT BOOLEAN,             —Trace requested Y/N?
  threshold           [2]  IMPLICIT INTEGER,             —Maximum SPs to cross
  pointCodesTraversed [3]  IMPLICIT PointCodeList,       —Recorded routes
  localReturnSP       [16] IMPLICIT PointCode OPTIONAL   —Send response to here
}
ACTIONRESULT          empty                              —Nothing if route ok
SPECIFICERRORS        [failure, partialSuccess}          —If error, the reason
```

Figure 12–3   Example of the use of primitives.

The parameters that must be passed by the user (shown as "Application" in the figure) to the MRVT ASE in the OM-CONFIRMED-ACTION primitive are (a) a transaction ID, (b) an invoke ID, (c) a resource class, (d) a resource instance, and (e) an action value. The first two parameters were explained in the TCAP chapter. The other parameters are coded according to the specific application running on top of OMAP.

Figure 12–3 also shows the ASN.1 coding for the MRVT query and response messages. I have added comments at the end of each line of coding to assist you in reading the code, and Appendix B provides more information on ASN.1 and the OSI presentation layer.

The receiving MRVT ASE receives the MRVT query message and passes it to the application. The application performs its functions (building a list, checking the list against the point codes in the message, etc.), and invokes the OM-EVENT-REPORT primitive. The MRVT uses this primitive to create the MRVT response message to send to the initiator. This message will contain nothing in the ACTIONRESULT parameter if the route is OK. If problems have occurred, the reason is cited in the SPECIFICERRORS parameter.

Examples of OMAP Messages

Figure 12–4 shows the type-length-value syntax for one of the OMAP messages: a response that indicates a failure (routing database problem is detected). Reading from the left of the figure to the right, the first column of information is a brief explanation of the purpose of the parameter in the message. The second column is the coding for the parameter. The notations a, b, c, and d are data-filled, depending upon the contents of the routing databases and the comparisons of the SP's list to the databases. The third column is the name of the parameter, and the right most notations (the arrows) show the presentation layer type-length value (TLV) structure of the message.

USE OF THE CMIP MODEL

The upper layers of SS7 are based on or actually use some of the OSI upper-layer protocols. We learned that TCAP is based on several of the OSI upper-layer protocols. In turn, OMAP uses TCAP and some of the OSI-based CMIP services. This section will explain these relationships.

An Example of a CMIP Operation

This section shows a CMIP operation that supports the EVENT-REPORT service. Since the ACTION service is quite similar, I do not describe it here. In the next section, I bring the ACTION service into the discussion.

One of the services provided in OSI network management is alarm management. As shown in Figure 12–5, alarm management is a user of the CMIP and uses service definitions defined in the Common Management Information Service Element (CMISE) to pass a primitive to CMIP. The primitive is an M-EVENT-REPORT and is used in this example because the SS7 OMAP uses this primitive, with modifications.

Explanation	Coding	
Explanation	**Coding**	
Response	1 1 1 0 0 1 0 0	Package Type Identifier
30 octets follow	0 0 0 1 1 1 1 0	Package Length
Responding	1 1 0 0 0 1 1 1	Transaction ID Identifier
4 octets follow	0 0 0 0 0 1 0 0	Transaction ID Length
Same as Query + P(MRVT)	a a a a a a a a	Transaction IDs
IAW T1.114.3	1 1 1 0 1 0 0 0	Component Sequence Identifier
22 octets follow	0 0 0 1 0 1 1 0	Component Sequence Length
Return error	1 1 1 0 1 0 1 1	Component Type Identifier
20 octets follow	0 0 0 1 0 1 0 0	Component Type Length
Invoke ID IAW T1.114.3	1 1 0 0 1 1 1 1	Component ID Identifier
1 octet follows	0 0 0 0 0 0 0 1	Component ID Length
Same as MRVT (correlation)	b b b b b b b b	Component ID Value
IAW T1.114.3	1 1 0 1 0 1 0 0	Error Code Identifier
1 octet follows	0 0 0 0 0 0 0 1	Error Code Length
Processing failure*	0 0 0 0 0 0 1 1	Error Code
Sequence type	0 0 1 1 0 0 0 0	Parameter Sequence Identifier
12 octets follow	0 0 0 0 1 1 0 0	Parameter Sequence Length
Error type*	1 0 0 0 0 0 0 0	Error Type Identifier
1 octet follows	0 0 0 0 0 0 0 1	Error Type Length
Failure	0 0 0 0 0 0 0 1	Error Type Code
Error parameter*	1 0 1 0 0 0 0 1	Error Parameter
7 octets follow	0 0 0 0 0 1 1 1	Error Parameter Length
Failure identifier*	1 0 0 0 0 0 0 0	Failure Type Identifier
2 octets follow	0 0 0 0 0 0 1 0	Failure Type Length
Failure string	c c c c c c c c	Failure Type Parameters
Trace sent*	1 0 0 0 0 0 0 1	Trace Sent Identifier
1 octet follows	0 0 0 0 0 0 0 1	Trace Sent Length
True=1, False=0	0 0 0 0 0 0 0 d	Trace Sent Parameter

Figure 12–4   Example of an OAMP message.

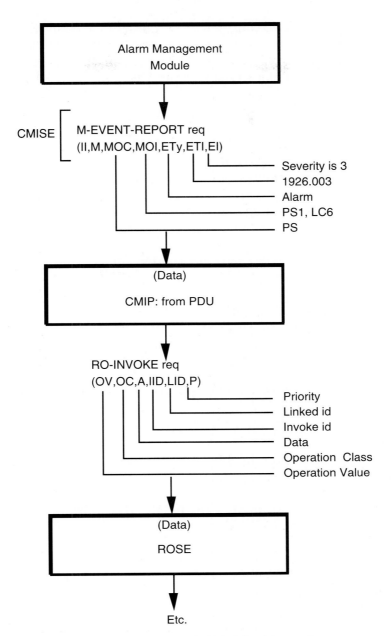

Figure 12–5   The OSI/CMIP approach.

The CMISE primitive contains the arguments used by CMIP to form the CMIP message, which is called a protocol data unit (PDU). CMIP forms the PDU, takes appropriate actions, depending upon the primitive, and passes a Remote Operations Service Element (ROSE) primitive to ROSE. ROSE then invokes its services, and passes the PDU to the presentation layer, and so on. (Recall from Chapter 11 that TCAP is based on several of the OSI upper-layer protocols, one of which is ROSE.)

The invoke identifier (II) parameter in the CMISE primitive is used to identify this specific invocation of the service. It must be unambiguous to distinguish it from other operations in progress. The mode (M) parameter specifies if the operation is to be confirmed or nonconfirmed.

All OSI network management PDUs are identified with the managed object class (MOC) and managed object instance (MOI), parameters that specify the class of the managed object and the instance within the class. The event type (ETy) parameter identifies which event and the type of event being reported. The event time (ETI) parameter is simply the time that an event occurs in the network.

The values of *event information (EI)* are not defined in any of the OSI network management standards. They are said to be application context specific, which, in OSI terms, means the value depends on the agreements reached between the communicating parties. This distinction is important, because it emphasizes that the OSI standards are interface and interworking standards and do not dictate the values of the user information carried within the user data field. However, it should also be remembered that the user data field might contain values from an upper layer protocol.

The *A (argument)* field in the CMIP to ROSE primitive contains the information passed from the alarm management module to CMIP. Therefore, MOC, MOI, ETy, ETI, and EI are encapsulated into the ROSE argument field. The other parameters in the RO-INVOKE.req primitive are used to identify the type of ROSE operation, and the identification of the operation. They are not pertinent to this discussion.

I have also included some possible values that could be coded into CMIP parameters, and they are shown to the right in Figure 12–5. The MOC value is coded as "PS" to identify the packet switch managed object class. The managed object instance (MOI) is "PS1.LC6" to identify line card 6 or packet switch 1. The event type (ETy) is an alarm. The time (ET1) of the alarm is 1926.003. And, the event type (EI) parameter is coded as 3, which in this specific application, means an alarm with a severity level of 3.

OMAP's Use of and Modification to the OSI/CMIP Approach

As represented in Figure 12–6, OMAP uses most of the OSI/CMIP EVENT-REPORT, and ACTION methods, with these changes (Table 12–2 provides summary of this discussion). The transaction ID (TI) used in OMAP is incorporated into OSI, CMIP at the ROSE layer. The invoke ID (II) serves the same functions in both protocol stacks. The OSI/CMIP

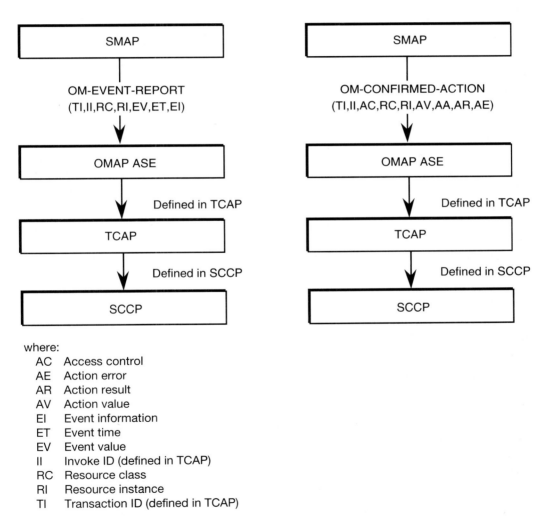

where:

AC	Access control
AE	Action error
AR	Action result
AV	Action value
EI	Event information
ET	Event time
EV	Event value
II	Invoke ID (defined in TCAP)
RC	Resource class
RI	Resource instance
TI	Transaction ID (defined in TCAP)

Figure 12–6   OMAP's use of OSI/CMIP operations.

Table 12–2 Comparison of OSI/CMIP and OMAP Parameters

EVENT REPORT		ACTION	
OSI	*OMAP*	*OSI*	*OMAP*
(1)	TI		(1)
II	II	II	II
M	(2)	M	(2)
MOC	RC	BOC	RC
MOI	RI	BOI	RI
ETy	EV	AT	AV
ETI	ET		
EI	EI	AR	AR
		Sy	
		F	
		AC	AC
		AA	AA
		E	AE

Notes:
1 Transaction ID (TI) used at ROSE, which TCAP incorporates into its protocol.
2 Mode is not needed in OMAP, since it is assumed confirmed mode is used for EVENT REPORT services.

stack includes some parameters that are not used in the OMAP stack for the ACTION service. They are scoping (Sc), filtering (F), and synchronization (Sy). These services are quite powerful, and allow a CMIP user to direct what part of a database is to be searched (scoping), to reduce the scoped traffic that is actually returned in the response message (filtering), and to establish if the remote operation is to be performed completely, not at all, or partially (synchronization). They are also complex and require substantial processing resources, and therefore are not deemed important enough to be used by OMAP.

MONITORING AND MEASUREMENTS FOR SS7 NETWORKS

In addition to the OMAP functions previously described thus far in this chapter, ANSI has published ANI T.115-1990, which describes many operations, maintenance, and administration parameters for monitoring

Table 12–3   MTP Signaling Link (SL)

MTP Signaling Link Performance
  Cumulative duration of link in the in-service state
  Failure—all reasons
  Failure—abnormal FIBR/BSNR
  Failure—excessive delay of acknowledgment
  Failure—excessive error rate
  Failure—excessive duration of congestion
  Alignment or proving failure
  Number of signal units received in error
  Number of negative acknowledgments received
  Local automatic changeover
  Local automatic changeback

MTP Signaling Link Availability
  Cumulative duration of SL unavailability (any reason)
  Cumulative duration of SL inhibition due to local management actions
  Cumulative duration of SL inhibition due to remote management actions
  Cumulative duration of SL unavailability due to link failure
  Cumulative duration of SL unavailability due to remote processor outage
  Start of remote processor outage
  Stop of remote processor outage
  Cumulative duration of local busy
  Number of local management inhibition occurrences
  Number of local management uninhibition occurrences
  Total number of local processor outages

MTP Signaling Link Utilization
  Number of SIF and SIO octets transmitted
  Octets retransmitted
  Number of MSUs transmitted
  Number of SIF and SIO octets received
  Number of MSUs received
  SL congestion indications
  Cumulative duration of SL congestions
  Stop of SL congestion
  MSUs discarded due to SL congestion
  Number of congestion events resulting in loss of MSUs

for SS7 networks. Most of the parameters deal with measurements, such as number of failures, duration of failure, and so on. This specification provides guidelines on the following aspects:

- Description of the measurement (signaling link failure, routing failure, etc.)
- The units used for the measurement (time in seconds, number of events, etc.)
- The duration of the measurement
- The level at which the measurement occurs (MTP 2, MTP 3, SCCP, etc.)
- Whether the measurement occurs on demand or on a permanent basis
- References to other ANSI SS7 specifications to obtain more information

Tables 12–3 to 12–7 are summaries of the measurements that are defined in ANSI T1.115-1990. I list the description of the measurement

Table 12–4   MTP Signaling Link Set, Route Set, and Signaling Point

MTP Signaling Link Set and Route Set Availability
  Cumulative duration of unavailability of signaling linkset
  Start of linkset failure
  Stop of linkset failure
  Indication of broadcast TFP and TCP due to failure of measured linkset
  MSUs discarded due to route set unavailability

MTP Signaling Point Status
  Cumulative duration of adjacent SP inaccessible
  Start of adjacent SP inaccessible state
  Stop of adjacent SP inaccessible state
  MSUs discarded due to a routing data error

MTP Signaling Traffic Distribution (Signaling Route Utilization)
  Number of SIF and SIO octets received with given OPC
  Number of SIF and SIO octets transmitted with given DCP
  Number of SIF and SIO octets handled with given SIO
  Number of SIF and SIO octets received with given OPC and SIO
  Number of SIF and SIO octets transmitted with given DPC and SIO
  Number of SIF and SIO octets handled with given OPC, DPC, and SIO

Table 12–5   SCCP

SCCP Performance
    Routing failure—No translation for address of this nature
    Routing failure—No translation for this specific address
    Routing failure—Network failure (point code is not available)
    Routing failure—Network congestion
    Routing failure—Subsystem failure
    Routing failure—Subsystem congestion
    Routing failure—Unequipped user
    Syntax error detected

SCCP Subsystem Availability
    Start of local SCCP unavailable—Failure
    Start of local SCCP unavailable—Maintenance made busy
    Start of local SCCP unavailable—Congestion
    Stop of local SCCP unavailable—(All reasons)
    Cumulative duration of local SCCP unavailable (All reasons)
    Subsystem out of service request granted
    Subsystem out of service request denied

SCCP Utilization
    UDTS messages sent
    UDTS messages received
    Total messages handled (from local or remote subsystems)
    Total messages intended for local subsystems
    Total messages requiring global title translation
    Total messages sent (for connectionless only)
    Total messages received (for connectionless only)
    Messages sent to a backup system

to give you an idea of the gist of this specification. If you have read the previous chapters in this book, most of the table entries should be familiar. I leave it to the reader to study ANSI T1.115-1990 for more detail, and recommend it highly to network managers and troubleshooters, but I will provide a few thoughts on these procedures.

The activities in Tables 12–3 and 12–4 pertain to the MTP signaling link (SL). These activities are concerned with network surveillance and are used to coordinate and assign priorities to OAM actions. Some measurements are made on an "on-occurrence" basis, and some are made on a periodic basis, ranging from every 5 to 30 minutes. Other activities identified in Tables 12–3 and 12–4 are concerned with congestion thresholds and checking that traffic discards are made within specifications.

Table 12–6   ISUP

ISUP Availability
Start of local ISUP unavailable—Failure
Start of local ISUP unavailable—Maintenance made busy
Start of local ISUP unavailable—Congestion
Stop of local ISUP unavailable—(All reasons)
Cumulative duration of local ISUP unavailable (All reasons)

ISUP Utilization
Total ISUP messages sent
Total ISUP messages received

ISUP Performance / Stability
No acknowledgment for circuit reset within one minute
No GRA received for GRS within one minute
Unreasonable message received
RLC not received within T1
Release initiated due to abnormal conditions

ISUP Circuit Availability
Circuit blocked
Circuit unblocked
Circuit group blocked (No release)
Circuit group blocked (Immediate release)
Circuit group unblocked (Any reason)
Circuit blocked in excess of five minutes
Circuits requiring automatic repeat attempt

ISUP Connection Performance
Total unsuccessful attempts (Calls cleared before an answer occurs)
Unsuccessful call attempt—Switching equipment congestion
Unsuccessful call attempt—No circuit available
Unsuccessful call attempt—Address incomplete
Unsuccessful call attempt—Temporary failure
Unsuccessful call attempt—Unallocated number
Unsuccessful call attempt—Busy
Unsuccessful call attempt—Destination out-of-service
Unsuccessful call attempt—Other causes
Second successive continuity check failure
Cross-office check failure

Table 12–7   TCAP

TCAP Availability
  Start of TCAP unavailable—Failure
  Start of TCAP unavailable—Maintenance made busy
  Start of TCAP unavailable—Congestion
  Stop of TCAP unavailable—(All reasons)
  Cumulative duration of local TCAP unavailable (All reasons)

TCAP Utilization
  Total number of TCAP messages sent by the node
  Total number of TCAP messages received by the node
  Total number of TCAP components sent by the node
  Total number of components received by the node

TCAP Performance
  Protocol error in transaction portion—Unrecognized package type
  Protocol error in transaction portion—Incorrect transaction portion
  Protocol error in transaction portion—Badly structured transaction portion
  Protocol error in transaction portion—Unrecognized transaction ID
  Protocol error in component portion—Unrecognized component
  Protocol error in component portion—Incorrect (mistyped) component portion
  Protocol error in component portion—Badly structured component portion
  Protocol error in component portion—Duplicate invoke ID
  Protocol error in component portion—Unrecognized correlation

The activities in Table 12–5 pertain to the Signaling Connection Control Part (SCCP) principally for (a) the monitoring of routing failures, (b) monitoring to the extent of unavailable service from SCCP or an SSN, and (c) accumulating usage statistics on SCCP operations.

The activities in Table 12–6 pertain to the ISDN User Part (ISUP). The information is similar to that of SCCP: usage statistics and the monitoring of failures.

Finally, the activities in Table 12–7 pertain to the Transaction Capabilities Applications Part (TCAP). Once again, the information deals with TCAP availability, utilization, and performance.

SUMMARY

The SS7 Operations, Maintenance, and Administration Part (OMAP) is responsible for MTP routing verification, SCCP routing verification, link verification, and link loopback testing. It assumes the operations of TCAP for support and incorporates many of the operations of the OSI network management's Common Management Information Protocol (CMIP). A separate specification, ANSI T1.115-1990, also contains valuable information on descriptions of the measurements on signaling link failure, routing failure, SCCP performance, ISUP performance, and many other aspects of SS7 operations.

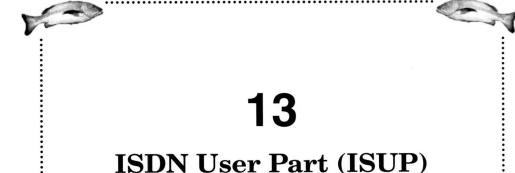

13

ISDN User Part (ISUP)

INTRODUCTION

This chapter examines the ISDN User Part (ISUP), one of several upper-layer applications supported by the SS7 network. The relationships of ISUP and SS7 are explained, as well as how they interwork with each other. Most of this chapter is devoted to an example of how ISUP and SS7 jointly set up and tear down a connection for an end user.

ISUP AND SS7 RELATIONSHIPS

This book has discussed SS7 and ISDN as separate subjects. Indeed, they are separate, and they perform different operations in the signaling network architecture. However, SS7 and ISDN can be "partners" in that ISDN assumes SS7 will set up the connections within a network and SS7 assumes ISDN will set up connections at network boundaries (outside the network). Therefore, as depicted in Figure 13–1, we can view ISDN as a user network interface (UNI) operating between the user device and the network node, and we can view SS7 ISUP as a network node interface (NNI) operating between the nodes within the network. SS7 also operates as an internetworking interface, allowing two networks to communicate with each other.

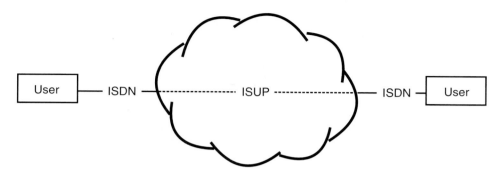

Figure 13–1   ISDN user part (ISUP).

THE ISUP MESSAGES

ISUP uses a wide variety of messages to support numerous features. Table 13–1 lists the mandatory (M) and (O) parameters that must be coded into the ISUP messages. This chapter concentrates on the mandatory parameters and some of the more commonly used optional parameters. The legend at the bottom of the table lists the names of the parameters that are associated with the numbers at the top of each column. The message types are shown on the left side of the table with the abbreviations of their names. The following list contains the abbreviations of the messages that are listed in Table 13–1. Later discussions in this chapter will make use of this table.

ACM	Address Complete Message
ANM	Answer
BLA	Blocking Acknowledgment
BLO	Blocking
CCR	Continuity Check Request
CFN	Confusion
CGB	Circuit Group Blocking
CGBA	Circuit Group Blocking Acknowledgment
CGU	Circuit Group Unblocking
CGUA	Circuit Group Unblocking Acknowledgment
COT	Continuity
CPG	Call Progress
CQM	Circuit Query
CQR	Circuit Query Response

Table 13–1 Parameters in ISDN User Part Messages

	1	2	3	4	5	6	7	8	9	10	11	12	13	14	15	16	17	18
IAM	M		M	M								M		O	M			M
INR	M													M				
INF	M			O									M					
CRA	M																	
CRM	M														M			
COT	M									M								
ACM	M	M			O								O					
EXM	M																	
ANM	M	O											O					
CPG	M	O			O						M		O					
FOT	M																	
REL	M				M													
CFN	M				M													
CVR	M					M			M									
CVT RLC	M																	
CCR RSC LPA	M																	
BLO UBL UCIC	M																	
BLA UBA	M																	
SUS RES	M																M	
CGB CGU	M						M									M		
CGBA CGUA	M						M									M		
GRS GRA CQM	M															M		
CQR	M							M								M		
FAC	M																	

1 Message type	10 Continuity indicators
2 Backward call indicators	11 Event information
3 Called party number	12 Forward call indicators
4 Calling party's category	13 Information indicators
5 Cause indicators	14 Information request indicators
6 Circuit group characteristic indicators	15 Nature of connection indicators
7 Circuit group supervision message type indicator	16 Range and status
8 Circuit state indicator	17 Suspend/resume indicators
9 Circuit validation response indicator	18 User service information

CRA   Circuit Reservation Acknowledgment
CRM   Circuit Reservation
CVR   Circuit Validation Response
CVT   Circuit Validation Test
EXM   Exit
FAC   Facility
FOT   Forward Transfer
GRA   Group Reset Acknowledgment
GRS   Group Reset
IAM   Initial Address Message
INF   Information
INR   Information Request
LPA   Loop-back Acknowledgment
REL   Release
RES   Resume
RLC   Release Complete
RSC   Reset Circuit
SUS   Suspend
UBA   Unblocking Acknowledgment
UBL   Unblocking
UCIC   Unequipped Circuit Identification Code

CONNECTION MANAGEMENT OPERATIONS

In this section we piece together some of the information explained in earlier chapters by providing an example of how the SS7 signaling procedures and call set-up occur. This example also shows the relationship of ISDN and SS7 connections.

Before we begin, some points should be clarified (Figure 13–2). In the systems that do not use digital signaling (ISDN and SS7), service tones (ringback, busy) are returned to the originating local exchange from the terminating local exchange. With ISDN and SS7, the tones can be generated locally upon the local exchange receiving an SS7 address complete (ACM) from the terminating exchange. Typically, this message is then used to generate the ringback to the user's terminal. At the distant end, the sending of the ACM signal means that the called party is being dialed.

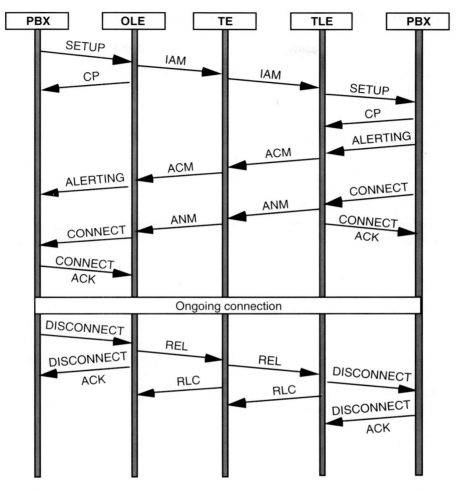

where:

ACM Address complete message
ANM Answer message
CP Call proceeding
IAM Initial address message
OLE Originating local exchange
PBX Private branch exchange
RLC Release complete
TE Transit exchange
TLE Terminating (destination)local exchange

Figure 13–2   Example of an ISDN/SS7 call.

THE INITIAL ADDRESS MESSAGE (IAM) OPERATIONS

Operations at the Originating Local Exchange

As shown in Figure 13–2, a call setup begins when a telephone or PBX (in this example) sends an ISDN SETUP message, which is used to create the SS7 initial address message (IAM). This message is formatted at the originating local exchange (OLE) and sent to a transit exchange (TE), or perhaps directly to the terminating local exchange (TLE). The originating exchange selects a suitable idle circuit during this process. The selection of the route for the call depends upon the called-party number, the transit network selection (if appropriate), and any special signaling capability that may be required to support the call, such as a data call. The selection of the route may be performed by the local exchange, or this exchange may obtain routing information from a remote database. It may also store information about the call locally or at a remote database.

The IAM should contain all the information required to set up and route the call, and it also initiates the seizure of the outgoing circuit. Therefore, the next (succeeding) exchange, upon receiving the IAM, assumes the preceding exchange has reserved the indicated circuit. All codes and digits that are required for the routing through a national or international network will be sent in this message.

Since the SS7 signaling does not pass over the speech path, it must provide facilities to provide a continuity check of the speech circuit to be used if the circuit does not provide inherent fault notification procedures. It also makes cross office checks to ensure the reliability of the connection through the various digital exchanges.

The originating exchange also places a call reference parameter in the IAM, as well as its SS7 point code, to provide the means for the terminating exchange to identify (and set up) an end-to-end connection.

Completion of Transmission Path (through connection). The rules for the originating exchange to complete the transmission path (the circuit for the call) in the backward direction are as follows: (a) for speech, 3.1 kHz audio, or unrestricted digital information (with tones and announcements), completion must be achieved no later than the receipt of the address complete message (ACM); (b) for any call, connection in both directions must be achieved no later than receipt of an answer or interworking indication (later discussions will explain this subject in more detail).

Operations at the Transit (Intermediate) Exchange (TE)

The transit exchange analyzes the IAM to determine: (a) a circuit to be seized; (b) routing through another country, if necessary; (c) the nature of the circuit (terrestrial or satellite); (d) if echo control is needed; (e) the calling party's category; and, (f) the need for continuity checks. The exchanges will disable any echo suppressers (if necessary) at this time.

If all the parameters in the IAM are acceptable, the transit exchange seizes a free circuit and sends an IAM to the next (succeeding) exchange. The fields in this message may be modified based on the characteristics of the outgoing circuit. For example, if the circuit is on a satellite, a parameter in the message will be changed to so indicate.

Operations at the Terminating Local Exchange (TLE)

Upon receipt of the IAM at the TLE, the called party number is examined to determine to which line the call should be connected. This line is then checked to determine if it is available. Other checks are made to decide if the call is allowed (call forward, do not disturb, etc.). If the call can be connected, the exchange sets up the connection to the called party (after a continuity check is done, if necessary). If the call is not allowed, this exchange must send back a release (REL) message to the originating exchange.

If the call is allowed, the terminating exchange creates an ISDN SETUP message and sends to the called party equipment (a PBX in this example). The called party responds with an ISDN CALL PROCEEDING (CP) message. This message is used by the exchange to set a field in the address complete message (ACM) to note an ISDN access has been made at the destination end (the field is called "ISDN access indicator"). But the ACM has not been sent. It is triggered by the receipt of the ISDN ALERTING message from the PBX.

THE ADDRESS COMPLETE MESSAGE (ACM) OPERATIONS

Operations at the Terminating Local Exchange (TLE)

The called party responds with an ISDN ALERTING message. Based on the contents of this message, the destination exchange sets a field in the ACM (called party's status indicator) to "subscriber is free". If the called party delays in responding beyond a set time, the exchange will set this field to "excessive delay". The terminating exchange must through-connect and apply the awaiting answer indicator (ringing-tone) to the transmission path to the calling party, if ringing tone emanates from the called end.

The ACM is sent in the backward direction to inform the originator of the call that all address signals have been received for routing the call to the receiving party. This message also indicates to the originating exchange that the path through the network is complete.

Operations at the Transit Exchange (TE)

Upon receipt of the ACM, the transit exchange must through-connect the path in the backward direction (if it has not yet performed this operation). It then forwards the IAM to the next exchange.

Operations at the Originating Local Exchange

Upon receipt of the ACM, the originating exchange checks the calling party's status indicator field. If it is set to "subscriber free", it sends an alerting indication to the calling party. For ISDN lines, it is an ALERTING message.

THE ANSWER (ANM) OPERATIONS

Operations at the Terminating Local Exchange (TLE)

When the terminating end answers the call, an ISDN CONNECT message is sent to the TLE, which maps this message into an SS7 answer message (ANM), which is then mapped into an ISDN CONNECT message and given to the originating caller.

When the called party answers with an ISDN CONNECT message (or going off-hook in a non-ISDN line), the TLE removes the ringing tone (if applicable), through-connects the transmission path, and sends the ANM to the preceding exchange. It also sends an ISDN CONNECT ACK message back to the called user.

Operations at the Transit Exchange

Upon receipt of the ANM, the transit exchange through-connects the path (if it has not already done so), and sends the ANM to the next preceding exchange.

Operations at the Originating Local Exchange

This exchange must also through-connect if it has not yet performed this operation. It then sends a connect indication (the ISDN CONNECT message) to the called party. This party responds with the CONNECT ACK message.

An ongoing connection is now in place, and the calling and called party can begin their conversation.

THE RELEASE (REL) AND RELEASE COMPLETE (RLC) OPERATIONS

Eventually one of the callers hangs up, which activates an ISDN DISCONNECT message, and in turn, the ISDN and SS7 messages shown in the bottom part of Figure 13–2. Upon receiving an ISDN DIS-CONNECT message from one of the parties, the originating exchange starts the release of the switched path, and sends the RELEASE (REL) message to the succeeding exchange, and an ISDN DISCONNECT message to the requesting party. At the transit exchange, the switched path is released, after which the release confirm (RLC) message is returned to the preceding exchange. At the transit exchange, the path is released, after which an ISDN DISCONNECT message is sent to the other party, which responds with the DISCONNECT ACK message.

After a designated period of waiting, if no other signals emanate from the end user, additional supervisory signals are exchanged between the two exchanges to make the circuit available for new traffic.

PARAMETERS IN THE MESSAGES

Parameters for the Initial Address Message (IAM)

Although a wide variety of parameters can be sent in the IAM, six parameters are mandatory (see Figure 13–3). The message type code is a one-octet field that identifies the type of message. For the IAM message the parameter is coded as 00000001.

The *called party number* (from 2 to 11 octets) contains the telephone number of the called party. It also identifies the addressing plan (E.164, for example) and a field to indicate the nature of the address (the number, such as a subscriber number, a test line number, an international number, a network-specific number. Each number is coded as 4-bit BCD codes (0000 is a 0, 0001 is 1 etc.).

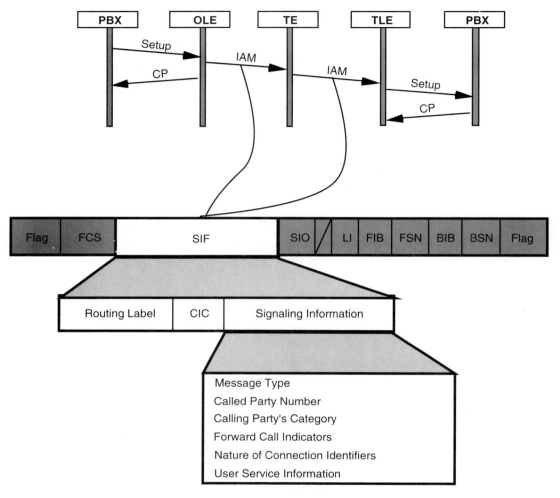

Figure 13–3   Parameters in the initial address message (IAM).

The *calling party's category* parameter is a one-octet field that contains information about: (a) the language used by the originating operator, (b) the type of call (test, data, regular voice, pay phone, emergency, high-priority, network-specific, etc.). Only one code is allowed in this parameter. So, one could not convey an emergency call with a Spanish operator (a bit restrictive, to be sure).

The *forward call indicators* parameter is a two-octet field that contains many parameters that are used to inform the receiving exchange about the services that are to be associated with the call. Information is coded to indicate if: (a) the call is of international origin, (b) the signaling method is pass-along or SCCP, (c) any intervening network is not SS7-based, (d) the IAM is segmented into more than one message, (e) ISUP is used end-to-end, (f) ISUP is required end-to-end, (g) originating access is ISDN, and (h) SCCP (and type [connectionless, connection-oriented]) is employed.

The *nature of connection* indicators parameter is a one-octet field that contains information about the circuit being set up (identified by the circuit identification code [CIC]). Information is coded to indicate if: (a) satellite circuits are in the connection, and if so, how many, (b) echo control devices are included, and (c) a continuity check is or is not needed.

The *user service information* parameter is variable-length (three to n octets). Its purpose is to provide information regarding a data call. It contains information about: (a) information transfer rate, (b) transfer mode (circuit/packet), (c) layer 1 employment, (d) use of various ITU-T rate-adaptation schemes (V.100, V.110, V.120), (e) use of V.6 modem negotiation parameters, (f) synchronous or asynchronous operations, (g) use of X.25 layer 3, and (h) several others.

Although not shown in this figure, the terminating exchange can send an *information message (INF)* back to the originating exchange if it needs more information about the call and/or the caller.

PARAMETERS IN THE ADDRESS COMPLETE MESSAGE (ACM)

The address complete message contains one mandatory parameter, the *backward call indicators* (see Figure 13–4). This parameter is two octets in length and contains these fields: (a) charge indicator: the indication if the call is free or is to be charged (if chargeable, the charged number is provided); (b) called party's status indicator: indication if party is available (if not available, a busy signal is returned to the caller; (c) called party's category indicator: indication of a called party's category, such as a pay phone or ordinary subscriber; (d) echo control device indicator: indication if echo control devices are included in connection; (e) IAM segmentation indicator: indication if message has been segmented; (f) end-to-end method indicator: indication of pass-along or SCCP operation; (g) interworking indicator: indication if another signaling network is involved in the call; (h) holding indicator: indication if holding the call is required; (i) ISDN user part indicator: indication if ISUP is used end-to-end; (j) ISDN access indicator: indication if terminating device uses ISDN; and (k) SCCP method indicator: indication of SCCP use (connection-oriented, connectionless).

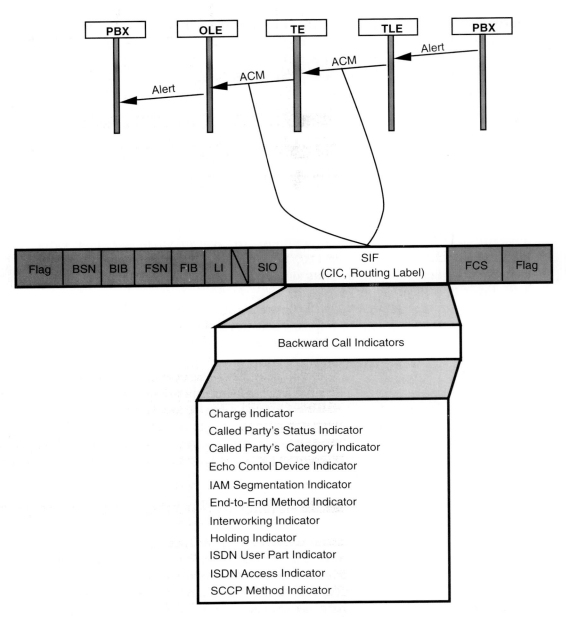

Figure 13–4   Parameters in the address complete message (ACM).

PARAMETERS IN THE ANSWER MESSAGE (ANM)

All the parameters in the answer message (ANM) are optional except for the CI and the routing label. This discussion explains some of these parameters (see Figure 13–5).

The optional *backward call indicator* parameter is sent in the backward direction to provide information regarding the call.

The *business group* parameter is used to code the characteristics and identifiers of business group. Examples of fields in this parameter

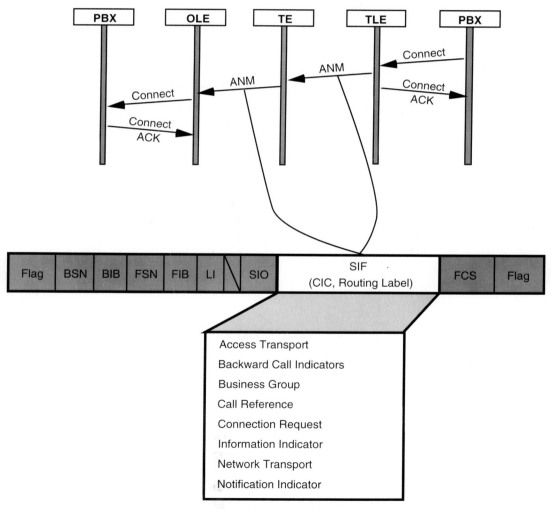

Figure 13–5   Parameters in the answer message (ANM).

are: (a) an identifier of the business group, (b) originating and terminating line privileges (e.g., unrestricted, fully restricted, customer defined), (c) party selector (e.g., calling party number, redirecting number, original called number), and (d) multilocation business group identifier.

The *connection request* parameter provides information on the terminal that originated the connection request. Examples of fields in this parameter are (a) the local reference number (b) the point code of the originator, and (c) a window size of the messages for the connection.

The *information indicator* parameter provides a wide variety of information: (a) calling party address is (not) available (included), (b) calling party address is held and not provided, (c) charge information and (d) information on a multilocation business group, if appropriate.

Parameters in the Release Message (REL)

The release message is used to disconnect the parties and free network resources that were reserved for the call (see Figure 13–6). It can be sent in either direction, when a party goes off-hook. The only mandatory part for this message is the *cause field*, which would usually be coded to indicate a normal clearing.

The access transport part is passed transparently by the SS7 network to users and local exchanges.

PARAMETERS IN THE RELEASE COMPLETE MESSAGE (RLC)

Finally, the release complete message is sent in response to the receipt of the release message or to a reset circuit message (see Figure 13–7).

OTHER EXAMPLES OF ISUP OPERATIONS

This section expands on the general explanations in the previous section. The calling and called party are not identified as to the specific type of instrument, which could a PBX, key set, terminal adapter, and so on. Also, additional transit exchanges (TEs) are shown in the next examples.

Figure 13–8 amplifies our earlier explanations on the call refusal at the called party and terminating local exchange end. The call may not be accepted because the called party is busy or is unavailable. Whatever the case may be, the switch path is removed between each exchange through the exchange of the release (REL) message. This message contains the

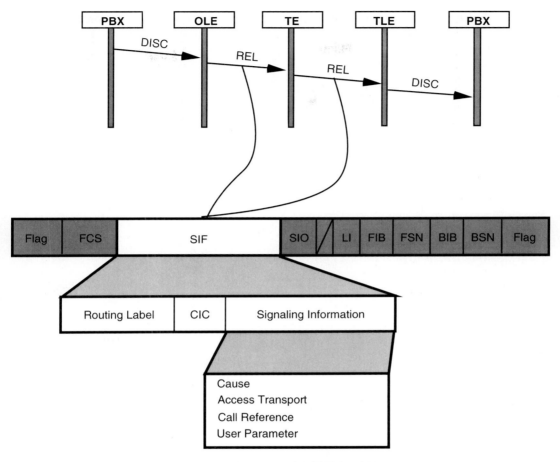

Figure 13–6   The release (REL) message.

message type, the cause indicators fields (in this example, a cause such as the called user is busy, no user responding, the call is rejected, and others). The procedure requires that the release complete (RLC) message acknowledge the REL message. The final part of the procedure is the invocation of Q.931 by the OLE and the calling party to exchange the ISDN disconnect request and disconnect ACK messages.

The last example (Figure 13–9) shows the operations when the called party hangs up (goes on-hook) during the active state of the call. For this example, the called party is not using ISDN. The on-hook signal alerts the TLE to begin the clearing procedure. The suspend (SUS) message is used for this activity. As the figure illustrates, the REL message is sent in the backward direction to the OLE. It contains the message

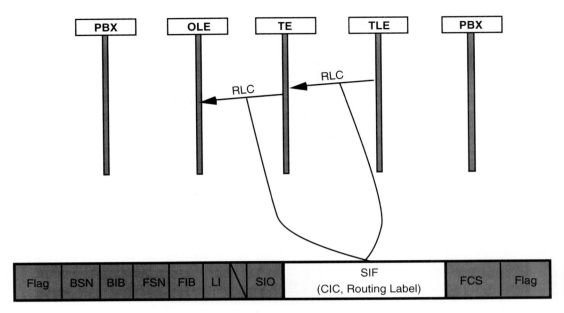

Figure 13–7   Parameters in the release complete (RLC) message.

type, the call reference value, the suspend indicators field, and several optional fields. The suspend indicators field uses one bit of the octet, which is set to 0 in the operation and was ISDN subscriber initiated, or set to 1 if it was network initiated.

CCS CALL SETUP WITHOUT ISDN

This section provides an example of a CCS intraLATA call setup with the customers using conventional telephones on the access lines (access line signaling is covered in Chapter 2). It is assumed you have read Chapter 2 and understand codes such as 0ZZ+XXX, and so on. As a brief review, we discussed the situation of when a trunk is not in use, the offices at both ends send an on-hook signal. A seizure of the trunk at the calling end means an off-hook signal is sent to the called end. At the called end, if a trunk is awaiting an answer to a call, it sends an off-hook signal to the calling end. An answer of the call results in an off-hook signal back to the calling end. A connect (or seizure) signal is a sustained off-hook signal and is forwarded to the called end of a trunk. The purpose of the signal is to request a service. Also recall that the wink is a toggle of the on-hook/off-hook signals to inform the originator of the call that it can

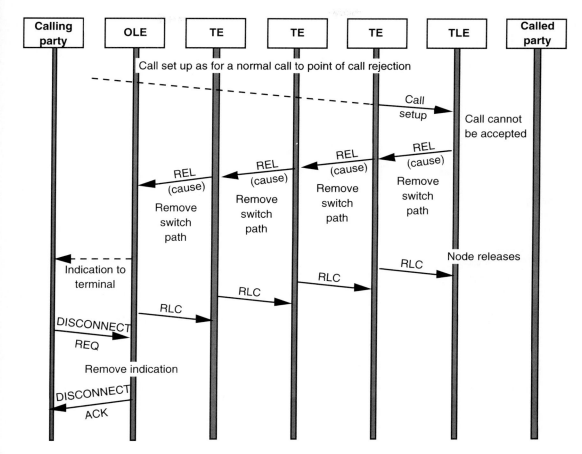

Figure 13–8   Called party cannot be reached.

begin sending to the called number. We also examined the key pulse (KP) and the start (ST) signals, which are placed at the beginning and ending of the dialed number or other pulsed digits, such as routing information.

Figure 13–10 is a general view of the operations with SS7. The originating local exchange accepts conventional dial tone multifrequency signaling from the calling party, and converts these signals into ISUP messages. At the terminating end, the local exchange performs a complementary service for the called party. One operation in Figure 13–10 has not yet been described; it is the continuity message (COT). This message is used to provide a continuity check of the circuit that will support this call. Each circuit in the end-to-end path is checked. Continuity checks are explained in Chapter 2.

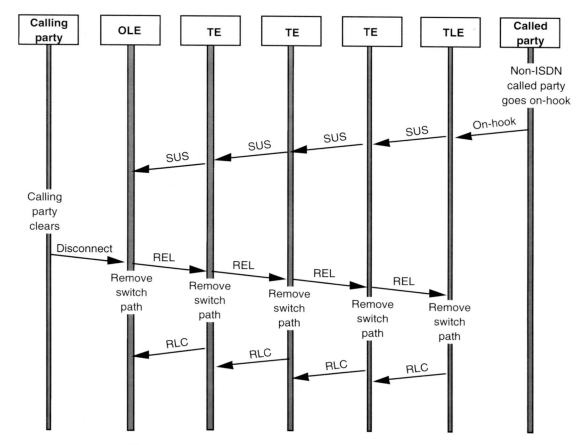

Figure 13–9   Called party goes on-hook during call.

Figure 13–11 shows these operations in more detail. To accommodate analog multifrequency (MF) signaling, the SS7 node (shown in this figure as the transit exchange or access tandem) provides the wink to the originating local exchange. This exchange then begins pulsing the called party number coded as KP+0ZZ+XXX+ST.

We learned earlier that SS7 signaling does not require that the entire transmission path to be reserved before the called party answers. It requires that the path be cut through (connected) in the backward direction no later than the receipt of the ACM. For multifrequency signaling, SS7 uses the following procedure to reserve the circuits in the SS7 part of the connection. The notes at the bottom of Figure 13–11 show at which points the SS7 timers are activated or deactivated.

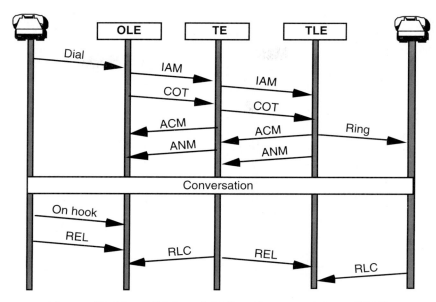

Figure 13–10   CCS intraLATA call setup without ISDN.

This procedure begins with the transit exchange in Figure 13–11 sending a circuit reservation message (CRM) to the succeeding exchange, which is an interexchange carrier in this example. The contents of the CRM is explained later, but for this analysis, it contains a request for a continuity check. The transit exchange sets a timer (T_{CRM}) upon sending the CRM (notation a in the figure).

Upon receiving the CRM, the interexchange carrier marks the circuit busy and sends back a circuit reservation acknowledgment message (CRA) (notation b in the figure), which allows the transit exchange to turn-off the T_{CRM} timer (notation c in the figure).

Since the CRM requested a continuity check, the interexchange carrier sets a timer (T_8, also shown as notation b in the figure) and awaits the receipt of a continuity message (COT). Once the interexchange carrier has sent the CRM, it is now expecting to receive not only a COT but an IAM as well. For the latter expectation, it turns on timer T_{CRA} (notation c in the figure). Therefore, at this point, it has two timers turned on: T_8 and T_{CRA}. When the COT is received, the interexchange carrier turns off timer T_8 (notation e in the figure). If this message indicates a good connection, this exchange then sends a COT to the next exchange for the outgoing circuit (this operation is not shown in Figure 13–11).

Back at the transit exchange, upon receiving the CRA, and completing any further continuity checking on the circuit, it sends an off-hook

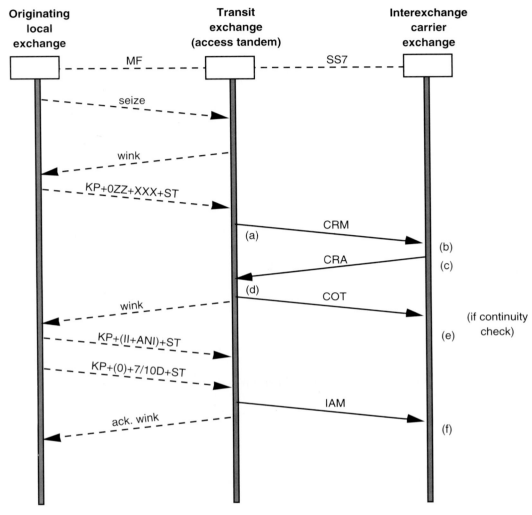

Notes:
  (a) Timer TCRM on
  (b) Timer T8 on
  (c) Timer TCRA on
  (d) Timer TCRM off
  (e) Timer T8 off
  (f) Timer TCRA off

Figure 13–11   Interworking multifrequency and SS7 signaling.

wink on the incoming circuit to the originating local exchange (the second wink in Figure 13–11). This signal prompts this exchange to send the routing and dialing information shown in the figure as KP+(II+ANI)+ST and KP+(0)+7/10D+ST. The receipt of this information prompts the transit exchange to send the wink ACK to the originating local exchange (the third wink in Figure 13–11).

The routing and dialing information received at the transit exchange is used to create and send the IAM. When the IAM is received at the interexchange carrier, it cancels timer T_{CRA} (notation f in the figure), and proceeds with normal SS7 call processing.

With this approach, the transit exchange becomes a gateway between the multifrequency signaling systems and the SS7 signaling system. The gateway function permits users to keep their ongoing analog equipment, so they do not have to move to ISDN.

Message Contents

The contents of the messages for this interworking operation are relatively simple, and contain few fields. The contents of these messages are:

CRM: Message type
Nature of connection indicators

CRA: Message type   ///U-both CRA and COT message types

COT: Message types

Continuity indicators (with one bit of an octet set to 0 for continuity check failed, and 1 for continuity check successful; the remaining seven bits are spares).

THE OTHER ISUP MESSAGES

ISUP is quite rich in its functions and the services it provides in the signaling network. We have examined the messages and operations that are invoked for several conventional operations, but have not examined all the ISUP messages. For the reader who wishes more to know about all the ISUP messages, Appendix 13–A provides a general description of them. For continuity, all messages (including those described in this chapter) are listed and described.

SUMMARY

While ISUP and SS7 are separate entities, they are "partners" in supporting the end users' connection. ISUP is a user network interface (UNI) operating between the user device and the network node, and SS7 is a network node interface (NNI) operating between the nodes within the network or between networks. ISUP is also employed as an internetworking interface allowing two networks to communicate with each other.

APPENDIX 13A—SUMMARY OF THE ISUP MESSAGES AND THEIR FUNCTIONS

This appendix lists and provides a general description of the ISUP messages. The reader is encouraged to read ANSI T1.113.4-1995 for the conventions and rules on how these messages are used. Each message and its acronym or initial is listed, followed by a short explanation of the function of the message.

Address Complete Message (ACM)

This message is sent in the backward direction to indicate that all addressing information has been received to complete the call of the called party. It also conveys that the call is being processed.

Answer Message (ANM)

This message is sent in the backward direction by the distant exchange. It signals that the call has been answered by the called party. Depending upon the specific implementation, it may start (which is usually the case) metering the charge to the bill party.

Blocking Message (BLO)

This message in typically used for maintenance purposes and is sent to the exchange at the other end of the circuit to block a circuit at that remote end.

Blocking Acknowledgment Message (BLA)

This message acknowledges the BLO and signals that the circuit has been blocked.

Call Progress Message (CPG)

This message indicates that an event has occurred in the processing of a call. It can be sent in the forward or backward direction and usually indicates that the call is being processed without problems.

Circuit Group Blocking Message (CGB)

This message is typically used for maintenance purposes and is sent to the exchange at the other end of the circuit to block a group of circuits at that remote end.

Circuit Group Blocking Acknowledgment Message (CGBA)

This message acknowledges the CGB and signals that the group of circuits has been blocked.

Circuit Group Reset Message (GRS)

If an exchange loses its knowledge about the state of a group of circuits (register problem, memory loss, whatever), it sends this message to the far-end exchange (in either direction). This message releases any calls in progress, any remotely blocked conditions, and aligns the state of the circuits as perceived by the far-end exchange.

Circuit Group Reset Acknowledgment Message (GRA)

This message acknowledges the GRS message.

Circuit Group Unblocking Message (CGU)

This message reverses the actions of the CGB message, explained earlier.

Circuit Group Unblocking Acknowledgment Message (CGUA)

This message acknowledges the CGU.

Circuit Query Message (CQM)

This message is sent in case an exchange wants the exchange at the far-end to give it status information about circuits in a particular range.

Circuit Query Response Message (CQR)

This message is sent in response to the CQM message.

Circuit Reservation Message (CRM)

This message is sent only to reserve a circuit when interworking with an exchange access that does not use SS7 (an exchange that uses multifrequency signaling). It is sent in the forward direction only and initiates any required continuity checking.

Circuit Reservation Acknowledgment Message (CRA)

This message is sent in the backward direction and acknowledges the CRM message and indicates that a circuit has been reserved for the call.

Circuit Validation Response Message (CVR)

This message is sent in response to the CVT message, explained next.

Circuit Validation Test Message (CVT)

This message is sent to request the distant exchange sent circuit translation information. Its purpose is to ensure that new translation parameters have been set correctly.

Confusion Message (CFN)

This message is a catch-all (which most software-based systems have) that is sent by an exchange in response to receiving a message that it does not understand—either the message, the fields in the message, or both.

Continuity Message (COT)

The message is used to give the status of a continuity check (that was requested in the IAM) on a circuit. It is sent in the forward direction to give the status of the preceding circuit as well as to select the circuit in the following exchange.

Continuity Check Request Message (CCR)

This message requests that continuity checking equipment be attached. It is sent to the exchange at the other end of the circuit and identifies the circuit to be checked.

Exit Message (EXM)

This message is sent by an outgoing gateway in the backward direction to signal that call setup has occurred to the adjacent network.

Facility Message (FAC)

This message is used in either direction by an exchange to request an action by another exchange. It can be used in any phase of the connection. It requests actions such as a billing verification, a reconnect request, coin collect, and so on.

Forward Transfer Message (FOT)

This message is sent in the forward direction on semi-automatic calls when the assistance of an operator is needed. The operator may be recalled when the call is completed.

Information Message (INF)

This message is sent in response to the information request message, described next.

Information Request Message (INR)

This message is sent by an exchange if it needs additional information to complete the call. For example it may need additional addressing information, a billing number, call forwarding information, or any parameters that are defined in the ISUP specification.

Initial Address Message (IAM)

This message is the first message sent to begin the call connection process. It initiates the seizure of the outgoing circuit.

Loop Back Acknowledgment Message (LPA)

This message is sent in the backward direction in response to a continuity check request message (CCR). It indicates that a loop has been connected.

Pass Along Message (PAM)

This message is sent in the forward or backward direction along the same path as the path used for the connection setup. The information that it contains can be any of the messages that are described in this appendix.

Release Message (REL)

When either party hangs up (goes on-hook), or the network brings the call down, this message is sent (in either direction) to begin the release of the circuit.

Release Complete Message (RLC)

This message acknowledges the REL message. It indicates that the circuit has been brought back into an idle condition.

Reset Circuit Message (RSC)

If an exchange loses its knowledge about the state of a circuit (register problem, memory loss, whatever), it sends this message to the far-end exchange (in either direction). This message releases any calls in progress, any remotely blocked conditions, and align the state of the circuit as perceived by the far-end exchange.

Resume Message (RES)

This message is sent in the backward direction and is used in two situations. First, it is used to indicate a reanswer from an interworking node. Second, it is used to indicate that a non-ISDN called party has gone off-hook, after having gone on-hook (for a specified time, which is network-dependent). The call is to stay active and the connection is to stay up.

Suspend Message (SUS)

This message is created in response to the on-hook signal of a user device. It alerts the next exchange to begin the clearing procedure.

Unblocking Message (UBL)

This message reverses the effect of the blocking message (BLO) described earlier.

Unblocking Acknowledgment Message (UBA)

This message acknowledges the UBL.

Unequipped Circuit Identification Code Message (UCIC)

This message is sent in response to a message that contains an unequipped circuit identification code.

14

Transaction Capabilities Applications Part (TCAP)

INTRODUCTION

This chapter examines the Transaction Capabilities Applications Part (TCAP) specification. The operations of TCAP are described, including the TCAP messages and the two major portions of TCAP, transaction and component. TCAP's relationships to the OSI Model are extensive, so they are examined, including the OSI presentation layer coding rules for the TCAP messages.

The coding examples of the TCAP message are based on ANSI T1 114 1992; and its use in the United States. Other codes are used in other countries (and in specific applications) that use TCAP.

TCAP FUNCTIONS

Prior to the implementation of TCAP, no standardized method existed for network providers to communicate with each other about matters pertaining to operations that did not relate directly to the establishment and termination of a voice call (non-circuit related information). The problem became evident as the 800 number service came into existence.

To solve the problem, TCAP was (and is) used in 800 number applications to allow different telephone companies to access centralized 800 number databases in a standardized manner. The term standardized is important, because TCAP defines the format and fields that allow a service switching point (SSP) or a service control point (SCP) to formulate a TCAP access request to another *node* and a *database*, regardless of the *node's architecture* and the *database structure* (see Figure 14–1(a)).

TCAP operates at the application layer of the OSI Model, but it may also include other lower-layer protocols needed to support it. It operates

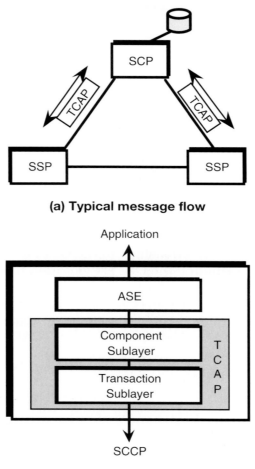

(a) Typical message flow

(b) Layer architecture

where:
    ASE   Application service element
    SCCP   Signaling connection control part

Figure 14–1 Transaction capabilities application part (TCAP).

on top of SCCP. TCAP supports database access by the SS7 switches, and the SS7 applications that reside in the switches use TCAP to access information.

TCAP provides other services to applications; this list provides examples of some of the new exchange services:

- *CLASS services.* Use TCAP to edit customer-programmable lists such as distinctive ringing/call waiting (DRCW).
- *ISDN queries.* Use TCAP to query remote ISDN switches about a customer's ability/desire to forward calls.
- *End office queries.* Use TCAP to query a remote end office to check the status of a telephone line without the need to set up a connection.
- *Subscriber profiles.* Use TCAP to access databases that contain information about subscriber's profiles (call forward, do not disturb, billing data, etc.).
- *Announcements.* Use TCAP to deliver instructions about the type of recorded message that should be played by an signaling point (SP).

TCAP and OSI

TCAP is a connectionless remote procedure call (RPC) and part of it is quite similar to the remote operation service element (ROSE), published in ITU's X.219 and X.229. Many of the ROSE features have been incorporated into TCAP (but it does not use ROSE, which would entail invoking redundant operations).

As Figure 14–1(b) shows, TCAP is divided into two sublayers. The transaction sublayer has services that are somewhat similar to the OSI commitment-concurrency-recovery (CCR) protocol and the component sublayer, which is modeled closely on ROSE. The transaction sublayer is organized around two types of dialogues that take place between peer entities in two machines operating in the transaction sublayer. The first dialogue is called the unstructured dialogue and is so named because no association is established between the users of this service. Additionally, no responses are provided from the receiver of this type of traffic. The second type of dialogue is the structured dialogue and requires the retention of information about the ongoing communications between the two transaction sublayers. A dialogue identifier is associated with each message pertaining to a specific dialogue.

The component sublayer an entity to issue invoke operations. It then returns results about what happened at the machine in which the invoke operation occurred.

Some of the TCAP operations are based on the OSI Red Book X.409 and X.410 applications layer standards. Four services are described in X.410, and are shown in Figure 14–2. An applications entity (AE) begins operations by transferring operation protocol data units (OPDUs). X.410 defines four types of OPDUs as:

- Invoke OPDU
- ReturnResult OPDU
- ReturnError OPDU
- Reject OPDU

X.409 describes the notation (structure for the PDUs). The general X.409 notation is:

$$\text{OPDU ::= choice \{[1] invoke, [2] Return Result,}$$
$$\text{[3] Return Error, [4] reject\}}$$

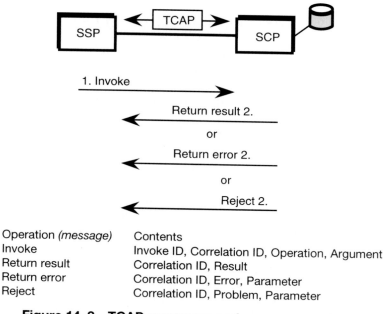

Operation *(message)*	Contents
Invoke	Invoke ID, Correlation ID, Operation, Argument
Return result	Correlation ID, Result
Return error	Correlation ID, Error, Parameter
Reject	Correlation ID, Problem, Parameter

Figure 14–2   TCAP messages and message contents.

The Invoke OPDU is used when an AE wishes to communicate with another AE. The OPDU contains an identifier that is used to ensure atomic actions of the OPDUs. The protocol data unit also specifies the operation to be performed. However, since the operation is application-specific, X.410 does not define this aspect of the AE-AE process.

The X.409 notation for the Invoke OPDU is:

Invoke ::= SEQUENCE {invokeID INTEGER,OPERATION,
argument ANY}

The ReturnResult OPDU reports the result of the AE-AE operation. It is sent if the result is successful. The ReturnError OPDU is sent if the operation is unsuccessful. The Reject OPDU is returned if the OPDU is rejected due to a content or formatting error. These OPDUs are coded in accordance with X.409:

Return Result ::= SEQUENCE {invokeID INTEGER, result ANY}
Return Error ::= SEQUENCE {invokeID INTEGER, ERROR,
parameter ANY}

The Reject OPDU is returned if the Invoke is not accepted. It is coded as:

Reject ::= SEQUENCE {invokeID INTEGER, Problem, parameter ANY}

CODING CONVENTIONS AND TRANSFER SYNTAX FOR TCAP

X.409/X.209 and ISO 8825 describe the encoding rules for the TCAP message. These basic encoding rules (BER) provide the conventions for the transfer syntax conventions.

The rules require that each TCAP message be described by a well-formed, specific representation. This representation is called a *data element* (or just an *element*). As shown below, it consists of three components: the identifier (also called type), the length of contents, and the contents (also called value). A common convention is to call this arrangement TLV for type, length, value, although TCAP does not use this convention. Messages are coded with this assembly:

Identifier (Type)   Length   Contents (Value)

The TLV convention, if adopted by the two communicating parties, allows the receiver to decode the incoming message with a standardized set of software. Of course, the transfer syntax protocol must be implemented in both machines for this type of operation to occur.

A number of transfer syntax protocols exist in the industry. Moreover, several vendors have established their own "closed system" transfer syntax protocols. Increasingly, vendors are moving away from proprietary solutions to the OSI approach as published by the ISO and the ITU-T.

The TCAP transfer data element is illustrated in Figure 14–3. It can consist of a single TLV or a series of data elements, described as multiple TLVs. The element consists of an integral number n of octets, written with the most significant bit (MSB) (H) on the left and the least significant bit (LSB) (A) on the right:

XXXXXXXX
HGFEDCBA

The TLV format of the TCAP message is also shown in Figure 14–4.

All identifiers use the two MSBs to indicate the identifier class. The identifier distinguishes one type from another (for example, a SEQUENCE of fields, a field that is coded as INTEGER, or a field that is a BIT STRING) and specifies how the remainder of the element is interpreted. The identifier distinguishes four classes of type (information): universal, application-wide, context-specific, and private-use. They are defined as:

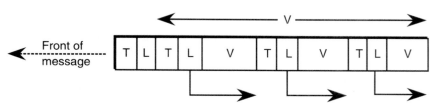

where:

  T Type (Identifier)
  L Length of Value (Contents)
  V Value (Contents)

Figure 14–3   The syntax for the TCAP message.

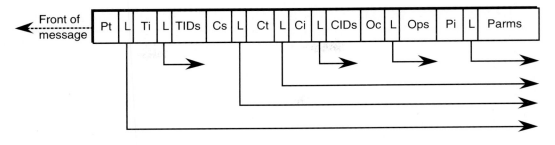

where:

Pt	Package type identifier	Ci	Component ID identifier
L	Length	CIDs	Component IDs
Ti	Transaction ID identifier	Oc	Operation code identifier
TIDs	Transaction IDs	Ops	Operation codes
Cs	Component sequence identifier	Pi	Parameter set/sequence identifier
Ct	Component type identifier	Parms	Parameters

Figure 14–4   TLV structure of TCAP message.

- *Universal.* These types are standardized identifiers (by the ITU-T), and application-independent types.
- *Application-wide.* These types are specific to an application. For TCAP, an application-wide type identifier is used to refer to the TCAP international standards.
- *Context-specific.* These types are specific to an application but also are limited to a set within the application.
- *Private-use.* These types are reserved for private use. TCAP uses this identifier for U.S. national and private applications.

The identifier is coded in the first octet of the message as depicted in Figure 14–5. In ANSI TCAP, bits HG identify the four type classes by the following bit assignments:

Universal:	00	
Application-wide:	01	International TCAP
Context-specific:	10	
Private-use:	11	National TCAP/Private TCAP

Bit F identifies the forms of the data element. Two forms are possible. A primitive element (bit F = 0) has no further internal structure of data elements. That is, it has one value (the structure is atomic). A constructor element (bit F = 1) is recursively defined in that it contains a series of data elements.

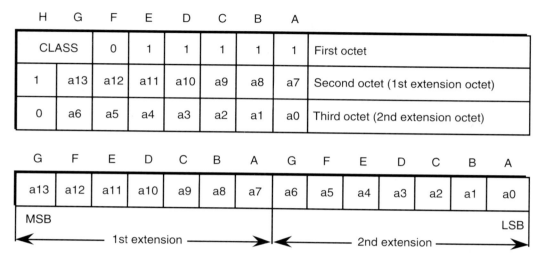

Figure 14–5   The identifier field and extension.

The remaining five bits (E, D, C, B, and A) distinguish one data type from another of the same class. For example, the field may distinguish BOOLEAN from INTEGER. Codes ranging between 00000 to 11110 are permitted.

If the system requires more than five bits, bits E, D, C, B, and A of the first octet are coded as 11111_2 and bit H of the subsequent octets are coded with a 1 to indicate more octets follow; a 0 in bit H of an extension octet indicates the last octet. The bottom part of Figure 14–5 shows how the extension octets are concatenated together; the first extension octet is the most significant octet, and so on.

The private class uses the extended formats for private TCAP and national TCAP extensions. The G bit in the first extension is used as follows: if G = 1, a private identifier is present; if G = 0, a national identifier is present.

The length (L) (shown in Figures 14–3 and 14–4) specifies the length of the contents. It may take one of three forms: short, long, or indefinite. The short form is one octet long and is used when L is less than 128 octets. Bit H is always 0, and bits A-G represent a binary number that indicates the length of the contents. The length value defines only the length of the contents (value) and does not include the octets that comprise the identifier and the length octets. The long form is used for a contents field greater than or equal to 128 and less than 2^{1008} octets. To identify the long form, bit H of the first octet in the L field is set to 1.

The contents (value) is the actual information of the element. The contents are interpreted based on the coding of the identifier (type) field.

Therefore, the contents are interpreted as bit strings, octet strings, or whatever they are.

TCAP OPERATIONS

During our analysis the TCAP operations, it will prove helpful for the reader to refer to Tables 14–1 and 14–2. Later discussions will examine additional aspects of these tables. TCAP operations revolve around

Table 14–1 Transaction Portion of Package Types

UNIDIRECTIONAL
Package Type Identifier
Total TCAP Message Length

Transaction ID Identifier
Transaction ID Length (=0)

Component Sequence Identifier
Component Sequence Length

QUERY WITH PERMISSION / QUERY WITHOUT PERMISSION

Package Type Identifier
Total TCAP Message Length

Transaction ID Identifier
Transaction ID Length
Originating Transaction ID

Component Sequence Identifier
Component Sequence Length

RESPONSE

Package Type Identifier
Total TCAP Message Length

Transaction ID Identifier
Transaction ID Length
Responding Transaction ID

Component Sequence Identifier
Component Sequence Length

CONVERSATION WITH PERMISSION / CONVERSATION WITHOUT PERMISSION

Package Type Identifier
Total TCAP Message Length

Transaction ID Identifier
Transaction ID Length
Originating Transaction ID
Responding Transaction ID

Component Sequence Identifier
Component Sequence Length

ABORT (P-Abort)

Package Type Identifier
Total TCAP Message Length

Transaction ID Identifier
Transaction ID Length
Responding Transaction ID

P-Abort Cause Identifier
P-Abort Cause Length
P-Abort Cause

ABORT (User Abort)

Package Type Identifier
Total TCAP Message Length

Transaction ID Identifier
Transaction ID Length
Responding Transaction ID

User Abort Information Identifier
User Abort Information Length
User Abort Information

Table 14–2   Component Portion of Package Types

INVOKE COMPONENT

Component Type Identifier
Component Length

Component ID Identifier
Component ID Length
Component IDs

Operation Code Identifier
Operation Code Length
Operation Code

Parameter Set/Sequence Identifier
Parameter Set/Sequence Length
Parameter Set/Sequence

RETURN RESULT COMPONENT

Component Type Identifier
Component Length

Component ID Identifier
Component ID Length
Component IDs

Parameter Set/Sequence Identifier
Parameter Set/Sequence Length
Parameter Set/Sequence

RETURN ERROR COMPONENT

Component Type Identifier
Component Length

Component ID Identifier
Component ID Length
Component IDs

Error Code Identifier
Error Code Length
Error Code

Parameter Set/Sequence Identifier
Parameter Set/Sequence Length
Parameter Set/Sequence

REJECT COMPONENT

Component Type Identifier
Component Length

Component ID Identifier
Component ID Length
Component IDs

Problem Code Identifier
Problem Code Length
Problem Code

Parameter Set/Sequence Identifier
Parameter Set/Sequence Length
Parameter Set/Sequence

PARAMETER

Parameter Identifier
Parameter Length
Parameter Contents

the use of transactions that operate between two application processes and two TCAPs. The application process passes a primitive to a TCAP, which contains the application traffic. This traffic is coded into parameters and placed in a TCAP transaction (transaction is a specific term used in TCAP). A transaction may actually consist of more than one TCAP message running between the two application processes. Additional application processes can become involved in the processing of these messages through an action called *handover,* which is discussed later in this chapter.

Transactions can be exchanged in one direction only or in both directions. The choice of these communications modes is determined by the applications process when it initiates the transaction. The application process is permitted to change the communication mode during the life of the transaction. When an application process initiates a transaction, a transaction ID is assigned and the same transaction ID is used for all messages pertaining to the transaction until the transaction is terminated. Termination can occur from either application process by its sending a primitive to its respective TCAP.

As stated earlier, more than one operation may take place within one transaction; and, within each operation, one or more components (again, a specific TCAP term) may be involved. The components are: invoke, return result, return error, and reject (which were discussed earlier in this chapter). The invoke component is correlated with the other components through a correlation ID that must be the same as the invoke ID that appears in the invoke component. It is possible for an invoke component to refer to another invoke component. If so, it must contain a correlation ID that is the same as the invoke ID of the correlated invoke component. It also must contain its own invoke ID (in other words, it contains two invoke component IDs).

Rules for the Dialogues between TCAP Entities

A TCAP user has the option of entering or not entering into a TCAP transaction. When not entering into a TCAP transaction, a message called the unidirectional package is used. This package type means that a component correlation is not needed nor is a transaction ID established.

For bidirectional cases, a transaction is established and a transaction ID must be reserved for these messages. This ID identifies the applications transaction process from the perspective of the local node.

In addition, the TCAP user must initiate one of two package types called query with permission to release and query without permission to release. This user selects the transaction ID, which then is used between both users. The query without permission to release means that the initiating TCAP user (user A) anticipates sending more components that are to be associated with the same transaction . Therefore, the receiving user B cannot release the transaction at its end. Conversely, the reception of a query with permission to release means the recipient need not expect any additional components regarding this transaction ID.

When the receiving TCAP user B receives a query message coded as a without permission to release package type, it must establish an application process transaction and respond to the sending party A. It may respond with a conversation package type that may be conversation with permission to release or conversation without permission to release. In either case, the conversation package type must include the same transaction ID value that was in the original TCAP transaction query. This transaction must also contain its own originating transaction ID. As in the case with the originating TCAP, this ID identifies the applications transaction process from the perspective of the local node.

If the message received is a query with permission to release, then the user at this node must decide if it wishes to establish an applications process transaction from its local standpoint. If it is decided to establish a transaction, it must respond to the originating party with either a conversation with permission to release or a conversation without permission to release. If it does not wish to establish a transaction from its own perspective, it simply responds with a response-type package that contains the transaction ID that was coded in the query transaction.

If a conversation mode is established, all messages must be coded as one of the two conversation package types until the TCAP transaction is terminated. The usual approach to terminating a TCAP transaction is for either party to receive a permission to release and for this party to return a response package type. In certain situations (which must be prearranged between the TCAP users), it is possible to terminate the TCAP transaction without the exchange of messages. This approach means that primitives are exchanged between the TCAP user and TCAP in each machine but messages are not exchanged between the application processes.

Purpose of the Query and Conversation Options. It is not difficult to become lost in the TCAP forest while searching for all these component/transaction trees. So, what is the purpose of these procedures? It gives either party the flexibility of extending a dialogue with the other party. In many situations, an initiating application process is not aware of the effect a query will have on another application process. When the query arrives at B, the TCAP user sends multiple messages back to A. Conversely, initiator A may know that its initial query to B will be one of several in a dialogue of messages. Therefore, TCAP messages allow the flexibility to extend or curtail the communications between two TCAP users.

Examples of TCAP Message Exchanges

Figure 14–6 depicts three examples of the exchange of messages between two TCAP processes. The parameters for the messages in these three examples are listed in Table 14–2. In example a, TCAP A sends a

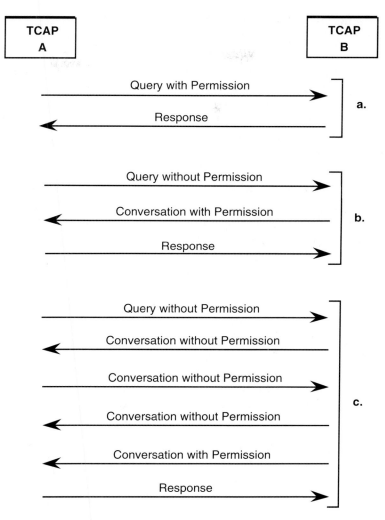

Figure 14–6   The TCAP communications.

query with permission to release to TCAP B. This type of message is sent because TCAP A does not anticipate sending any more components. TCAP B sends back a response message, which indicates that it does not wish to establish an application process transaction from its perspective.

In Figure 14–6, TCAP A sends a query without permission to release to TCAP B, because it anticipates sending more components that it wishes TCAP B to treat as the same transaction. TCAP B responds with a conversation with permission to release message, which from its perspective means it does not anticipate sending any more components. TCAP A returns a response to TCAP B.

In Figure 14–6, neither TCAP A nor TCAP B wants to release the transaction, at least initially. Later in the dialogue, TCAP B sends a conversation with permission to release to TCAP A, and TCAP B returns a response.

HANDOVER PROCEDURES

During the exchange of TCAP messages between two nodes, it may become necessary to request services from another node. From the perspective of TCAP, this operation means that one or more components will be transferred to this third node. This transfer of component processing is called a handover (see Figure 14–7). A handover may be permanent, which lasts for the remainder of the transaction, or temporary, which lasts for a part of the transaction.

The initiating user (TACP B) decides when a handover is required. It begins the process by sending an invoke TCAP message (to TCAP C) that specifies a temporary handover operation is taking place. Next, the initiating user sends the components that it wishes this third node to process. These parameters must contain the transaction ID of party B, as well as B's SCCP calling party address and the package type of that party C should use when it returns the message to party A.

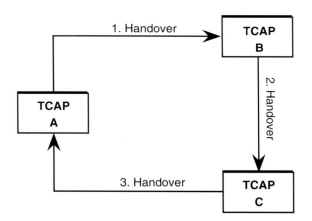

Figure 14–7   Example of a handover operation.

GENERAL LAYOUT OF THE TCAP MESSAGE

Figure 14–8 shows a general layout for the TCAP message. A description of the fields follows. The length fields are not explained, since they simply depict the length of the field or fields that follow. The arrows on the right side of the figure show the part of the message covered by each length field.

- *Package type identifier*. This field is an identifier field coded as national (11) in bits HG and constructor (1) in bit F. It is coded in one of seven forms, as depicted in Table 14–1, to identify the specific package type.
- *Transaction ID identifier*. Transaction IDs are placed in each TCAP message to correlate the messages associated with a transaction. It is coded as national and primitive with bits A-E set to 7.

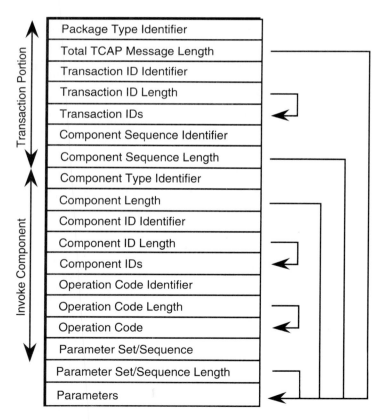

Figure 14–8   General structure of the TCAP message.

- *Transaction IDs.* This field contains one or more transaction IDs unless the package type is unidirectional. The rules for the use of transaction IDs in the seven package types are listed in Table 14–3. The originating transaction ID is assigned by the originator of the message. It must always be the first transaction ID if more than one is present. The responding transaction ID is assigned by the recipient of the message and it must be the same value as the originating transaction ID.
- *Component sequence identifier.* This field identifies a component sequence and is coded as national constructor with bits A-E set to 8.
- *Component type identifier.* This field can be coded in one of six values as a national constructor type to identify: (a) Invoke (last), (b) Return Result (last), (c) Return Error, (d) Reject, (e) Invoke (not last), and (f) Return Result (not last).
- *Component ID identifier.* This field is one octet in length and is used to indicate that components follow in the message. It is coded as national primitive with A-E set to 15.
- *Component IDs.* The component ID identifies each component. The number that exists in the message is determined by the component type of: (a) invoke (last), (b) return result (last), (c) return error, (d) reject, (e) invoke (not last), or (f) return result (not last).
- *Operation code identifier.* This field is one octet and can be coded to indicate either a national TCAP (A-E set to 16) or a private TCAP (A-E set to 17).
- *Operation code.* Operation codes are application specific and are not examined by the TCAP software. For ANSI specifications, the operation codes are encoded in accordance with Table 14–4.

Table 14–3   Transaction IDs and Package Types

Package Type	Originating ID	Responding ID
Unidirectional	No	No
Query with permission	Yes	No
Query without permission	Yes	No
Response	No	Yes
Conversation with permission	Yes	Yes
Conversation without permission	Yes	Yes
Abort	No	Yes

Table 14–4   TCAP National Operations

Operation Name Family	Specifier	GFEDCBA Family Code	HGFEDCBA Specifier Code
All families	Reserved	0000000	11111111
All families	Not used	0000000	00000000
Parameter	Provide value	0000001	00000001
Parameter	Set value	0000001	00000010
Charging	Bill call	0000010	00000001
Provide instructions	Start	0000011	00000001
Provide instructions	Assist	0000011	00000010
Connection control	Connect	0000100	00000001
Connection control	Temporary connect	0000100	00000010
Connection control	Disconnect	0000100	00000011
Connection control	Forward disconnect	0000100	00000100
Caller interaction	Play announcement (PA)	0000101	00000001
Caller interaction	PA and collect digits	0000101	00000010
Caller interaction	Indicate information waiting	0000101	00000011
Caller interaction	Indicate information provided	0000101	00000100
Send notification	When party free	0000110	00000001
Network management	Automatic code gap	0000111	00000001
Procedural	Temporary handover	0001000	00000001
Procedural	Report assist termination	0001000	00000010
Operation control	Cancel	0001001	00000001
Report event	Voice message available	0001010	00000001
Report event	Voice message retrieved	0001010	00000010
Spare			
Miscellaneous	Queue call	1111110	00000001
Miscellaneous	Dequeue call	1111110	00000010
Reserved		1111111	

- *Parameter set/sequence identifier.* This field identifies either the type sequence or type set depending on how the following parameters are organized. Both identifiers are coded as national constructor with bits A-E set to 18 for Set and set to 16 for Sequence.
- *Parameters.* The reason the TCAP message is exchanged between fields is to convey the values in the parameter field. Currently, the ANSI TCAP specification defines twenty-five national parameters. It is beyond the scope of this book to describe each of these parameters but a summary is provided in the section titled, "TCAP parameters."

TCAP OPERATIONS, PARAMETERS, AND ERROR CODES

Operations

The TCAP operations depend upon how they are implemented in each network, but ANSI T1.114 1992 defines eleven operations. They are summarized in this section.

TCAP operations are divided into two parts, the operation family and the operation specifier. The operation family is a broad category pertaining to the more specific operations. Our approach will be to first explain an operation family, and then to describe the operation(s) associated with the family (operation specifier). Table 14–5 provides a summary of the parameter family and the associated operations (and operation codes).

Parameter Family.   This family indicates how the parameters in the message will be used at the receiving entity. The two options are:

- *Provide value specifier.* The values in the parameter set are to be provided to the receiver.
- *Set value specifier.* The values in the parameter set are to be set by the receiver.

Charging Family.   One option exists for this family—the *bill call specifier*—that indicates that a billing record pertaining to the transaction should be created for the party indicated in the calling party address parameter.

Provide Instructions Family.   This family is used during an assist operation. The two options are:

- *Start specifier.* This operation initiates the interpretation of the service; its specific operations are not yet defined (for further study).
- *Assist specifier.* This operation is used to request instructions from the sender.

Connection Control Family.   This family provides information about connection control operations. Four options are:

- *Connect specifier.* This operation indicates that the connection is to be established.

- *Temporary connect specifier.* In the event another operation must transpire with another database, a temporary connect is made to that database. This operation contains the parameters (addresses, subsystem number, etc.) to accomplish the task.
- *Disconnect specifier.* This operation indicates that the connection is to be terminated.
- *Forward disconnect specifier.* This operation must follow the temporary connect specifier.

Caller Interaction Family. This family is used to provide guidance on how an exchange interacts with a caller with regard to playing announcements and requesting services of another application. Four options are:

- *Play announcement specifier.* This operation identifies which announcement is to be played to the caller.
- *Play announcement and collect digits specifier.* This operation is the same as the previous operation, except that it entails the collection of digits from the caller.
- *Indicate information waiting specifier* and *indicate information provided specifiers.* These two operations allow one applications process to inform another that information is waiting and, upon transferral, that it has been provided.

Send Notification Family. This family contains one operation called *when party free specifier.* It is used to notify a caller that the called party, while previously busy, is now free and will be notified if it is still available. This operation permits a busy party to be redialed and is also known as the ring again operation. After sending an ISUP initial address message (IAM), the calling exchange may receive a busy signal (for example, an ISUP release [REL] message) from the called exchange. The calling exchange can then send a TCAP message as invoke network ring again request. The called exchange will ACK the invoke, and upon the calling party going on-hook, will send a TCAP message indicating this party is now idle. The calling exchange will send a TCAP end dialogue message, and then resend an initial address message (IAM) to try again.

Network Management Family. This family contains one operation, called *automatic code gap transfer.* It is used to inhibit specific codes for a given time period.

Procedural Family. This family indicates that the procedure identified in the specifier is to be performed. Presently it controls two types of procedures with two options:

- *Temporary handover specifier.* This operation notifies a node that a temporary handover is in progress, and the node can release all resources for the identified transaction after the completion of the handover.
- *Report assist termination specifier.* This operation simply indicates the end of an assist.

Operation Control Family. This family contains one operation, called *cancel specifier.* It is used to cancel an operation. For example, it can cancel the send notification operation.

Report Event Family. This family is presently used for VMSR operations in which the messaging service for a subscriber is located at a remote exchange. The two options are:

- *Voice message available specifier.* This operation indicates to the subscriber's exchange that a message is available from the VMSR.
- *Voice message retrieved specifier.* This operation removes the message available indicator for the VMSR subscriber.

Miscellaneous Family. As the name implies, this family does not fit under the other headings. The options are:

- *Queue call specifier* and *dequeue call specifier.* These two operations request that a call be placed and removed in/from a queue of calls, respectively.

Parameters

I mentioned earlier that the parameters in the TCAP message are specific to an application and are not examined by TCAP. They are passed transparently to the application supported by TCAP. This section describes the parameters published in ANSI T1.114–1992, and Table 14–5 lists them and their identifier codes. Be aware that each parameter name is identified with an identifier code consisting of eight bits, which we have described in previous material as bits H, G, F, E, D, C, B, A.

Timestamp. As this name implies, this parameter reflects the difference between the local time and universal coordinated time (that is, Greenwich Mean Time) and is used to record the time an event occurred.

Table 14–5   TCAP National Parameters

Parameter Name	Identifier Code HGFEDCBA
Timestamp	00010111
ACG indicators	10000001
Standard announcement	10000010
Customized announcement	10000011
Digits	10000100
Standard user error code	10000101
Problem data	10000110
SCCP calling party address	10000111
Transaction ID	10001000
Package type	10001001
Service key	10001010
Busy/Idle status	10001011
Call forwarding status	10001100
Originating restrictions	10001101
Terminating restrictions	10001110
DN-to-line service type mapping	10001111
Duration	10010000
Returned data	10010001
Bearer capability requested	10010010
Bearer capability supported	10010011
Reference ID	10010100
Business group	10010101
Signaling networks identifier	10010110
Reserved	10010111
Message waiting indicator type	10011000

ACG Indicators.   This parameter contains fields that indicate the reason for applying automatic code gap (ACG) control. It is used to suspend an activity and/or apply flow control to an ongoing operation. Suspension can last from 1 to 2048 seconds, with intervals between the suspensions ranging from .1 to 600 seconds. Currently five reasons exist for initiating ACG control.

- *Vacant code.* Calls are being received for an unassigned code.
- *Out-of-band.* Calls are being received for a band to which a customer does not subscribe.

- *Database overload.* Operations must be suspended because of insufficient resources at the database.
- *Destination mass calling.* Too many calls are being received for a specific destination.
- *Operations support system (OSS) initiated.* An external OSS has generated ACG control.

Standard Announcement. Several types of standard announcements can be applied to a user call. They are as follows:

- *Not used.* The code value is not used.
- *Out-of-band.* The customer has not subscribed to this band.
- *Vacant code.* A call was received for an unassigned code.
- *Disconnected number.* The called number is not available due to being disconnected.
- *Reorder.* All trunks are busy.
- *Busy.* The called number is busy.
- *No circuit available.* No available circuits exist to the called number.
- *Miscellaneous reorder.* A reorder announcement such as, "Call cannot be completed, please try again."
- *Audible ring.* The called party is being alerted.

Customized Announcement. This service is dependent on the specific implementation and is not defined in the standards. Its ASN.1 coding is context specific, which means bits H-G are set to 10.

Digits. The digits parameter is used by TCAP to determine the type of digits (i.e., a calling party number, a routing number, etc.), the nature of the number (i.e., national or international), the encoding scheme (i.e., BCD, IA5), the numbering plan (i.e., ISDN, Telex, telephony), the number of digits, and the digits themselves.

Standard User Error Code. If a TCAP transaction operation is unsuccessful, the standard user error code parameter is coded in a result message. This parameter covers only two types of user errors: caller abandon (the calling party hangs up before the completion of the TCAP transaction) and improper caller response.

Problem Data. This parameter contains the data that has caused a problem in a TCAP transaction. Its contents depend on the nature of the problem and it is not defined in the specifications.

SCCP Calling Party Address.   This parameter is used to identify the SCCP calling party address during a temporary handover. It is used by the node that receives a temporary handover message. It can consist of a global title, a subsystem number, or a signaling point code.

Transaction ID.   This parameter contains the transaction ID that must be used by the receiving node for the temporary handover operation.

Package Type.   This parameter is also used in a temporary handover operation and specifies the package type that is to be used during this operation. The package type was explained earlier in this chapter.

Service Key.   This parameter contains values used to access a record in the database. It is implementation specific and therefore coded as a context-specific.

Busy/Idle Status.   This parameter indicates if a line is busy or idle.

Call Forwarding Status.   This parameter indicates if the call forwarding service option is active, inactive, or not supported. The parameter is coded to indicate (a) call forwarding is variable (call is forwarded immediately without ringing the called party), (b) call forwarding on busy, (c) call forwarding on "don't answer," (d) selective forwarding (call is forwarded based on a user-defined number).

Originating Restrictions.   Originating restrictions apply only to outgoing calls. This parameter is used to indicate any restrictions that are assigned to a line. In essence, it defines the type of call a station is permitted to use. Currently, this parameter is coded to indicate four types of restrictions: (a) denied origination (DO) (calls cannot be originated from a specific line), (b) fully restricted originating (FRO) (allows a user to call numbers within a business group but blocks calls outside the business group), (c) semi-restricted originating (SRO) (restricts direct outgoing access to parties outside the business group but allows indirect access to parties outside the business group through an attendant), (d) unrestricted originating (UO) (allows a line to call any number inside or outside the business group).

Terminating Restrictions.   Terminating restrictions apply only to incoming calls. Currently this parameter is coded to indicated five types of restrictions: (a) denied terminating (DT) (no incoming calls are permitted for this line), (b) fully restricted terminating (FRT) (all calls are blocked from parties outside the business group), (c) semi-restricted terminating (SRT) (blocks direct incoming access from parties outside the business group, but allows incoming access from parties outside the business group via an attendant, (d) unrestricted terminating (UT) (no restrictions are placed on incoming calls), and (f) call rejection applies (CRA) (the call has been requested to be rejected by the called party).

DN to Line Service Type Mapping.   This parameter identifies what type of line service is associated with a directory number (DN). It also indicates whether the DN pertains to originating and terminating services. The following line service types have been defined:

- *Individual.* Single party service
- *Coin.* A pay station line
- *Multiline hunt.* Call to a busy line can be redirected to other lines
- *PBX.* A PBX line
- *Choke.* Traffic to an identified DN is subject to network-specific constraints
- *Series completion.* Calls to a busy line are redirected to another line in the same office
- *Unassigned DN.* A valid DN, but is not assigned to a customer
- *Multiparty.* Multiparties share a line
- *Non-specific.* Other line categories
- *Temporary out-of-service.* DN not in service

Duration.   This parameter indicates the duration requirements for an operation. The parameter identifies the time for monitoring the status of the called party (i.e., until the called party is free). Typically, if the called party remains busy after the time has expired, the timer is restarted.

Returned Data.   This parameter contains the data that caused a problem (including header and traffic) and is used for troubleshooting purposes.

Bearer Capability Requested.   Bearer capability is a term used in many systems (ATM, frame relay, etc.) to describe the service profile a network provides to the user. A wide variety of options exist in providing the user with services. The major services available to the user are set up as profiles that are stored in the database. The profile information that is available includes:

- The information transfer capability that describes the type of signal the user wishes supported (speech, digital information, video, and various bandwidths of audio, etc.)
- A user profile with regards to information transfer rate (i.e., 64 kbit/s, 1536 kbit/s, etc.), as well as the transfer mode (circuit mode or packet mode)
- The requirements for unidirectional or bidirectional transfer of the user's information
- An indication if the transfer is to be symmetric or asymmetric
- What types of protocols the user needs at the lower three layers of the OSI Model
- What type of companding is required for voice transmissions
- An indication, if any, of the type of rate adaptation that is required (allows a user to run with conventional modem rates yet be supported by the higher bandwidth networks)

Bearer Capability Supported. This parameter indicates if a requested bearer capability is supported. A TCAP message may request a bearer capability that is not supported because it is not profiled in the user's file in the database.

Reference ID. This parameter is used to identify the transaction that is exchanged between the database and an exchange during an assist service.

Business Group. This parameter identifies the multilocation business group (MBG) information associated with each number type contained in the message. The parameter may refer to (a) calling-party number, (b) called-party number, (c) connected-party number, (d) redirecting number, (f) original called-party number.

The contents contain information about (a) attendant status, (b) business group identifier (BGID), (c) fixed or customer-defined line privileges, (e) party selector (number to which this parameter applies, (f) business group ID, (g) sub-group ID, (f) line privileges for the party identified by the party selector.

Signaling Networks Identifier. The parameter identifies (at least) one signaling network (with a point code). This address is used by the sending application to inform the receiving application about the networks the sending application anticipates the transaction will traverse.

Message Waiting Indicator Type. The value of this parameter is determined by the service provider and the customer and is used to provide more information to the customer about a waiting message.

Error Codes

Error codes are placed into a TCAP transaction to indicate a problem, such the cause of an unsuccessful operation. Error codes can be specified for national or private use. The national error codes (U.S.) are listed and explained in Table 14–6.

Table 14–6   The TCAP Error Codes

VMSR system ID did not match user profile	Voice message storage retrieval (VMSR) not available because destination DN is not a customer of identified VMSR system
Notification unavailable to destination DN	Due to a short term problem (unavailable line, for example), notification cannot be provided to destination
Unassigned DN	Destination DN is not assigned to an active interface
Not queued	Application decided not to queue an operation
Unexpected component sequence	Component sequence is incorrect (for example, a disconnect sequence followed by a play announcement sequence)
Unexpected data value	Received data value does not match expected value (for example, expected a routing number, but received a billing number
Unavailable resource	Requested rescue is not available
Missing customer record	Requested customer record is not available
Data unavailable	Data specified in requested operation is not available
Task refused	Task refused by an entity (no reason given)
Queue full	Required queue is full
No queue	No queue available
Timer expired	Timer associated with this specific service has expired
Data already exists	Parameter already exists, and a parameter change operation is needed
Unauthorized request	User is not authorized to access the database

THE ASN.1 CODE FOR TCAP

In several chapters of this book, it has been explained that ASN.1 is used in many of the SS7 protocols to describe the signal units (messages), contents (fields), and syntax (coding of the fields). Appendix B provides a tutorial on ASN.1, and contains enough information for you to be able to read the ASN.1 code for TCAP, which is coded below. If you find it necessary to study this chapter in more detail, or reread it, it would be a good idea to refer back to this code.

```
TCAPPackage   {ansiTCAPObjectIdentifier} DEFINITION::=

BEGIN
              —defining a module called TCAPPackage which contains type
              —definitions for the contents of any generic TCAP message
EXPORT OPERATION ERROR
              —this allows various TCAP-based applications to use
              —the Error and Operation macros defined in this module

ansiTCAPObjectIdentifier OBJECT IDENTIFIER ::=?  --not yet defined

PackageType ::=CHOICE  {

          unidirectional          [PRIVATE 1] IMPLICIT TransactionPDU
          queryWithPerm           [PRIVATE 2] IMPLICIT TransactionPDU
          queryWithoutPerm        [PRIVATE 3] IMPLICIT TransactionPDU
          response                [PRIVATE 4] IMPLICIT TransactionPDU
          conversationWithPerm    [PRIVATE 5] IMPLICIT TransactionPDU
          conversationWithoutPerm [PRIVATE 6] IMPLICIT TransactionPDU
          abort                   [PRIVATE 22] IMPLICIT Abort }

TransactionPDU ::=SEQUENCE { TransactionID, ComponentSequence }
TransactionID  ::=[PRIVATE7] IMPLICIT OCTETSTRING
              --0 octets for the Unidirectional, 4 octets for Query,
                Response & Abort
              --8 octets for Conversation in the order Originating
                then Responding TID

Abort          ::=SEQUENCE { TransactionID,
                   CHOICE { P-Abort-cause,
                      UserAbortInformation OPTIONAL } }
              --When the Abort package is generated by the Transac-
                tion sublayer,
              --the P-Abort-cause must be present

P-Abort-cause  ::=[PRIVATE23] IMPLICIT INTEGER {
                   unrecoginizedPackageType(1),
                   incorrectTransactionPortion(2),
```

```
                        badlyStructuredTransactionPortion(3),
                        unrecognizedTransactionID(4),
                        permissionToReleaseProblem(5), --for further study
                        resourceUnavailable(6) }

UserAbortInformation ::=[PRIVATE 24] EXTERNAL

ComponentSequence    ::=[PRIVATE 8] IMPLICIT SEQUENCE OF ComponentPDU


--Component Portion specification starts below

ComponentPDU ::=CHOICE { invokeLast       [PRIVATE 9] IMPLICIT
                                            Invoke
                         returnResultLast  [PRIVATE 10] IMPLICIT
                                            |ReturnResult
                         returnError       [PRIVATE 11] IMPLICIT
                                            |ReturnError
                         reject            [PRIVATE 12] IMPLICIT
                                            |Reject
                         invokeNotLast     [PRIVATE 13] IMPLICIT
                                            |Invoke
                         returnResultNotLast [PRIVATE 22] IMPLICIT
                                            ReturnResult }

    Invoke       ::=SEQUENCE  { ComponentID,
                               operationCodeOperationCode,
                               parameter ANY DEFINED BY operationCode
                                OPTIONAL }
ReturnResult     ::=SEQUENCE  { ComponentID,
                               parameter ANY OPTIONAL }
ReturnError      ::=SEQUENCE  { ComponentID,
                               errorCodeErrorCode,
                               parameter ANY DEFINED BY errorCode
                                OPTIONAL }
    Reject       ::=SEQUENCE  { ComponentID,
                               problem,
                               parameter ANY OPTIONAL }

ComponentID      ::=[PRIVATE 15] IMPLICIT OCTETSTRING
                 --0, 1, or 2 octets long for INV Component, 0, or 1
                   octets long for RR, RE,
                 --REJ Components

OperationCode    ::=CHOICE    { nationalOperation [PRIVATE 16]
                               OPERATION,
                               privateOperation [PRIVATE 17] OPERATION }
ErrorCode        ::=CHOICE    { nationalError [PRIVATE 19] ERROR,
                               privateError [PRIVATE 20] ERROR }

--PROBLEMS, the specification of Problems follows
```

```
Problem          ::=CHOICE     { GeneralProblem,
                                 InvokeProblem,
                                 ReturnResultProblem,
                                 ReturnErrorProblem,
                                 TransactionPortionProblem }

GeneralProblem       ::=[PRIVATE 21] IMPLICIT INTEGER {
                             unrecognizedComponentType(257),
                             incorrectComponentPortion(258),
                             badlyStructuredComponentPortion(259) }
InvokeProblem        ::=[PRIVATE 21] IMPLICIT INTEGER {
                             duplicateInvokeID(513),
                             unrecognizedOperationCode(514),
                             incorrectParameter(515)
                             unrecognizedCorrelationID(516) }
ReturnResultProblem  ::=[PRIVATE 21] IMPLICIT INTEGER {
                             unrecognizedCorrelationID(769)
                             unexpectedReturnResult(770),
                             incorrectParameter(771) }
ReturnErrorProblem   ::=[PRIVATE 21] IMPLICIT INTEGER {
                             unrecognizedCorrelationID(1025)
                             unexpectedReturnError(1026),
                             unrecognizedError(1027)
                             unexpectedError(1028),
                             incorrectParameter(1029) }
TransactionPortionProblem ::=[PRIVATE 21] IMPLICIT INTEGER {
                             unrecognizedPackageType(1281),
                             incorrectTransPortion(1282),
                             badlyStructuredTransPortion(1283),
                             unrecognizedTransID(1284),
                             permissionToReleaseProblem(1285),
                             resourceUnavailable(1286) }


--definition of Operation Macro follows; when operations are specified,
--the valid parameter set/sequence, results and error codes are
  indicated

OPERATION MACRO  ::=BEGIN

TYPE NOTATION    ::=ArgumentResultErrors
VALUE NOTATION   ::=LocalValue | GlobalValue

Argument         ::="PARAMETER"NamedType --if no parameters, SET/
                     SEQUENCE is still --present

Results          ::=empty | "RESULT"NamedType --the expected results
                     for this operation
Errors           ::=empty | "ERRORS" "{"ErrorNames"}" --possible er-
                     rors indicated here
```

```
NamedType          ::=identifier type | type
ErrorNames         ::=empty | IdentifierList
IdentifierList     ::=identifier | IdentifierList "," identifier
LocalValue         ::=value (VALUE INTEGER)
GlobalValue        ::=value (VALUE OBJECT IDENTIFIER) --not yet defined

END --end of Operation Macro

--Definition of Error Macro follows.

ERROR MACRO        ::=
BEGIN

TYPE NOTATION      ::=Argument
VALUE NOTATION     ::=LocalValue | GlobalValue

Argument           ::="PARAMETER"NamedType --if no parameters, SET/
                       SEQUENCE still --present

NamedType          ::=identifier type | type
LocalValue         ::=value (VALUE INTEGER)
GlobalValue        ::=value (VALUE OBJECT IDENTIFIER) --not yet defined

END --end of Error Macro

END --end of the TCAPPackage Module
```

SUMMARY

TCAP is used in many applications to allow different service providers to communicate with each other in a standardized manner. TCAP defines the format and fields that allow SS7 nodes to exchange TCAP messages without expensive protocol conversion. TCAP is a generic protocol and is not aware of the specific application that it supports. TCAP operates at the application layer of the OSI model, and it operates on top of SS7's SCCP.

15
Intelligent Networks

INTRODUCTION

This chapter introduces the concept of the intelligent network. The subject warrants a complete book (and one is being written as part of this series), but the focus for this chapter is how SS7 supports the intelligent network. We also examine the emerging advanced intelligent network (AIN) and focus of the Bellcore AIN call model.

WHAT IS AN INTELLIGENT NETWORK?

The term intelligent network has different meanings to different people. Some view it as a network that offers many features to the user that can be provisioned quickly and customized to the user's individual needs. Others view it as the implementation of the Bellcore or ITU-T intelligent network standards. Still others view it as a network that employs SS7 features. All these views are correct—an intelligent network provides all these features and services.

But the term intelligent network apparently is not sufficient for some of the creators of these systems. The term they prefer is the advanced intelligent network, or AIN. Let us take a look at the AIN, and show how it came about.

THE ADVANCED INTELLIGENT NETWORK (AIN)

The advanced intelligent network (AIN) is an evolving concept, based on the implementation of a service independent and machine independent architecture from which network service providers can create new services for the customer.

One of the key components to the success of network and customer satisfaction with the network is the allowance and support of new services in a flexible and expeditious manner. In a nutshell, future architecture is focused on faster provisioning and customized services for the user.

Service Creation in an AIN

A fundamental component of AIN is the ability to support the creation of services for the end customer in a rapid manner. While this goal is laudable and, on the surface, appears to be a simple task, it is in fact difficult and complex to achieve. The difficulty stems from the breadth of some customers' requests, and the ability to create the services to support these requests (through the modification and/or addition to the network's existing hardware and software architecture). Just consider, a service request may impact hundreds of hardware components and thousands of software modules containing millions of lines of code. Therefore, service creation requires a structured and disciplined approach, and usually entails modeling, building generic blocks for simulation, specifying the service through special languages. In other words, it requires the development of a formal method or model.

EVOLUTION TOWARD THE INTELLIGENT NETWORK

There are different opinions in the industry regarding the difference between an intelligent network (IN) and an advanced intelligent network (AIN), but some people use the two terms to describe the same concept. This part of the chapter will explain how the terms came into use and how we can describe their differences.

As discussed in many parts of this book, common channel signaling (CCS) partitions the signaling (call processing) part of the network from the user traffic part. SS7 is the prominent CCS system in operation today. In the early 1980s, a switch contained not only switching capabilities but call processing and database processing (the "control data") as well (see Figure 15–1). With some exceptions, all switches in the public switched network housed these three functions.

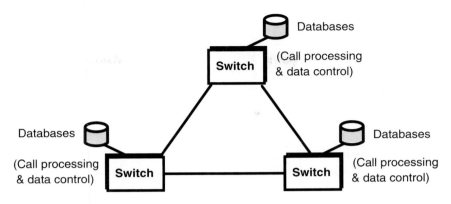

Figure 15–1   Foundation architecture for the intelligent network.

Of course, this all-in-one approach created duplication in the switches; many switches were configured with identical control databases. It also made change control cumbersome and complex, because multiple copies of the data and supporting software had to be maintained.

During this period, each vendor had a different approach about how to handle certain tasks at a switch, which made the interworking of heterogeneous equipment a very difficult task. In addition, this monolithic approach led to large and hard-to-change systems, which resulted in the inability to respond to the customers' requests in a timely manner.

THE INTELLIGENT NETWORK (IN)

The vendor-specific systems cited in the previous paragraphs provided a rich variety of services and were quite powerful. One could say they were intelligent. Yet, they were cumbersome to use, maintain, and change.

As shown in Figure 15–2, the network providers decided to implement a slightly different approach to the CCS architecture: move and distribute functions into specialized modules and specialized machines and reduce the duplication of user services by placing them in one (or a few) processor(s). This approach led to the off-loading of many services and resources from the switch and permitted their being shared by a community of users.

In the mid-1980s, the so-called intelligent network (IN) began to be implemented when services, such as the 800 directory, were moved from

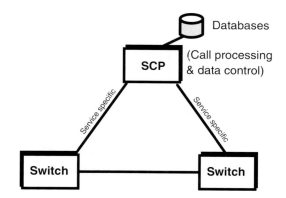

Figure 15–2   Intelligent network architecture.

the network switch to a service control point (SCP). This approach represented considerable progress, but at this stage of the development, the interface (and messages) between the switch and the SCP were tailored to each service. Customized messages at the switch and the SCP were created for each service.

Nonetheless, it provided a platform from which multiple vendors could access a common resource, and, with the publication of SS7, it provided standardized interfaces between the vendors' equipment and software. Single (or at least fewer) copies of databases and software lead to reduced costs and less complexity in maintenance.

THE ADVANCED INTELLIGENT NETWORK (AIN)

The next step in this evolution is called the advanced intelligent network (AIN) in some countries (see Figure 15–3). Instead of tailored messages for a specific service, the AIN uses a common set of standardized messages for a variety of services. Thus, the switch call processing and the service switching point (SSP) database processing support a common interface. This concept is certainly not revolutionary, as the software industry has been using this approach for over two decades. The publication and acceptance of SS7 in 1984 at last provided a common (and powerful) platform to implement these concepts in the telephone network.

AIN is much more than just standardized messages between SSPs and SCPs. AIN is published as a standard by the ITU-T, Bellcore, ETSI, and ANSI, and contains an extensive set of rules and procedures stipu-

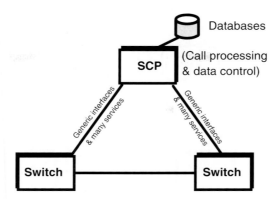

Figure 15–3   Architecture for the advance intelligent network.

lating how the information is exchanged between the AIN components. In addition, AIN defines several other components that may be employed in the network. The next section describes these components.

OTHER AIN COMPONENTS

During the evolution from a conventional service-specific environment to a service-independent environment, it was recognized that the implementation of other components would enhance and improve the network, mainly by aiding in the rapid creation of services and in the efficient maintenance of these services. As shown in Figure 15–4, these components are called the service creation environment (SCE), the service management system (SMS), the intelligent peripheral (IP), the adjunct and the network access point (NAP). Their position in the AIN topology is illustrated in this figure. Notice that I have included a "cloud" that depicts the SS7 backbone. Inside this cloud are the STPs and their associated links. With a few exceptions (explained shortly), the AIN does not impose additional tasks for the STPs.

The SCE provides design and implementation tools to assist in creating and customizing services in the SCP. The SMS is a powerful database management system. It is used to manage the master database that controls the AIN customer services. This service includes ongoing data-

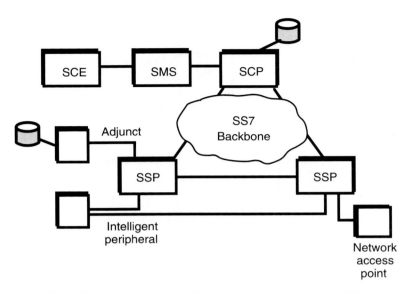

Note: The SCP, adjunct, and intelligent peripheral house the AIN appli-
      cations programs.
where:
   SCE   Service creation environment
   SMS   Service management system

Figure 15–4   Other parts of the AIN.

base maintenance, backup and recovery procedures, log management, and audit trails.

The intelligent peripheral can connect to an AIN call. It provides the following services: (a) tone generation, (b) voice recognition, (c) playback, (d) compression, (e) call control, (f) record, and (g) dual-tone multifrequency (DTMF) detection and collection. As this figure illustrates, the IP is connected to one or more SSPs. It is designed to be application-independent, and to support generic services for more than one application.

The adjunct performs the same operations as an SCP, but it is configured for one (or few) services for a single switch. The connection is through a high-speed link in order to support user requests that need a fast response. Other switches that wish to use the services of the adjunct must come through the SSP to which the adjunct is directly connected.

The NAP is a switch that has no AIN functions. It is connected from an SSP and connects to trunks with SS7 or frequency tones. Based on the called and calling number received at the NAP, it may route the call to its attached SSP for AIN services.

The AIN STPs perform two functions beyond their usual operations. First, they can employ pseudo-addressing, which enables them to balance the load between two or more SCPs. Second, they can employ alternate routing in the event of a problem in the network.

ITU-T vs. BELLCORE VIEW

The ITU-T and Bellcore Models are similar. Most of their differences pertain to terminology. This section provides a summary of these differences (see Figure 15–5).

The *service switching function (SSF)* provides the means to recognize calls requiring (A)IN service processing and to interact with call processing and the service logic on behalf of those calls.

The *call control function (CCF)* (or call processing) provides the means for establishing and controlling bearer services on behalf of network users.

The *call control agent function (CCAF)* provides users with access to the services and represents the users to call processing. The CCAF represents the interface between the user and the network control functions.

The *service control function contains (SCF)* (A)IN service logic providing the logical control to be applied to a call involving an (A)IN service. The SCF handles service related processing activities such as analysis, translation, screening, and routing.

The *service data function (SDF)* handles service-related and network data. It provides the SCF with a logical view of the data. The SDF contains data that directly relates to the provision or operation of (A)IN services, and may include access to user defined service related data.

The *specialized resource function (SRF)* provides end-user interaction with the (A)IN through control over resources such as DTMF receivers, voice recognition capabilities, protocol conversion, and announcements.

The *service management function (SMF)* provides the service provisioning, deployment, and management control. The SMF allows access to all (A)IN functional entities for the transfer of information related to service logic and service data.

The *service management access function (SMAF)* controls access to service management functions.

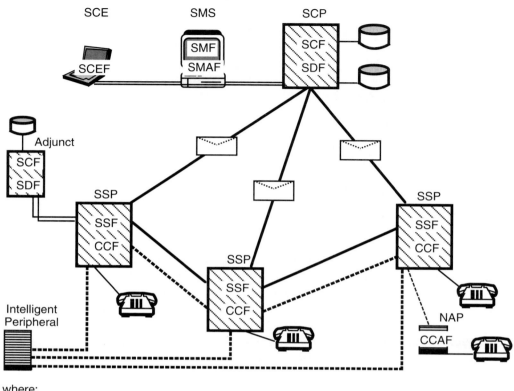

Figure 15–5   The ITU-T and Bellcore views.

where:
SSF	Service switching function
CCF	Call control function
CCAF	Call control agent function
SCF	Service control function
SDF	Service data function
SRF	Specialized resource function
SMF	Service management function
SMAF	Service management access function
SCEF	Service creation environment function

The *service creation environment function (SCEF)* supports the creation, verification, and testing of new AIN services.

As Figure 15–6 shows, several AIN components may be combined in one node or may be actually combined together in a node. For example, the service node can combine the functions of an IP and an SCP, which means that the SCF, SDF, and SRF components are combined into this

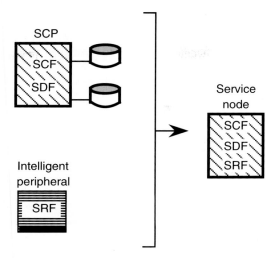

Figure 15–6   Alternate configurations.

one node. The idea behind these options is to give vendors and service providers flexibility in implementing the AIN technology.

EXAMPLE OF AN AIN SERVICE

Figure 15–7 shows an example of how an AIN application can be implemented to provide simple but powerful services to an end user. We assume that a customer wishes to order a pizza, and consults his yellow pages to find Pizza-a-Go-Go, who is willing and able to provide the service. In event 1, the customer dials the number furnished in the yellow pages (800-1234), which is forwarded to the local central office. This office serves as a SSP office and, under the SSP function, analyzes the number. It discovers that it must route a *query* message to another office that services this telephone number. Therefore, in event 2, the SSP office forms an AIN query and sends the message to an SSP/adjunct node. The calling and called addresses in this message are SS7 destination and source point codes and the message itself is coded as a TCAP message.

The SCP/adjunct node uses these addresses to make a query to a database to discover the location of the nearest Pizza-a-Go-Go outlet. In event 3, it sends this information back to the SSP office. Upon receipt of this message, in event 4 the SSP places a call to the pizza parlor, thus connecting the customer to the pizza parlor.

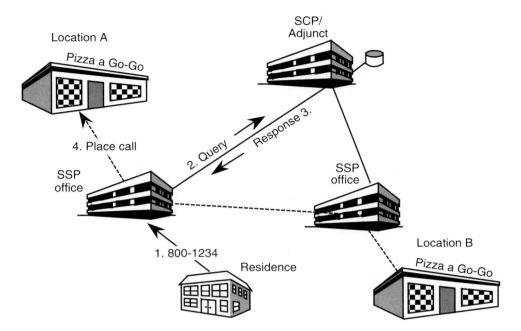

Figure 15–7   Example of an AIN Service.

THE AIN CALL MODEL

I have made the point previously regarding the importance of having a formal method for service creation operations. In this section of the chapter, we will discuss an example of how a model is created and examine some tools for supporting this model.

The AIN call model is a generic representation of a sequence of procedures executed by an AIN to set up, manage, and clear a connection between users. It allows both ends of a connection, regardless of the specific vendor's machine, to share a common view of the ongoing phases and operations of a call. In simple words, it defines the interfaces, states, and events that are associated with each type of call (i.e., each type of AIN service).

The AIN call model has three goals:

- Provide a simple model for AIN calls that is independent of switch type or manufacturer's architecture.
- Depict, in an unambiguous manner, the states and events that should be visible to AIN machines, but not states and events that are specific to a vendor's architecture.

- From the first two goals, provide an environment for the fast creation of services, independent of vendor-specific architectures.

States and the Point in Call (PIC)

All AIN operations are based on an AIN call model. As depicted in Figure 15–8, the model is organized around actions or a collection of actions called a point-in-call (PIC). The PIC represents the external view of the AIN operations. By external I mean that the AIN implementor is free to choose the method of implementation for the actual software, just as long as the software behaves according to this external representation. However, each vendor is required to support the interfaces depicted by the PICs. As the figure shows, a PIC is described by an entry point and an exit point. We shall see shortly that the PIC contains other informa-

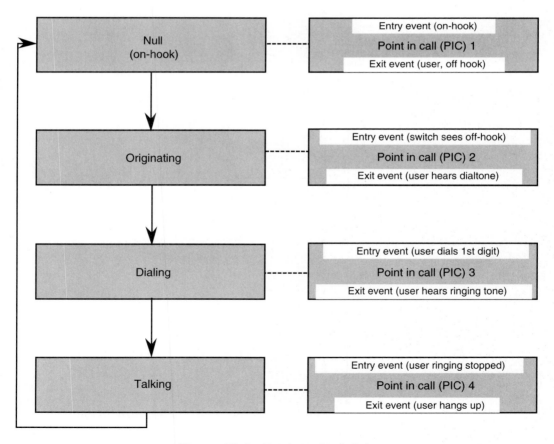

Figure 15–8   Basic call model.

tion at the entry and exit points. The entry and exit events in the PICs represent a typical (abbreviated) sequence of events in a telephone connection.

Detection Point (DP)

Detection points (DPs) operate between the PICs. They delineate the points in the model at which call processing is suspended and other actions invoked, for example, an action of sending a message to another AIN node. Query messages are associated with specific DPs. When a specific query message is received by an AIN node, it knows the exact stage of a call that has been completed in the transmitting AIN node. As Figure 15–9 illustrates, the DP is located between PICs (acting as transition points) in the call model.

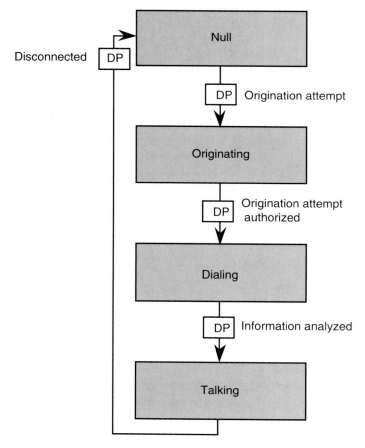

Figure 15–9   Detection point.

Triggers

DPs are associated with triggers. As Figure 15–10 illustrates, a trigger lists a set of criteria that contain a condition(s) that must be satisfied before a message is generated. In addition, the trigger point must include the address of the AIN node that is to receive the message if it is generated. Trigger criteria are either satisfied or not satisfied, and, as this figure shows, DPs can consist of one-to-many operations and their associated triggers. A combination of the DP and trigger criteria, if satisfied, results in the suspension of call processing at the AIN node. The suspension results in the creation and sending of a message to the relevant recipient node and operations remain suspended until a response is returned from the remote node. If none of the trigger criteria are satisfied, call processing proceeds directly to the next PIC.

The Originating and Terminating Call Model

As depicted in Figure 15–11, the AIN call model is divided into two parts: the originating call model (OCM) and the terminating call model (TCM). Both models describe a state machine for the call processing logic. As this figure depicts, the OCM and TCM each operate in the AIN node. Obviously, an AIN operation begins with the invocation of the OCM, then the TCM is started based on the satisfaction of trigger criteria. Once the TCM starts, both the OCM and TCM operate in parallel.

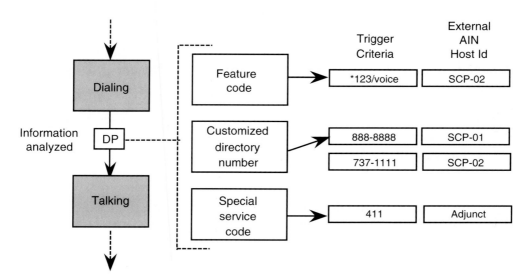

Figure 15–10   Detection points and triggers.

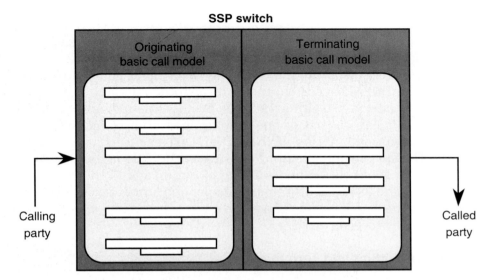

Figure 15–11   The call model at a single switch.

Although the specific instance of the OCM may be suspended when the TCM is operating.

The OCM initiates the call, performs call validation of the calling party, and is responsible for controlling the call to its completion. The TCM validates the call party and is responsible for terminating the call.

I made the point earlier that both the OCM and TCM operate in an AIN node. Consequently, if a customer call involves the operations of more than one AIN node, both models are active in both nodes. As depicted in Figure 15–12, the majority of the operations will occur as follows:

- The switch serving the calling party (switch A) executes most of the OCM logic.
- The switch serving the called party (switch B) executes most of the TCM logic.

One of the most important aspects of the AIN call model is the standardization of a protocol operating between the AIN nodes (see Figure 15–13). The protocol is organized around the SS7 TCAP, which has been explained in earlier chapters. The contents of the message are defined in the Bellcore, ANSI, and ITU-T standards and contain information on source and destination code points, the detection point where a query is

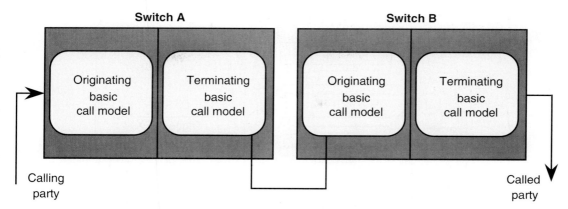

Figure 15–12   The call model at multiple switches.

detected, trigger criteria information, and information on the type of TCAP transaction such as query, response, or notification.

Execution of the Call Model

The AIN call model defines the exchange of information between an SSP and an SCP. As Figure 15–14 depicts, an incoming call is processed through the originating call model (OCM) module by executing the state logic with points in call (PICs) and detection points (DPs). This figure shows the four basic events to execute the model leading to the invocation of trigger operations. In event 1, the SSP receives information (i.e. dialed digits, E.164 addresses). In event 2, it executes the PICs until (for example) the information analyze detection point is reached that invokes the trigger logic, which is depicted in event 3. The various trigger criteria are analyzed and, in event 4, trigger 3 and its criteria are satisfied.

Based on the trigger 3 criteria, the AIN node assembles the required information to build a query message (see Figure 15–15, event 5). As described earlier, this message contains all the fields necessary to identify

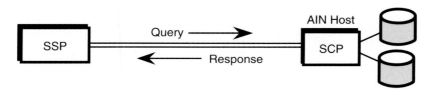

Figure 15–13   AIN messages.

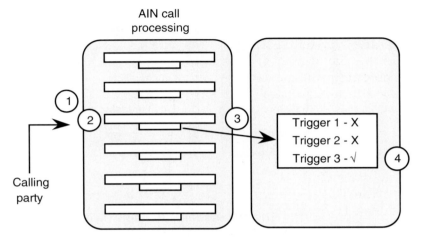

AIN call
processing

Figure 15–14   Matching a trigger.

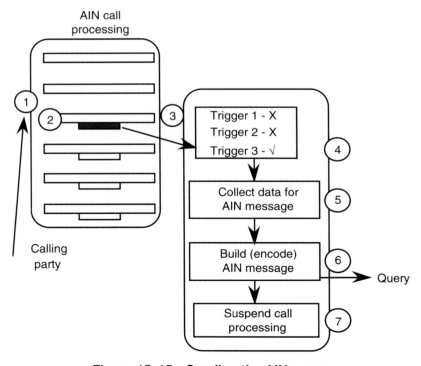

AIN call
processing

Figure 15–15   Sending the AIN query.

the message (addresses, type of message, etc.). In event 6, this message is coded into the SS7 TCAP query message and sent to the relevant SCP. After the query is sent, event 7 shows that the SSP suspends call processing on this particular call to await the response from the SCP node.

The operations at the SCP are quite straightforward. In event 8 (see Figure 15–16) the SCP decodes the incoming AIN TCAP message. Based on the analysis of the fields in the message, it executes the specific software module to service the query (event 9). This module executes the operation and generates the parameters that are used to create the response message (event 10). Finally, in event 11, the SCP creates a TCAP response message and sends this message to the originating SSP.

When the TCAP response arrives at the SSP, the suspended call is activated. The TCAP message is decoded as depicted in event 12 (in Figure 15–17), which may entail the execution of other actions (such as "do not charge for this call," "replace the dialed number with a different

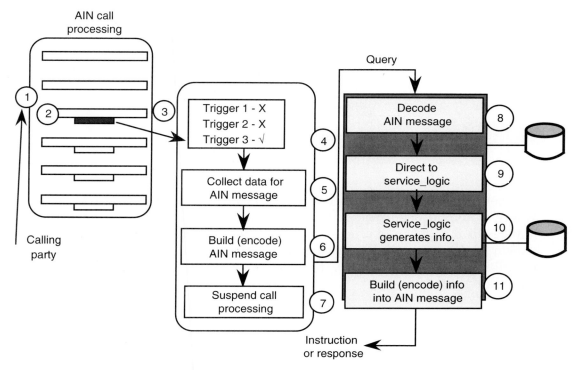

Figure 15–16   The AIN external host responds.

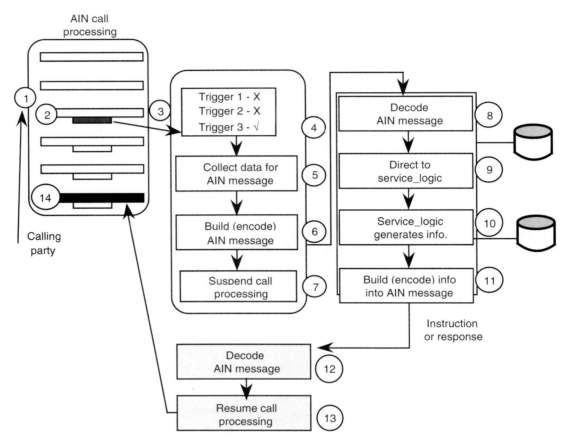

Figure 15–17   Processing resumes at query site.

number"). The information processed in event 12 also instructs the SCP where it should begin the activation of the call processing. In some instances, it may assume processing at a different point in the call than is shown in the sequential state diagram. The activation of a different PIC is called warping. Whatever the case, processing is resumed as illustrated in event 13.

BELLCORE BASIC CALL MODEL

Figures 15–18 and 15–19 show the Bellcore basic call model for AIN, release 0.1 (AIN 0.1). The PICs in the originating call model are:

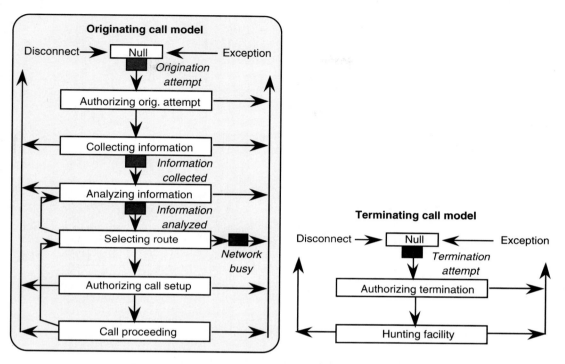

Figure 15–18 The originating basic call model.

Setup:

- *Null.* Line or trunk interface is idle (no call exists), and switch provides supervision
- *Authorizing origination attempt.* Switch verifies authority of the user to place a call with the given properties (e.g., line restrictions)
- *Collecting information.* Switch collects initial information (e.g., service codes, address information) from the user according to a specified dialing plan
- *Analyzing information.* Switch interprets and translates the collected information according to the specified numbering plan, determining the called party ID, type of call, carrier, and (when applicable) route index
- *Selecting route.* Switch interprets and analyzes the results to select the outgoing route (e.g., point-to-a-local DN, point-to-a-list of trunk names)
- *Authorizing call setup.* Switch verifies that the calling party is authorized to place the call (e.g., checks toll restrictions)

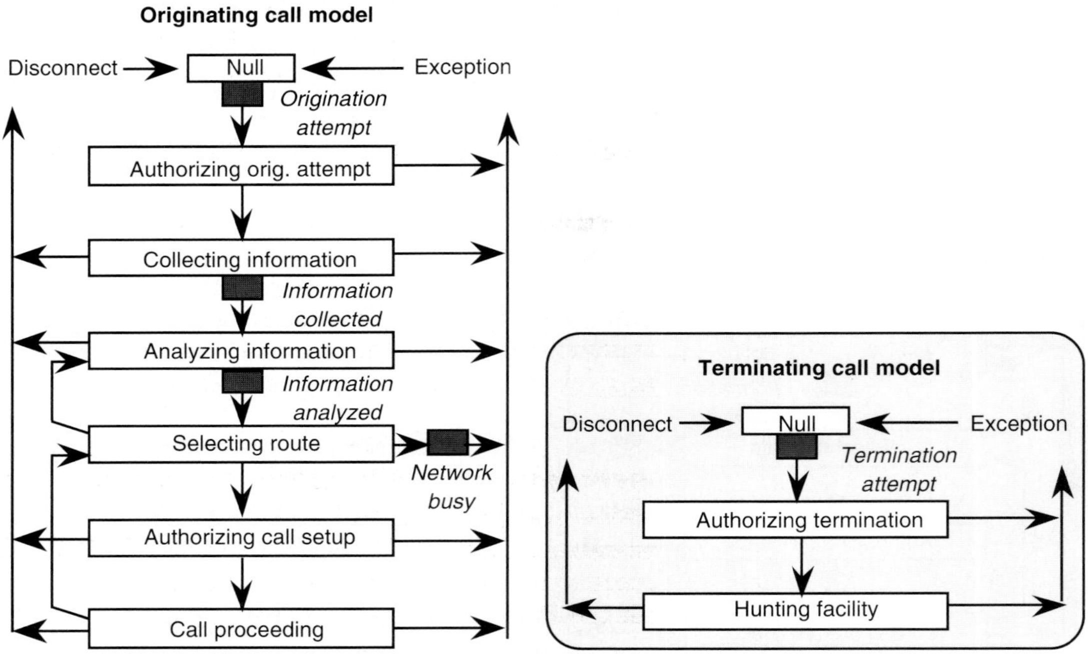

Originating call model

Figure 15–19   The terminating basic call model.

Stable:

- *Call proceeding.* Originating-call portion notifies terminating-call portion of desire to terminate on a DN or on a trunk group name

The DPs in the originating call model are:

- *Origination attempt.* Used for situations where a message is to be sent to the SCP as soon as user goes off hook (hot line type services)
- *Information collected.* Used for situations where a message is to be sent to the SCP unless an escape code is dialed or for incoming trunk receiving only public DNs
- *Information analyzed.* Used for situations where the type of digits dialed (feature code, public DN, special service code) must be ascertained before message can be sent to SCP
- *Network busy.* Used to send a message to the SCP requesting overflow routes (when all routes known to this SSP are busy)

The PICs in the terminating call model are as follows:

Setup:

- *Null.* Line or trunk interface is idle (no call exists) and switch provides supervision
- *Authorizing origination.* Switch verifies authority to route this call to the terminating access (e.g., check business group restrictions)
- *Hunting facility.* The busy/idle status of the terminating access of the call is determined

The DP, in the terminating call model follows:

- *Termination attempt.* Used in situations where a message is to be sent to the SCP before the SSP attempts to terminate the call

BASIC CALL MODEL AIN RELEASE 1, UPDATE 1992

The basic call model was modified in 1992 and now consists of more PICs and PDs, but it has not seen much implementation. Another book in this series, *The Advanced Intelligent Network,* will pick up on this topic and explain both call models in more detail.

TOLL-FREE SERVICE USING AIN

As discussed earlier in this chapter, when a user dials the 800 Service Access Code (SAC), it indicates that the call is toll free to the caller. The digits that follow the 800 number are then used to determine the routing for the call. The routing information is stored in a database, where translations are made to select an LEC or IXC to support the call. We also learned that the industry has designated the 888 numbering plan area (NPA) code for new toll-free numbers.

Two approaches are used for supporting new toll-free services and both entail the use of centralized databases. One approach is to expand the current arrangement, and the other approach is to use AIN functions to support these services. This latter approach is the subject of this section.

The AIN toll-free services builds on the basic functionality of AIN and SS7. It establishes numerous requirements that a vendor must im-

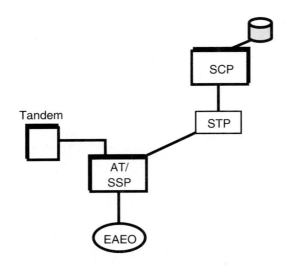

Figure 15–20   AIN toll-free service arrangements.

plement in its AIN nodes. For example, each MTP, SCCP, and TCAP message (and contents) is identified, and the responsibilities of each AIN node is defined in relation to how these messages must be processed.

Figure 15–20 shows the topology and architecture for the AIN toll-free service. Since this service must be provided to all calls that have access to the public network, ubiquitous service is provided using SSP operations at the Equal Access End Office (EAEO) and at the Access Tandem (AT). All AIN functionality for toll-free service is provided at the SSP node. If a toll-free call is originated from offices that do not have SSP functionality, the call must be routed to the EAEO for processing.

THE VIRTUAL PRIVATE NETWORK

SS7 networks can be configured to provide for Private Virtual Networks (PVN). PVN service allows calls to be carried over the public network at a price lower than with standard toll calling systems. In addition, remote user offices can also be connected to the PVN, which might otherwise be too expensive via standard toll services. PVN offers shared trunking (with other customers using the lines), but PVN customers can still use private number prefixes and access other private networks, WATS, 800, and so on.

Figure 15–21 shows an example of how a PVN can be used. An end user's central office (end office in figure) does not have SSP capability

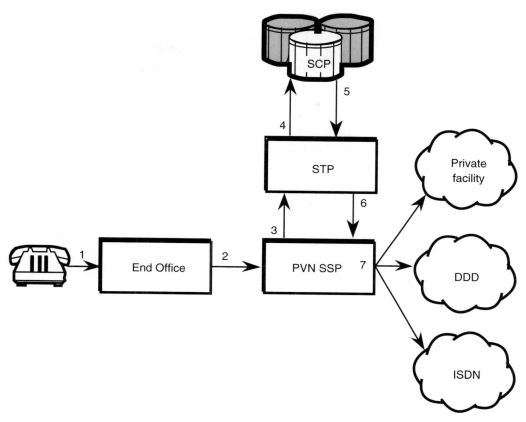

where:
DDD   Direct distance dial
ISDN Integrated Services Digital Network
SCP   Service control point
SSP   Service switching point
STP   Signalling transfer point

Figure 15–21   Private virtual networks (PVNs).

(event 1), so it routes the call to a SSP (event 20, which sends a TCAP query to the SCP database. The call may contain information such as a called number, calling number, account code, or caller's privileges. The SCP checks the database to determine if the caller is allowed to make the call, perhaps translates the number to another number, and determines how the call is to be routed. A TCAP response is sent back to the STP, then to the SSP. For example, the route may be to a private network, the direct distance dial network (DDD), or an ISDN interface. Moreover, the SCP can determine a least-cost route, if needed.

SUMMARY

The intelligent network is an evolving concept that is being refined as service providers and standards organizations become more experienced with its operations and with customer requirements. As it matures, it will continue to add many features for the user that can be provisioned quickly and customized to the user's requirements. SS7 technology is its technical underpinnings.

Appendix **A**

The OSI Model in ISDN and SS7

INTRODUCTION

ISDN and SS7 relay heavily on the Open Systems Interconnection (OSI) Model. This appendix introduces OSI and describes aspects of OSI that are used by ISDN and/or SS7. The specific functions of each OSI layer are not covered in this appendix, but are explained in relation to ISDN and SS7 in the main body of the book.

BASIC CONCEPTS

Machines communicate through established conventions called protocols. Since computer systems provide many functions to users, more than one protocol is required to support these functions. A convention is also needed to define how the different protocols of the systems interact with each other to support the end-user. This convention is referred to by several names: network architecture, communications architecture, or computer-communications architecture. Whatever the term used, most systems are implemented with layered protocols, and ISDN and SS7 are no exceptions to this statement.

In the OSI Model, a layer is considered to be a service provider to the layer above it. As shown in Figure A–1, this upper layer is considered to be a service user to its lower layer. The service user avails itself of the

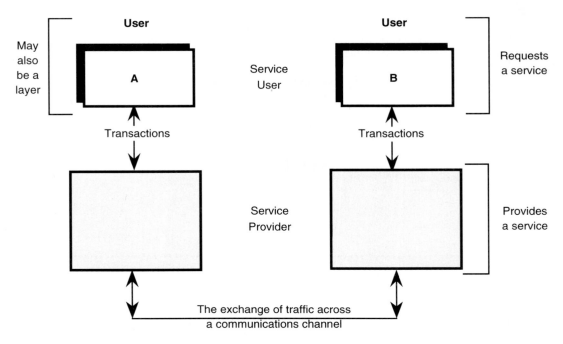

Figure A–1   The layer as a service provider.

services of the service provider by sending a transaction to the provider. This transaction informs the provider as to the nature of the service that is to be provided (at least, requested). In so far as possible, the service provider does provide the service. It may also send a transaction to its user to inform it about what is going on.

At the other machine (B in this figure), the operation at A may manifest itself by the remote service provider accepting the traffic from service provider A, providing some type of service and informing the remote user about the operation. This user may be allowed to send a transaction back to its provider, which may then forward traffic back to A. In turn, service provider A may send a transaction to user A about the nature of the remote operation. The OSI Model provides several variations on this general scenario.

As shown in Figure A–2, the end user rests on top (figuratively speaking) of the application layer. Therefore, the user obtains all the services of the seven layers of the OSI Model.

Neither ISDN nor SS7 use all the layers of the OSI Model, even though according to the rules of the OSI Model, a layer cannot be bypassed. Even if an end user does not wish to use the services of a particu-

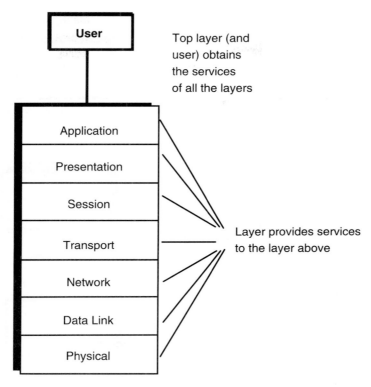

Figure A–2   Services of the full OSI Model.

lar layer, the user must still "pass through" the layer on the way to the next adjacent layer. This pass-through may only entail the invocation of a small set of code, but it still translates to overhead. However, every function in each layer need not be invoked. A minimum subset of functions may be all that is necessary to "conform" to the standard.

RELATIONSHIPS OF THE LAYERS

The OSI Model refers to layers with the terms N, N+1, and N-1 (see Figure A–3). The particular layer that is the focus of attention is designated as layer N. Thereafter, the adjacent upper layer to layer N is designated as layer N+1 and the adjacent lower layer to layer N is designated as layer N-1.

For example, if the network layer is the focus of attention, it is layer N. The transport layer is designated as layer N+1 and the data link layer is designated as layer N-1.

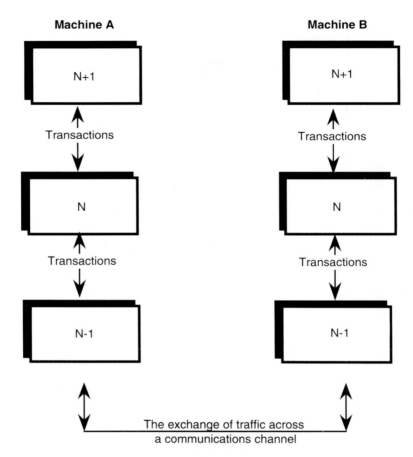

Figure A–3   The N, N+1, and N-1 layer concept.

In this manner, designers can use generic terms in describing the OSI layers. Moreover, the transactions between the layers can be developed in a more generic sense as well.

Layered network protocols allow interaction between functionally paired layers in different locations without affecting other layers. This concept aids in distributing the functions to the layers. In the majority of layered protocols, the data unit, such as a message or packet, passed from one layer to another is usually not altered, although the data unit contents may be examined and used to append additional data (trailers/headers) to the existing unit. With a few minor exceptions, ISDN and SS7 use these concepts.

As depicted in Figure A–4, each layer contains entities that exchange data and provide functions (horizontal communications) with

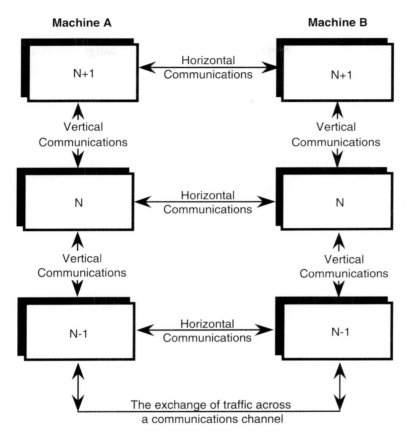

Figure A–4   Horizontal and vertical communications.

peer entities at other computers. For example, layer N in machine A communicates logically with layer N in machine B, and the N+1 layers in the two machines follow the same procedure. Entities in adjacent layers in the same computer interact through the common upper and lower boundaries (vertical communications) by passing parameters to define the interactions.

Typically, each layer at a transmitting station (except the lowest in most systems) adds "header" information to data. The headers are used to establish peer-to-peer sessions across nodes, and some layer implementations use headers to invoke functions and services at the N+1 or N adjacent layers. The important point to understand is that, at the receiving site, the layer entities use the headers created by the *peer entity* at the transmitting site to implement actions.

Figure A–5 shows an example of how machine A sends data to machine B. Data is passed from the upper layers or the user application to layer N+1. This layer adds a header to the data (labeled N+1 in the figure). It performs actions based on the information in the transaction that accompanied the data from the upper layer.

Layer N+1 passes the data unit and its header to layer N. This layer performs some actions, based on the information in the transaction, and adds its header N to the incoming traffic. This traffic is passed across the communications line (or through a network) to the receiving machine B.

At B, the process is reversed. The headers that were created at A are used by A's *peer layers* at B to determine what actions that are to be taken. As the traffic is sent up the layers, the respective layer "removes"

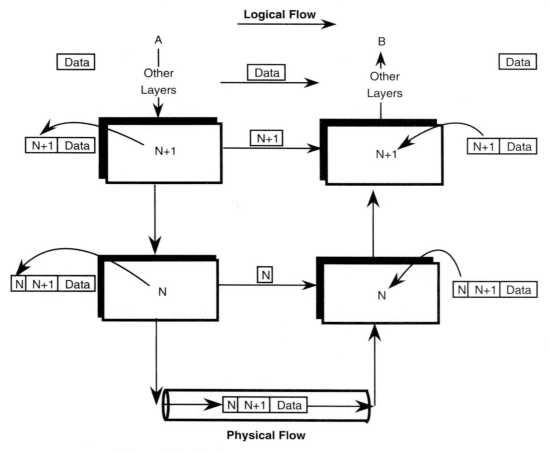

**Figure A–5	Machine A sends data to machine B.**

its header, performs defined actions, and passes the traffic on up to the next layer.

The receiving user application (at B) is presented only with user data—which was created by the sending user application (A). These user applications are unaware (one hopes) of the many operations in each OSI layer that were invoked to support the end user data transfer.

PRIMITIVES—KEY COMPONENTS IN OSI, ISDN, AND SS7

The services invoked at a layer are dictated by the upper layers' passing primitives (transactions) to the lower layer. In Figure A–6, users A and B communicate with each other through a lower layer.

Services are provided from the lower layer to the upper layer through a service access point (SAP). The SAP is an identifier. It identi-

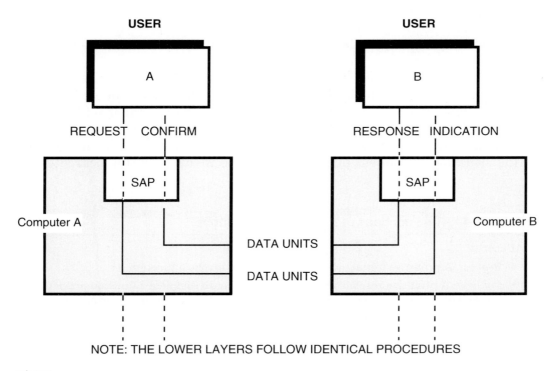

Figure A–6   Communications between adjacent layers.

fies the entity in N+1 that is performing the service(s) for layer N. Be aware that ISDN uses SAPs, but SS7 does not.

An entity in machine A can invoke some services in machine B through the use of SAPs. For example, a user that sends traffic can identify itself with a source SAP ID (SSAP). It identifies the recipient of the traffic with a destination SAP value (DSAP).

It is the responsibility of the receiving lower layer N (in concert of course with the operating system in the receiving machine) to pass the traffic to the proper destination SAP in layer N+1. If multiple entities (e.g., processes) exist in the machine, the DSAP serves to properly identify the process.

Some people view the SAP as a software "port." It is akin to the socket concept found in the UNIX operating system environment.

A primitive is used by the layer to invoke the service entities and create any headers that will be used by the peer layer in the remote station. This point is quite important. The primitives are received by adjacent layers in the local site and are used to create the headers used by peer layers at the remote site.

At the receiving site, the primitive is used to convey the data to the next and adjacent upper layer, and to inform this layer about the actions of the lower layer.

The OSI Model uses four types of primitives to perform the actions between the layers, which are summarized in Table A–1. The manner in which they are invoked varies. Not all four primitives must be invoked with each operation. For example, if the remote machine has no need to respond to the local machine, it need not return a response primitive. In this situation, a request primitive would be invoked at the local site to

Table A–1   The Functions of the Service Definitions

At user A:

- *Request*. A primitive initiated by a service user to invoke a function.
- *Confirm*. A primitive response by a service provider to complete a function previously invoked by a request primitive. It may or may not follow the response primitive.

At user B:

- *Indication*. A primitive issued by a service provider to (a) invoke a function, or (b) indicate a function has been invoked.
- *Response*. A primitive response by a service user to complete a function previously invoked by an indication primitive.

---

get the operation started. At the remote site, the indication primitive would be invoked to complete the process.

Of course, if the remote station were to send traffic back, it would invoke the operation with a response primitive, which would be mapped to the confirm primitive at the local machine.

SUMMARY

The OSI Model uses the concepts of layered protocols; ISDN and SS7 are based on this OSI feature. Two key aspects of the OSI Model are service definitions for vertical communications between layers in the same machine, and protocol specifications for horizontal communications between the same layers in different machines.

OSI is organized around the concepts of encapsulation and decapsulation. Service access points (SAPs) form the basis for OSI identifiers. They are used in ISDN operations but not in SS7 networks. SAPs are used in ISDN operations, but not in ISDN networks.

Appendix **B**

The OSI Presentation Layer and SS7

INTRODUCTION

Most of the SS7 upper layers, such as the Transaction Capabilities Applications Part (TCAP) and the ISDN User Part (ISUP), make extensive use of the OSI presentation layer. This appendix provides an overview of the OSI presentation layer and describes it in the context of SS7 usage.

FUNCTIONS OF THE PRESENTATION LAYER

The presentation layer is concerned with the representation of the data in a data communications system. It provides a means to define how the bits are structured within protocol data units (PDUs) and within the fields in the PDUs. As a simple example, it defines if the bits are positioned in a field in high or low order. It also allows two end users in two different machines to negotiate the type of syntax that will be used between two applications in those machines. For example, one user might use ASCII and the other user might use EBCDIC code. The presentation layer allows these two users to negotiate how the data will be represented. It also supports the conversion of the data to a syntax that is acceptable to both programs. Figure B–1 provides an illustration of this idea.

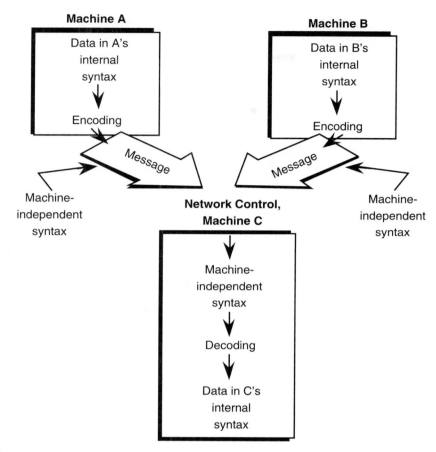

Figure B–1   Machine independent syntax.

The presentation layer uses Abstract Syntax Notation One (ASN.1) to define the types of data, such as integer, real, octet, or bit string. It also employs a standard (X.209) to define the structure of the data for the communications channel. X.209 is based on Courier, a Xerox Network System (XNS) protocol.[1]

The ASN.1 language is used to describe data structures (structured information). In addition, the ASN.1 notations are coded into machine-

---

[1]Two documents by ISO pertaining to the use of this layer by SS7 are: ASN.1, described in ISO 8824; and the basic encoding rules (BER), described in ISO 8825. These standards were republished in 1988 by ITU-T as ASN.1—Recommendation X.208 and BER—Recommendation X.209.

independent messages at the sender. These messages are conveyed across the communications channel to the receiver in a machine-independent format. At the receiver, this format is decoded into the receiver's machine-dependent format.

ASN.1 TYPES

ASN.1 defines a number of "built-in" types. This term means that certain types are considered an essential part of the ASN.1 standard; they are predefined. They are called built-in because they are defined within the standard itself. Table B–1 provides a summary of some of the more common built-in types.

One might wonder what is a "non-built-in" type. That kind of type is not defined in the standard and is considered to be a type that is defined by an enterprise. For example, in the Internet (as published by the Internet Activities Board [IAB]) a non-built-in type is network address. This type is always identified as a 32-bit Internet Protocol (IP) address, in which the type must be coded as either *network address.host address* or *network address.subnetwork address.host address.*

Table B–1   Built-in Types (other types are also defined)

Boolean	Identifies logical data (true or false conditions)
Integer	Identifies signed whole numbers (cardinal numbers)
Bit string	Identifies binary data (ordered sequence of 1s and 0s)
Octet string	Identifies text or data that can be described as a sequence of octets (bytes)
Null	A simple type consisting of a single value
Sequence	A structured type, defined by referencing an ordered list of various types
Set	A structured type, similar to the Sequence type except that Set is defined by referencing an unordered list of types that allows data to be sent in any order
Choice	Models a data type chosen from a collection of alternative types that allows a data structure to hold more than one type
Tagged	Models a new type from an existing type but with a different identifier
Object Identifier	A distinguishable value associated with an object, or a group of objects, like a library of rules, syntaxes, and so on.
Character String	Models strings of characters for some defined character set
Real	Models real values (for example: $M * B^e$, where M = the mantissa, B = the base, and e = the exponent)

The ASN.1 built-in types offer a wide array of types for the enterprise to use. Indeed, many organizations (in order to reduce the complexity of the presentation layer) choose to implement a subset of the build-in types.

THE BASIC ENCODING RULES (BER)

X.209 and ISO 8825 describe the encoding rules for the types and their values in contrast to X.208 and ISO 8824, which are concerned with the description of objects. These basic encoding rules (BER) provide the conventions for the transfer syntax conventions, illustrated in Figure B–2.

The rules require that each type be described by a well-formed, specific representation. This representation is called a *data element* (or just an *element*). As shown here, it consists of three components, type, length, and value (TLV), which appear in the following order:

Type   Length   Value

The *type* is also called the identifier. It distinguishes one type from another (for example, SEQUENCE from OBJECT IDENTIFIER) and specifies how the remainder of the element is interpreted.

The length (L) specifies the length of the contents. It may take one of three forms: short, long, or indefinite. The short form is one octet long and is used when L is less than 128 octets. Bit 8 is always 0, and bits 7 through 1 indicate the length of the contents. The length value defines only the length of the contents (value) and does not include the octets

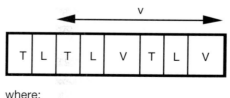

where:
T   Type (identifier)
L   Length
V   Value (contents)

Figure B–2   Basic encoding rules (BER) format for the transfer element.

that comprise the identifier and the length octets. The long form is used for a longer contents field: greater than or equal to 128.

The contents (value) is the actual information of the element. The contents are interpreted based on the coding of the identifier (type) field. Therefore, the contents are interpreted as bit strings, octet strings, and so on.

The transfer element can consist of a single TLV or a series of data elements, described as multiple TLVs.

SUMMARY

Most of the SS7 upper layers make use of the OSI presentation layer. The presentation layer is concerned with the representation of the data in a communications system. It provides a means to define how the bits are structured within SS7 signal units and within the fields in the signal units.

The use of the presentation layer provides a generic protocol for the exchange of traffic between different manufacturers' equipment and software.

Appendix **C**

The ISDN Terminal Adapter (TA)

INTRODUCTION

This appendix provides a more detailed explanation of the ISDN terminal adapter (TA). The material is meant for the reader who is familiar with physical layer interfaces. The ITU-T standards X.30 and X.31 are highlighted here as examples of the operations of these machines.

HOW RATE ADAPTATION WORKS

Since different transfer rates must be accommodated on each side of the terminal adapter, and the R interface may see rates ranging from 300 bit/s to 56 kbit/s, ISDN uses a mapping scheme in which a frame of a fixed size is used for all data rates. This approach simplifies the design of the TA.

Later discussions in the appendix show how the frame is coded. For this introduction, Table C–1 shows how two data rates (2.4 kbit/s and 4.8 kbit/s) are mapped into the X.30 frame. For the lower transfer rates, some of the bits in the frame are not utilized; they are padded to create a standardized frame.

Table C-1   Mapping Schemes

2400 bit/s:

- 8000 bit/s / 80 bits per frame = 100 frames per second
- 100 frames per second * 48 user bits per multiframe = 4800 bit/s
- Every other bit data bit position contains a data bit; therefore, the data rate is 2400 bit/s

4800 bit/s:

- 8000 bit/s / 80 bits per frame = 100 frames per second
- 100 frames per second * 48 user bits per multiframe = 4800 bit/s

X.30

X.30 describes the connections of X.21 and X.21 bis devices to an ISDN. These devices must operate within specified user classes of service, according to Recommendation X.1.[1] X.30 also describes the connections of X.20-based devices with an ISDN utilizing asynchronous data rates of 600, 1200, 2400, 4800 and 9600 bit/s. The recommendation stipulates the use with both circuit switched and leased line systems.

X.30 covers the rate adaptation scheme between the user device through the user ISDN terminal adapter (TA). It does not cover the requirements for the data transfer speed conversion in the event of internetworking—for example, between ISDNs and circuit switched networks. X.30 also defines the mapping of X.21 and X.21 bis signals to/from the ISDN network layer messages.

---

[1]X.1 defines sixteen classes of service. The classes of service depend on whether the user station operates as (a) an asynchronous start/stop device, (b) a synchronous device, or (c) a packet mode device. The user classes of service and the data signaling rates range from 300 bit/s start/stop asynchronous modes to 64 kbit/s modes. A vendor or administration may not support all classes of service. Common classes of service are:

Synchronous Mode :		*Asynchronous Mode:*	
8	2400 bit/s	20	50–300 bit/s
9	4800 bit/s	21	75–1200 bit/s
10	9600 bit/s	22	1200 bit/s
11	48000 bit/s		
12	1200 bit/s		
13	64000 bit/s		

Figure C–1 shows the X.21 mapping functions utilizing the X.21 interface between the DTE and TA and the S/T interface from the TA to the ISDN node. The X.21 operations begin with the DTE issuing the DTE ready signal to the TA. The X.21 DTE ready signal is conveyed across the X.24 interface with circuits t and c in the following states: t = 1 and circuit c = OFF. The terminal adapter receives the DTE ready signal and then waits for the DTE call request. As seen in the figure, this occurs with the DTE transmitting the call request signal. The call request signal is conveyed by the following signal across the X.24 circuits: t = 0, c = ON. (Hereafter in our description of this operation, we are not going to describe the ON/OFF and 0/1 relationships of the X.24 interfaces.)

Continuing our analysis, the TA receives the call request signal and returns a proceed to select signal. In turn, the DTE sends the selection signals to the TA.

By this time, the TA has enough information to map the selection signals into an ISDN call establishment with an ISDN I.450/451 SETUP message. The DTE then informs the TA that it is in a DTE waiting state. During this time, the TA receives status messages across the S/T reference point. The status messages are shown as CALL PROCEEDING and ALERTING.

To continue the analysis, note that the ALERTING signal is mapped back the X.21 call progress signal. Note also that the TA takes it upon itself to return an X.21 DCE waiting signal to the DTE (the TA is playing the role of the DCE). Finally, an ISDN CONNECT message—a Call Accepted signal from the remote entity—is received by the TA, and it is sent to the DTE in a DCE provided information signal. Thereafter, the TA sends to the DTE the connection in progress signal.

Eventually, the TA receives the end-to-end sync signal, which it maps to the X.21 ready for data signal.

After all these activities, the data transfer occurs. To clear the connection, the DTE issues the X.21 clear request signals. These signals are mapped by the TA into an ISDN DISCONNECT. The TA takes it upon itself to return the DCE clear confirmation. Next, the ISDN RELEASE message is transferred back to the TA, which maps this message to an X.21 DCE ready. To complete the process, the DTE transfers to the TA an X.21 DTE ready signal. The TA issues an ISDN RELEASE COMPLETE to its peer entity.

The mapping of X.21 bis interface to and from ISDN is somewhat simpler. This operation is depicted in Figure C–2. The ready signal is created by the V.24 108.2 being set to OFF. This signal is received by the TA and held until the call request signal is received (a V.24 108/1 = ON). This signal is used by the TA to create an ISDN SETUP message. No

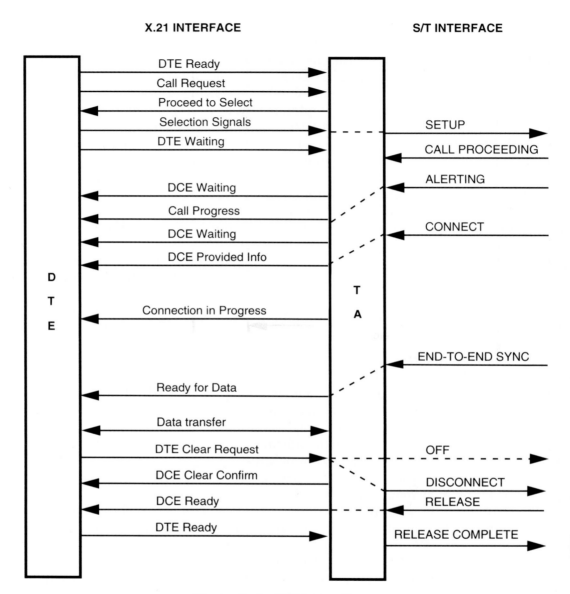

Figure C–1   X.30 operations.

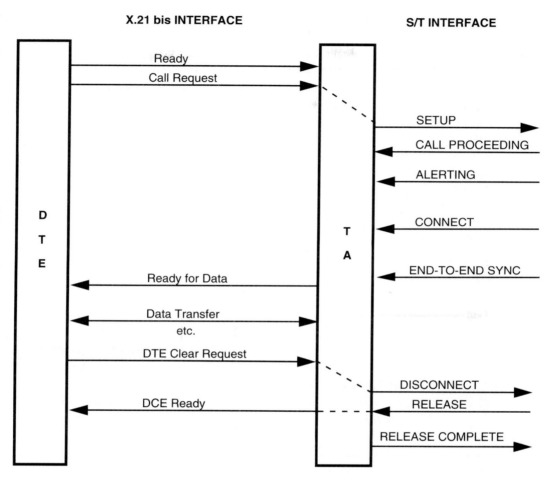

Figure C–2   Mapping X.21 bis and ISDN.

more activities occur between the TA and the DTE while the TA is receiving an ISDN call proceeding, alerting, connect and finally an end-to-end sync.

Upon receiving this last message, the TA turns on the ready-for-data signal to its DTE (V.24 107 = ON). Upon receiving the signal, the DTE enters the data transfer mode and transfers data. Eventually the DTE clears the connection by a DTE Clear Request (V.24 108/1 = OFF). This signal begins the ISDN disconnect operations depicted in the bottom of the figure.

A system using X.30 must go through some rather elaborate operations to interface with ISDN. These operations are accomplished through an ISDN terminal adapter (TA). An X.30 terminal adapter is shown in Figure C–3. It is quite similar to terminal adapters found in other ISDN interworking operations (for example, V.110 has a similar terminal adapter). The TA consists of two functions, rate adaptation 1 (RA1) and rate adaptation 2 (RA2). The purpose of RA1 is to convert the X.21 or X.21 bis data rate to an intermediate rate (IR) of either 8 or 16 kbit/s. It uses ITU-T Recommendation X.1 to define the classes of service and the data signaling rate.

X.1 rates for user classes 3, 4, and 5 are converted to a 8 kbit/s and user class 6 is converted to a 16 kbit/s rate. The intermediate rate is then input into RA2, which is responsible for placing the data onto the ISDN 64 kbit/s basic channel.

The RA1 Frame

The output of the RA1 function is in the form of a 40 bit-frame. The structure of this frame is shown in Figure C–4. This frame is similar to the frame used in V.110 terminal adapters. The frame, although described in 40 bits, actually consists of two multi-frames. The odd numbered frames set the octet position 1 to all 0s. The even numbered frames use this octet for the E bits (which are described later).

This figure also shows the position of the data bits in the odd and even frames. The data bits are placed in the data positions, low-order bit first, in three octets in each of the frames. Therefore, each frame carries 24 data bits in the P, Q, and R bit positions.

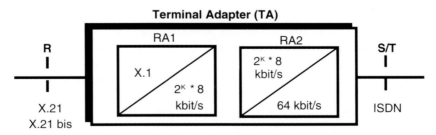

Figure C–3   The X.30 terminal adapter (TA).

| Bit Position | | | | | | | | Octet | |
1	2	3	4	5	6	7	8	Position	
0	0	0	0	0	0	0	0	0	
1	P1	P2	P3	P4	P5	P6	SQ	1	
1	P7	P8	Q1	Q2	Q3	Q4	X	2	Odd
1	Q5	Q6	Q7	Q8	R1	R2	SR	3	Frame
1	R3	R4	R5	R6	R7	R8	SP	4	
1	E1	E2	E3	E4	E5	E6	E7	0	
1	P1	P2	P3	P4	P5	P6	SQ	1	
1	P7	P8	Q1	Q2	Q3	Q4	X	2	Even
1	Q5	Q6	Q7	Q8	R1	R2	SR	3	Frame
1	R3	R4	R5	R6	R7	R8	SP	4	

Figure C–4   The X.30 frame.

The status bits are labeled SQ, SR, SP, and X. The status bits provide a mapping from the local X.21 interface to the remote X.21 interface. We shall see shortly that the mapping occurs by the X.30 protocol establishing a relationship between the SP, SQ, SR, and the data bit groups of P, Q, and R. For our present analysis, it is sufficient to note that the S bits are used on the transmit side (local side) to reflect the state of the X.21 interchange circuit. These bits are then conveyed across an ISDN node to the remote receiver, where they are used to create the signals on the X.21 i interchange circuit. (In all cases during this discussion the c and i circuits represent an ON condition with binary 0 and OFF condition with binary 1. The contents of the SQ, SR, and SP bits are: 0 = ON, 1 = OFF.)

X.30 uses a 17-bit frame alignment pattern with eight 0s in the first octet of the odd frame and the first bit positions of subsequent octets in the odd and even frames. These bit values are set to one.

Circuit Mapping

Figure C–5 shows the relationships of the X.24 circuits (at the transmit and receive side) and the SQ, SR, and SP bits. Notice that the ON and OFF signals at the transmit side c interchange circuit are mapped into the SQ, SR, and SP bits, which are then used to set the proper signal on the receive i interchange circuit.

Figure C–6 shows the mapping of the transmit c interchange circuit to the receive i interchange circuit. The timing for the mapping occurs

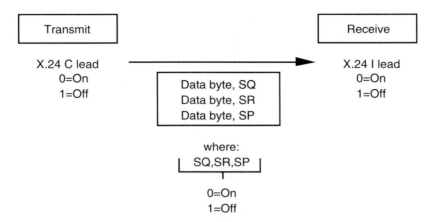

Figure C–5   The *c* and *i* interchange signals.

through the eighth bit position of the R, P, and Q data octets. The arrows in the figure show that the sampling of the *c* lead occurs in the middle of the eighth bit of the respective preceding R, P, or Q bit group. At the receive side, the SQ, SP, and SR status bits are used to create the signals on the *i* interchange circuit. In essence, on the receive side, the values of status bits SP, SQ, and SR are adapted by the *i* lead.

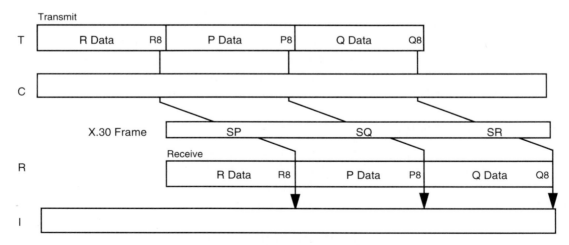

Figure C–6   Mapping operations.

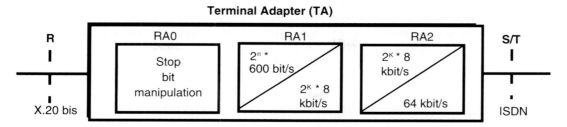

Figure C–7   The X.30 RA0 TA.

Asynchronous Support

X.30 also supports terminal adaptation operations from terminals using X.1 user classes of service 1 and 2. The reader may recall from previous discussions of X.1 that user classes of service 1 and 2 define asynchronous operations. The adaptation is provided through yet another terminal adapter as depicted in Figure C–7. This terminal adapter has another stage labeled RA0 (rate adapter 0). This stage functions as an asynchronous-to-synchronous converter and uses the conversion techniques defined in ITU-T V.14.

X.31 AND THE TERMINAL ADAPTER

In parts of the world (notably Europe), X.25 has been prevalent in systems since the mid-1970s. The ITU-T publishes the X.25 Recommendations and has been a strong supporter of the technology. It then comes as little surprise that ITU-T would publish specifications on the interworking of X.25 and ISDN. X.31 is this standard. It offers a wealth of options; for simplicity, I will furnish one example.[2]

Figure C–8 shows an example of how X.31 defines the mapping of the X.25 protocol and IDSN messages. Table C–2 provides an explanation of the terms used in Figure C–8. The top "boxes" represent the components that participate in the operation:

---

[2]An explanation of the X.25 operations is beyond the scope of this book. The interested reader can study *X.25 and Related Protocols,* by Uyless Black, and published by the IEEE Computer Society Press.

Table C–2   Explanation of Terms in Figure C–8

SABME   Set asynchronous balanced mode extended. Sets up the ISDN link, clears the
buffers, and sets sequence numbers to 0.

SABM   Performs the same functions as LAPD on the X.25 interface. In this configuration, the TA also sends the LAPB traffic across the ISDN link to the packet
handler (PH).

PH   Packet handler. Used to process the X.25 layer two (LAPB) and layer three
(packets) traffic.

UA   Unnumbered acknowledgment. Acknowledges the SABME frame in LAPD and
the SABM frame in LAPB. It also acknowledges the disconnect from (DISC).

DISC   Disconnect. Used in both LAPD and LAPB to terminate the layer two traffic
session

Note 1: The following entries in Figure C–8 are X.25 layer three packets:

Call request   Sent by local TE2 A to set up an X.25 connection

Incoming call: Sent by remote TE3 B in response to an incoming call

Call confirm: Upon receiving a call accepted, sent by PH to local TE2 A

Clear request: Sent by either TE2 A or TE2 B (TE2 A in this example) to terminate
an X.25 connection

Clear indication: Upon receiving a clear request, PH sends to TE2 B

Clear confirm: Acknowledges the clear request

Note 2: The other entries in Figure C–8 are ISDN layer three messages (Q.931) and are
explained in Chapter 5 of this book.

- TE2 A/TE2 B: The originating and receiving user devices, respec-
tively
- TA1 and TA2: The originating and receiving TAs, respectively
- NT1: The ISDN physical connections between the TA and the
ISDN node
- LE: The ISDN local exchanges
- PH/NW: The ISDN packet handler and the packet network

The top left part of the figure shows the TA setting up a LAPD connection with the LE with SABME and UA. This illustration assumes the
X.21 or X.21 bis operations between TE1 A and TA1 have been com-

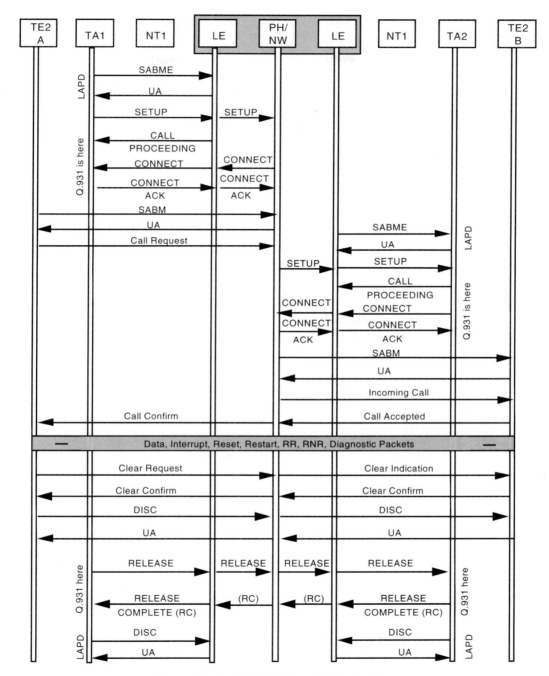

Figure C–8 An X.31 terminal adapter.

pleted. Therefore, the physical level interface between TE2 A and TA1 is (and the remote TE and TA as well) is:

- For X.21: States 13S, 13R, or 13
- For X.21 bis: V.24 circuits 105 through 109 in ON condition
- For EIA-232-D: circuits CA, CB, CC, CD, and CF in ON condition

Abbreviations

2B+D: B, B and D channels
2B1Q: 2 binary 1 quaternary

A/D: Analog-to-digital
ABM: Asynchronous balanced mode
AC: Access control
AC: Authentication center
ACD: Automatic call distributor
ACG: Automatic code gap
ACK: Positive acknowledgment
ACM: Address complete message
ACO: Additional call offering
ADSL: Asymmetrical digital subscriber line
AE: Application entity
AI: Address indicator
AIN: Advanced intelligent network
ANM: Answer message
ANSI: American National Standards Institute
AR: Action result
AR: Aligned/ready state
ARS: Automatic route selection
ASE: Application service element
AT: Access tandem
ATM: Asynchronous transfer mode
AV: Action value
BCD: Binary coded decimal
BER: Basic encoding rules
BIB: Backward indicator bit
BLA: Blocking acknowledgment
BLO: Blocking
BOC: Bell Operating Companies
BRI: Basic rate interface
BSDB: Business services database

BSN: Backward sequence number
C/R: Command/response
CAMA-ANAI: Centralized automatic message accounting-automatic number id
CC: Connection confirm
CCAF: Call control agent function
CCF: Call control function
CCIS: Common Channel Interoffice Signaling
CCITT: Now named ITU-T
CCR: Commitment-concurrency-recovery
CCR: Continuity check request
CCS: Common channel signaling
CCS6: Common channel signaling #6
CCSSO: CCS switching office
CFN: Confusion
CGB: Circuit group blocking
CGBA: Circuit group blocking acknowledgment
CGU: Circuit group unblocking
CGUA: Circuit group unblocking acknowledgment
CID: Component ID
CMIP: Common Management Information Protocol
CMISE: Common Management Information Service Element
CMSDB: Call management service database
CNIS: Calling number ID services
CO: Central office
COT: Continuity
CP: Call proceeding
CPE: Customer premises equipment
CPG: Call progress
CQM: Circuit query message

CQR: Circuit query response
CR: Command/Response bit
CR: Connection request
CRA: Call rejection applies
CRA: Circuit reservation acknowledgment
CRC: Cyclic redundancy check
CRM: Circuit reservation:
CUG: Closed user group
CVR: Circuit validation response
CVT: Circuit validation test
DB: Databases
DCS: Digital Cellular System
DDD: Direct distance dial
DECT: Digital European Cordless Telephony
DISC: Disconnect
DLCI: Data link connection identifier
DLR: Destination local reference
DM: Disconnect mode
DN: Directory number
DO: Denied origination
DOD: Direct outward dialing
DP: Detection point
DPC: Destination point code
DRCW: Distinctive ringing/call waiting
DSU: Data service unit
DT: Connection-oriented data (DT)
DT: Denied terminating
DTMF: Dual-tone multifrequency
E800: Enhanced 800 (E800
EA: Extended address
EAEO: Equal access end office
EC: Exchange carrier
EI: Event information
EIR: Equipment Identity Register
EKTS: Electronic key telephone service
EO: End office
ET: Event time
ET: Exchange termination
EV: Event value
EXM: Exit message
F: Framing bit
FAC: Facility
FCC: Federal Communications Commission
FCS: Frame check sequence
FGB: Feature group B
FIB: Forward indicator bit
FISU: Fill-in signal unit
FOT: Forward transfer
FRMR: Frame reject
FRO: Fully restricted originating
FRT: Fully restricted terminating
FSN: Forward sequence number
FTA: Facility test acknowledgment
FTL: Facility test loopback
FTR: Facility test results
FTU: Facility test underway
FX: Foreign exchange
GRA: Group reset acknowledgment
GRS: Group reset

GSM: Global System for Mobile Communications
GT: Global Title
HDLC: High level data link control
HFC: Hybrid fiber coaxial cable
HLR: Home location register
Hz: Hertz
I: Information
IA5: International Alphabet #5
IAM: Initial address message
IC: Interexchange carrier:
IE: Information elements
II: Invoke ID
IN: intelligent network
INF: Information
INR: Information Request
INWATS: Inward-wide area telecommunications service
IOC: ISDN ordering codes
IP: intelligent peripheral
ISDN: Integrated Service Digital Network
ISNI: Intermediate Signaling Network Identification
ISP: International signaling point
ISP: Internet Service Providers
ISUP: ISDN user part
IXC: Interexchange carrier
ITU-T : International Telecommunication Union–Telecommunication Sector
kbit/s: Kilobits per second
KP: Key pulse
L: Balancing bit
LAPB: Link access procedure, balanced
LAPD: Link access procedure for the D channel
LATA: Local access and transport area
LEA: Link equipment available
LEC: Local exchange carrier
LEF: Link equipment failure
LEU: Link equipment unavailable
LFS: Link fault sectionalization
LI: Length indicator
LIDB: Line information database
LME: Layer management entity
LMI: Layer management interface
LR: Local reference number
LSB: Least significant bit
LSSU: Link status signal unit
LSTP: Local signaling transfer point
LT: Line termination
M bit: More data bit
MAN: Metropolitan Area Network
MAP: Mobile Application Part
Mbit/s: Megabit per second
MF: Multifrequency
MFJ: Modification of Final Judgment
MHS: Message handling services
MIB: Management information base
MOC: Managed object class
MOI: Managed object instance

MRVA: MTP routing verification acknowledge
   message
MRVR: MTP routing verification result
MRVT: MTP routing verification test
ms: Microsecond
MSB: Most significant bit
MSC: Mobile Switching Center
MSU: Message signal unit
MTP: Message transfer part
MTS: Message telecommunications service
N(R): Receive sequence number
N(S): Send sequence number
NA: Not aligned state
NA: Numbering plan area
NAK: Negative acknowledgment
NANP: North American Numbering Plan
NAP: Network access point
NI-1: National ISDN-1
NIDs: Network IDs
NNI: Network node interface
NSP: National signaling point
NT: Network termination
Oc: Operation code identifier
OCM: Originating call model
OCU: Office channel unit
OLE: Originating local exchange
OMAP: Operations, maintenance, and adminis-
   tration part
OPC: Origination point code
OPDU: Operation protocol data unit
Ops: Operation codes
OSI: Open Switching Intervals
OSI: Open Systems Interconnection
OSS: Operations support system
OSS: Operator service signaling
OSS: Operator service system
OUTWATS: Outward-wide area telecommuni-
   cations service
P: Proving state
Parms: Parameters
PBX: Private branch exchange
PC: Point code
PCM: Pulse code modulation
PCR: preventive cyclic retransmission
PCS: Personal Communications System
PDU: Protocol data unit
PHF: Packet-handling function
Pi: Parameter set/sequence Identifier
PIC: Point in call
POP: Point of presence
POT: Point of termination
PPP: Point-to-point
PRI: Primary rate interfaces
Pt: Package type identifier:
PVN: Private virtual networks
QOS: Quality of service
RA: Rate adapter
RBOC: Regional Bell Operating Company
RC: Resource class

REJ: Reject
REL: Release
RES: Resume
RI: Resource instance
RLC: Release complete
RNR: Receive not ready:
ROH: Receiver-on-hook
ROSE: Remote operations service element
RPC: Remote procedure call
RR: Receive ready
RREJ: Receive reject
RSC: Reset circuit
RSTP: Regional signaling transfer point
SABME: Set asynchronous balanced mode,
   extended
SAC: Service Access Code
SAP: Service access point
SAPI: Service access point identifier
SCCP: Signaling connection control part
SCE: Service creation environment ,
SCEF: Service creation environment function
SCF: Service control function
SCLC: SSCP connectionless control
SCMG: SCCP management
SCOC: SCCP connection-oriented control
SCP: Service control point
SCRC: SSCP routing control
SDF: Service data function
SDLC: Synchronous data link control
SEP: Signaling end point
SF: Status field (SF)
SI=E: Status indicator emergency(SI=E)
SI=N: Status indicator normal (SI=N)
SI=N/E: Status indication set to normal or
   emergency alignment
SI=O: Status indication set to out of alignment
SIF: Signaling information field
SIO: Service indicator octet
SL: Signaling link
SLR: Source local reference
SLS: Signaling link selection
SMAE: System management application entity
SMAF: Service management access function
SMAP: System management application process
SMF: Service management function
SMS: Service management system
SMSI: System management service interface
SONET: Synchronous Optical Network
SP: Signaling point
SPI: Service profile ID
SRF: Specialized resource function
SRO: Semi-restricted originating
SRT: Semi-restricted terminating
SRVT: SCCP routing verification test
SS6: Signaling System No. 6
SS7: Signaling System No. 7
SSF: Service switching function
SSN: Subsystem number
SSP: Service switching point

ST: Start
STP: Signaling transfer point
SU: Signal unit
SUS: Suspend
SVCs: Switched virtual calls
SWF-DS1: Switched DS1/Switched Fractional
  DS1 Service
TA: Terminal adapter
TCAP: Transaction capabilities application part
TCM: Terminating call model
TDM: Time division multiplexing
TE: Terminal equipment
TE: Transit exchanges
TEI: Terminal endpoint identifier
TI: Transaction ID
Ti: Transaction ID Identifier:
TIDs: Transaction IDs:

TLE: Terminating local exchange
TLV: Type-length value
TR: Terminating resistor
TUP: Telephone user part
UA: Unnumbered acknowledgment
UBA : Unblocking Acknowledgment
UBL: Unblocking
UCIC: Unequipped circuit identification code
UDT: User data traffic
UI: Unnumbered Information
UNI: User network interface
UP: User parts
USID: User service ID
UT: Unrestricted terminating
VLR: Visitor location register
XID: Exchange identification
XUDT: extended unit data (XUDT)

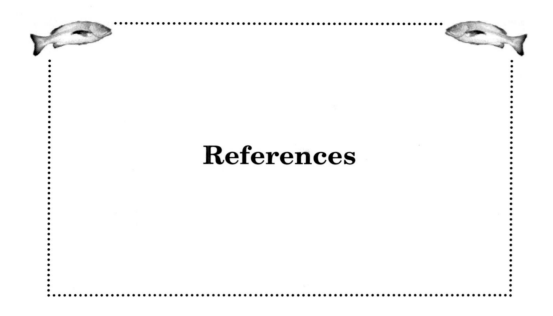

References

ANSI STANDARDS

ANSI

T1.109
1990   Telecommunications—Exchange—Interexchange Carrier Interfaces—950+XXXX EC-to-IC Access Signaling Protocols

T1.110
1992   Telecommunications—Signaling System No. 7 (SS7)—General Information

T1.111
1992   Telecommunications—Signaling System No. 7 (SS7)—Functional Description of the Signaling System Message Transfer Part (MTP)

T1.111a
1994   Telecommunications—Signaling System No. 7 (SS7)—Message Transfer Part (MTP) (Numbering of Signaling Point Codes)

T1.112
1992   Telecommunications—Signaling System No. 7 (SS7)—Signaling Connection Control Part (SCCP)

T1.113
1992   Telecommunications—Signaling System No. 7 (SS7)—Integrated Services Digital Network (ISDN) User Part

T1.113a
1993   Telecommunications—Signaling System No. 7 (SS7)—Integrated Services Digital Network (ISDN) User Part (NxDS0 Multi-Rate Connection)

T1.114
1992   Telecommunications—Signaling System No. 7 (SS7)—Transaction Capability Application Part (TCAP)

T1.115
1990   Telecommunications—Monitoring and Measurements for Signaling System Number 7 Networks

T1.116
1990   Telecommunications—Signaling System Number 7 (SS7)—Operations, Maintenance and Administration Part (OMAP)

T1.117
1991   Telecommunications—Digital Hierarchy Optical Interface Specifications (Short Reach)

T1.118
1992   Telecommunications—Signaling System Number 7 (SS7)—Intermediate Signaling Network Identification (ISNI)

T1.119
1994   Telecommunications—Synchronous Optical Network (SONET)—Operations, Administration, Maintenance, and Provisioning (OAM&P) Communications

T1.201
1987   Telecommunications—Information Interchange—Structure for the Identification of Location Entities for the North American Telecommunications System

T1.202
1988   Telecommunications—Internetwork Operations—Guidelines for Network Management of the Public Switched Networks Under Disaster Conditions

T1.203
1988   Telecommunications—Operations and Maintenance—Human—Machine Language

T1.204
1993   Telecommunications—Operations, Administration, Maintenance, and Provisioning (OAM&P)—Lower-Layer Protocols for Telecommunications Management Network (TMN) Interfaces between Operations Systems and Network Elements

T1.205
1988   Telecommunications—Information Interchange—Representation of Places, States of the United States, Provinces and Territories of Canada, Countries of the world, and Other Unique Areas for the North American Telecommunications System

T1.206
1994   Telecommunications—Digital Exchanges and PBXs—Digital Circuit Loopback Test Line with N x DS0 Capability

T1.207
1989   Telecommunications—Operations, Administration, Maintenance and Provisioning (OAM&P)—Terminating Test Line Capabilities and Access Arrangements

T1.208
1993   Telecommunications—Operations, Administration, Maintenance, and Provisioning (OAM&P)—Upper-Layer Protocols for Telecommunications Management Network (TMN) Interfaces between Operations Systems and Network Elements

T1.209

1989 Telecommunication—Operations, Administration, Maintenance, and Provisioning (OAM&P)—Network Tones and Announcements

T1.210

1993 Telecommunications—Operations, Administration, Maintenance, and Provisioning (OAM&P)—Principles of Functions, Architectures, and Protocols for Telecommunication Management Network (TMN) Interfaces

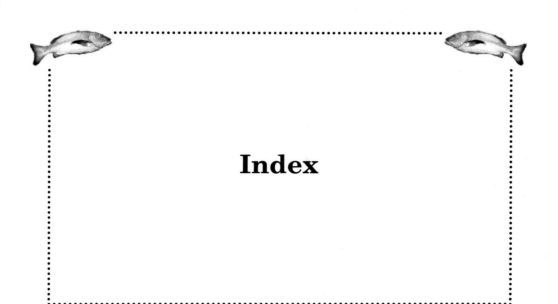

Index